PELICAN BOOKS

ILLUSTRATED ENGLISH SOCIAL HISTORY I

George Macaulay Trevelyan, O.M., C.B.E., F.B.A., born in 1876, was the third son of Sir George Otto Trevelyan and a great-nephew of Lord Macaulay. He was educated at Harrow and at Trinity College, Cambridge. In the First World War he was awarded the Silver Medal for Valour (Italy) and the Chevalier of the Order of St Maurice and St Lazarus (Italy).

He was an Hon. D.C.L., Oxford, and Hon. LL.D., St Andrews and Edinburgh, a Fellow of Trinity College, Cambridge, and an Honorary Fellow of Oriel College, Oxford. From 1927 to 1940 he was Regius Professor of Modern History at Cambridge and from 1940 to 1951 he was Master of Trinity. He was also a Trustee of the British Museum and the National Portrait Gallery. He was President of the Youth Hostels' Association from 1930 to 1950, and was Chairman of the Estates Committee of the National Trust. He died in 1962.

Among his books on British history are: *England in the Age of Wycliffe*, *England under the Stuarts*, *The English Revolution 1688*, *England under Queen Anne*, *British History in the Nineteenth Century*, and *History of England. Lord Grey of the Reform Bill*, *Lord Grey of Fallodon*, *The Life of Bright*, and the famous Garibaldi trilogy are his biographical works.

ILLUSTRATED ENGLISH SOCIAL HISTORY

G. M. TREVELYAN

VOLUME ONE: CHAUCER'S ENGLAND AND THE EARLY TUDORS

WITH 180 ILLUSTRATIONS, SELECTED BY RUTH C. WRIGHT

PENGUIN BOOKS

Penguin Books Ltd, Harmondsworth,
Middlesex, England
Penguin Books Australia Ltd, Ringwood,
Victoria, Australia

First published in the U.S.A. and Canada
by Longmans, Green 1942
Published in Great Britain 1944
Illustrated edition in four volumes first
published 1949–52
Published in Pelican Books 1964
Reprinted 1966, 1968, 1973
English Social History copyright ©
Longmans, Green, 1942, 1944
Illustrated English Social History copyright ©
Longmans, Green, 1949–52, 1954, 1960

Made and printed in Great Britain by
Brightype litho at Flarepath Printers Ltd
St Albans, Herts
Set in Monotype Imprint

TO THE MEMORY OF EILEEN POWER

ECONOMIC AND SOCIAL

HISTORIAN

CONTENTS

PREFATORY NOTE
TO THE ILLUSTRATIONS

In selecting these illustrations to form a pictorial commentary on the text, I have been guided by two considerations, first, that they should be drawn as far as might be from English sources as distinct from European sources generally, and secondly, that they should be as nearly contemporary as possible with the scenes they represent. It has not been possible to adhere strictly to these two principles in every example; for instance, I have had to turn to French chronicles (with Flemish illumination) for such illustrations as those of the Peasants' Revolt [11–13],[1] where the chronicler's miniaturist is endeavouring to portray the actual historical events of some eighty years before; again, I have used Flemish sources for the medieval garden [92] and the medieval farm [96] and French sources for the medieval dramas [122–4], since no such suitable miniatures are available for that period from English sources. But these illustrations, while affording useful parallels at a time when the practices of chivalry, the minutiae of everyday life and entertainment, or the methods of agriculture and industry, had doubtless much in common throughout Europe, must inevitably betray local differences: the architecture of the farm [96], for instance, or the elaborate formalism of the garden scene [92]. Similarly, it has been sometimes necessary to draw examples from an apparently faithful copy of an earlier original now lost, as in John Doharty's 1744 copy of Blagrave's map of Feckenham [125] or S. H. Grimm's 1785 water-colour copy

1. Figures in square brackets refer to illustrations in the text.

of the Cowdray picture of Edward VI's Riding from the Tower in 1547 [130], which was destroyed in the disastrous Cowdray fire of 1793.

Modern photographs and eighteenth- and nineteenth-century engravings have been used freely to illustrate places (as distinct from social scenes), even though the purist might, I suppose, complain that I have used Loggan's engravings of Trinity or Christ Church to show in full maturity the foundations of Henry VIII and Wolsey, instead of confining myself to plans of the stage which they had actually reached in Tudor times.

I cannot hope to reflect in entirety the many-sided picture presented by Dr Trevelyan, but I have endeavoured to cover as representative a selection as possible of all the places and activities mentioned.

Detailed descriptive notes on the illustrations will be found at the end of the book; these give a summary account of the source of each illustration, its authorship, date, and provenance and its present whereabouts, together with an indication of any particular noteworthy features either in its subject-matter or manner of treatment.

RUTH C. WRIGHT

INTRODUCTION TO
COMPLETE EDITION

Although I have attempted to bring this book up to date in
the light of the most recent publications (1941), it was nearly
all written before the war. I then had in view a social history
of England from the Roman times to our own, but I left to the
last the part that I would find most difficult, the centuries
preceding the fourteenth. The war has rendered it impossible
for me to complete the work, but it has occurred to me that
the chapters which I have already finished constitute a con-
secutive story of six centuries, from the fourteenth to the
nineteenth, and as such some readers may give it welcome.

Social history might be defined negatively as the history of
a people with the politics left out. It is perhaps difficult to leave
out the politics from the history of any people, particularly the
English people. But as so many history books have consisted of
political annals with little reference to their social environment,
a reversal of that method may have its uses to redress the
balance. During my own lifetime a third very flourishing sort
of history has come into existence, the economic, which greatly
assists the serious study of social history. For the social scene
grows out of economic conditions, to much the same extent
that political events in their turn grow out of social conditions.
Without social history, economic history is barren and political
history is unintelligible.

But social history does not merely provide the required link
between economic and political history. It has also its own posi-
tive value and peculiar concern. Its scope may be defined as the

daily life of the inhabitants of the land in past ages: this includes the human as well as the economic relation of different classes to one another, the character of family and household life, the conditions of labour and of leisure, the attitude of man to nature, the culture of each age as it arose out of these general conditions of life, and took ever-changing forms in religion, literature and music, architecture, learning and thought.

How far can we know the real life of men in each successive age of the past? Historians and antiquarians have amassed by patient scholarship a great sum of information, and have edited innumerable records, letters, and journals, enough to provide reading for whole lifetimes; yet even this mass of knowledge is small indeed compared to the sum total of social history, which could only be mastered if we knew the biographies of all the millions of men, women, and children who have lived in England. The generalizations which are the stock-in-trade of the social historian, must necessarily be based on a small number of particular instances, which are assumed to be typical, but which cannot be the whole of the complicated truth.

And small as is the mass of accumulated knowledge in proportion to the vastness of the theme, how pitifully small is the selection from that mass which I have been able to set down in 200,000 words dealing with six whole centuries of the variegated and wonderful life of England. Yet even a millionth part of a loaf may be better than no bread. It may at least whet the appetite. If it makes a few people more eager to study the literature and records of the past, this book will have served its turn.

Disinterested intellectual curiosity is the life-blood of real civilization. Social history provides one of its best forms. At bottom, I think, the appeal of history is imaginative. Our imagination craves to behold our ancestors as they really were, going about their daily business and daily pleasure. Carlyle called the antiquarian or historical researcher 'Dryasdust'. Dryasdust at bottom is a poet. He may find difficulty in expressing to his neighbour the poetry he finds for himself in the muniment room. But the main impulse of his life is the desire to feel the reality of life in the past, to be familiar with 'the chronicle of wasted time' for the sake of 'ladies dead and lovely knights'.

Scott began life as Dryasdust – as an antiquarian – because that way he could find most poetry, most romance. Carlyle, like every great historian, was his own Dryasdust. Indeed he is really the greatest defender of Dryasdust in the whole field of literature. He declared, with a striking exaggeration, that the smallest real fact about the past of man which Dryasdust could unearth was more poetical than all Shelley and more romantic than all Scott.

Consider all that lies in that one word *Past*! What a pathetic, sacred, in every sense *poetic*, meaning is implied in it; a meaning growing ever the clearer the farther we recede in time — the more of that same Past we have to look through! History after all is the true poetry. And Reality, if rightly interpreted, is grander than Fiction.

It is the detailed study of history that makes us feel that the past was as real as the present. The world supposes that we historians are absorbed in the dusty records of the dead; that we can see nothing save –

> The lost-to-light ghosts, grey-mailed
> As you see the grey river mist
> Hold shapes on the yonder bank.

But to us, as we read, they take form, colour, gesture, passion, thought. It is only by study that we can see our forerunners, remote and recent, in their habits as they lived, intent each on the business of a long-vanished day, riding out to do homage or to poll a vote; to seize a neighbour's manor-house and carry off his ward, or to leave cards on ladies in crinolines.

And there is the 'fair field full of folk'. Generation after generation, there is the ploughman behind the oxen, or the horses, or the machine, and his wife busy all day in the cottage, waiting for him with her daily accumulated budget of evening news.

Each one, gentle and simple, in his commonest goings and comings, was ruled by a complicated and ever-shifting fabric of custom and law, society and politics, events at home and abroad, some of them little known by him and less understood.

13

Our effort is not only to get what few glimpses we can of his intimate personality, but to reconstruct the whole fabric of each passing age, and see how it affected him; to get to know more in some respects than the dweller in the past himself knew about the conditions that enveloped and controlled his life.

There is nothing that more divides civilized from semi-savage man than to be conscious of our forefathers as they really were, and bit by bit to reconstruct the mosaic of the long-forgotten past. To weigh the stars, or to make ships sail in the air or below the sea, is not a more astonishing and ennobling performance on the part of the human race in these latter days, than to know the course of events that had been long forgotten, and the true nature of men and women who were here before us.

Truth is the criterion of historical study; but its impelling motive is poetic. Its poetry consists in its being true. There we find the synthesis of the scientific and literary views of history.

Since, however rashly and inadequately, some attempt is to be made in this work to imagine the life of our ancestors in such partial light as modern research can afford, in what form can the story best be told? It cannot, like the web of political history, be held together by the framework of well known names of kings, Parliaments, and wars. These indeed have their influence on social development which has often to be noted. The Puritan Revolution and the Restoration were social as well as political events. But, on the whole, social change moves like an underground river, obeying its own laws or those of economic change, rather than following the direction of political happenings that move on the surface of life. Politics are the outcome rather than the cause of social change. A new king, a new Prime Minister, a new Parliament often marks a new epoch in politics, but seldom in the life of the people.

How then is the tale to be told? Into what periods shall social history be divided up? As we look back on it, we see a continuous stream of life, with gradual change perpetually taking place, but with few catastrophes. The Black Death is perhaps one, and the Industrial Revolution another. But the Industrial Revolution is spread over too many generations to be rightly regarded either as a catastrophe or as an event. It is not, like the Black Death, a fortuitous obstruction fallen across the river of life and temporarily diverting it; it is the river of life itself in the lower part of its course.

In political history one king at a time reigns; one Parliament at a time sits. But in social history we find in every period several different kinds of social and economic organization going on simultaneously in the same country, the same shire, the same town. Thus, in the realm of agriculture, we find the open-field strip cultivation of the Anglo-Saxons still extant in the eighteenth century, side by side with ancient enclosed fields of the far older Celtic pattern, and modern enclosures scientifically cultivated by methods approved by Arthur Young. And so it is with the varieties of industrial and commercial organization – the domestic, the craft, the capitalist systems are found side by side down the centuries. In everything the old overlaps the new – in religion, in thought, in family custom. There is never any clear cut; there is no single moment when all Englishmen adopt new ways of life and thought.

These things being so, it has seemed to me best to tell the story as life is presented on the stage, that is to say by a series of scenes divided by intervals of time. There will be a good deal in common between one scene and the next, between the age of Chaucer and the age of Caxton, the age of Dr Johnson and the age of Cobbett – but there will also be a good deal that is different.

To obtain a true picture of any period, both the old and the new elements must be borne in mind. Sometimes, in forming a mental picture of a period in the past, people seize hold of the new features and forget the overlap of the old. For example, students of history are often so much obsessed by the notorious political event of the Peterloo massacre that they imagine the Lancashire factory hand as the typical wage-earner of the year 1819; but he was not; he was only a local type, the newest type, the type of the future. The trouble was that the rest of old-fashioned society of the Regency period had not yet adjusted itself to the change heralded by his advent. They were annoyed with him, they could not place him, because he was not then, as he is now, the normal.

So then the method of this book is to present a series of successive scenes of English life, and the first of these scenes presented is the lifetime of Chaucer (1340–1400). I have already confessed that the reason why the book begins at that point is personal and accidental. But in fact it is a good starting-point. For in Chaucer's time the English people first clearly appear as a racial and cultural unit. The component races and languages have been melted into one. The upper class is no longer French, nor the peasant class Anglo-Saxon: all are English. England has ceased to be mainly a recipient of influences from without. Henceforward she gives forth her own. In the age of Chaucer, Wyclif, Wat Tyler, and the English bowmen, she is beginning to create her own island forms in literature, religion, economic society, and war. The forces moulding England are no longer foreign but native. She no longer owes her progress to great foreign churchmen and administrators, to Norman ideas of the feudal manor, to Angevin lawyer kings, to cavalry armed and trained on French models, to the friars coming over from Latin lands. Henceforward England creates her own types and her own customs.

When, in the Hundred Years War (1337–1453), the 'Goddams' (as Joan of Arc called them) set out to conquer France, they went there as foreign invaders, and their successes were due to the fact that England was already organized as a nation and conscious of her nationhood, while France as yet was not. And when that attempted conquest at length failed, England was left as a strange island anchored off the Continent, no longer a mere offshoot or extension of the European world.

It is true that there was nothing sudden in this growth of our distinctive nationhood. The process neither began nor ended in the lifetime of Chaucer. But during those years the principle is more active and more observable than in the three previous centuries, when the Christian and feudal civilization of Europe, including England, was not national but cosmopolitan. In the England of Chaucer's time we have a nation.

The publishers' grateful thanks are due to all those who have given permission for photographs to be taken of the MSS., printed books, pictures or antiquities in their care or ownership, or have allowed photographs in their possession to be reproduced. Full details of such ownership, etc., will be found in the descriptive notes for each item.

CHAUCER'S ENGLAND

FIELD, VILLAGE, AND MANOR-HOUSE

In Chaucer's England we see for the first time the modern mingling with the medieval, and England herself beginning to emerge as a distinct nation, no longer a mere oversea extension of Franco-Latin Europe. The poet's own works register the greatest modern fact of all, the birth and general acceptance of our language, the Saxon and French words happily blended at last into 'English tongue' which 'all understanden', and which is therefore coming into use as the vehicle of school teaching and of legal proceedings. There were indeed various provincial dialects of English, besides the totally distinct Welsh and Cornish. And some classes of society had a second language: the more learned of the clergy had Latin, and the courtiers and well-born had French, no longer indeed their childhood's tongue but a foreign speech to be learnt

after the school of Stratford-atte-Bowe.[1]

Chaucer, who spent long hours of his busy day in Court circles, had the culture of medieval France at his fingers' ends:

1.   Some can French and no Latin
That have used courts and dwelled therein:
And some can of Latin a party
That can French full febelly:
And some understandeth English
That neither can Latin nor French:
But lerid and lewid [learned and ignorant], old and young
All understanden English tongue.

So, in Chaucer's day, wrote William Nassyngton.

when therefore he set the pattern of modern English poetry for centuries to come, he set it in forms and metres derived from France and Italy, in both of which countries he had travelled several times on business of State. None the less he struck a new English note. It was he who, in the *Canterbury Tales*, gave the first full expression of 'the English sense of humour', one quarter cynical and three quarters kindly, that we do not look for in Dante, Petrarch, or the *Roman de la Rose*, and do not find even in Boccaccio or Froissart.

Other characteristics of the new-born nation were expressed in Langland's religious allegory, *Piers Plowman*. Though he too was a learned poet and a Londoner most of his life, he was by origin a Malvern man, and used the form still common in the West country, the alliterative blank verse derived from Anglo-Saxon poetry. That native English form was soon to be generally displaced by Chaucer's rhymings, but the spirit of *Piers Plowman* lived on in the religious earnestness of our fathers, their continual indignation at the wrongdoing of others and their occasional sorrow for their own. English Puritanism is much older than the Reformation, and the two 'dreamers', Piers the Plowman and Bunyan the tinker, are more alike in imagination and in feeling than any other two writers divided by three centuries.

While Langland and Gower, without straying into heresy, bewailed the corruptions of medieval society and religion, looking back to the ideals of the past rather than forward to a different future, Wyclif hammered out red-hot a programme of change, most of which was long afterwards put into force by English anti-clericalism and English Protestantism. An open Bible in the new common tongue of England was part of this programme. Meanwhile John Ball asked in medieval terms the most modern question of all:

When Adam delved and Evé span
Who was then a gentleman ?

For in the economic sphere also the medieval was beginning to yield to the modern, and England was beginning to develop social classes peculiar to herself. The break-up of the feudal manor and the commutation of field-serfdom were proceeding apace. The demand advanced by the rebellious peasants that all Englishmen should be freemen has a familiar sound today, but it was then a novelty and it cut at the base of the existing social fabric. Those workmen who already enjoyed this boon of freedom, were constantly on strike for higher pay in approved modern English fashion. Moreover, the employers against whom these strikes were directed were not so much the old feudal lords as new middle classes of leasehold farmers, manufacturers, and merchants. The cloth trade, destined to make the wealth and remould the society of England, was already in the reign of Edward III fast encroaching on the medieval marketing of our raw wool overseas. And the State was already making intermittent attempts to unite the interests of the mutually jealous medieval towns in a common policy of protection and control for the trade of the nation.

In pursuit of this policy, sea-power must be maintained in home waters, and Edward III's new gold coinage represents him standing armed and crowned in a ship [1]. Chaucer's merchant

> Wold the see were kept for anything
> Betwixt Middleburgh and Orewell

1. Edward III's new gold coinage

(namely, between Holland and Suffolk). National self-consciousness is beginning to dissolve the local loyalties and the rigid class divisions which had characterized the cosmopolitan society of the feudal age. And so, in the Hundred Years War to plunder France, the King and nobles find themselves supported by a new force, a democratic jingoism of the modern type, taking the place of feudal polity and warfare. At Crécy and Agincourt, that 'stout yeoman', the archer, is in the forefront of his country's battle, fighting shoulder to shoulder with the dismounted knights and nobles of England and shooting down, in heaps of men and horses, the antiquated chivalry of France [2].

The institution of justices of the peace, local gentry appointed by the Crown to govern the neighbourhood in the King's name, was a move away from inherited feudal jurisdictions. But it was also a reversal of the movement towards bureaucratic royal centralization: it recognized and used local connexions and influence for the King's purposes, a compromise significant of the future development of English society as distinct from that of other lands.

All these movements – economic, social, ecclesiastical, national – are reflected in the proceedings of Parliament, a characteristically medieval institution in origin, but already on the way to be modernized. It is not merely a council of great nobles, churchmen, judges, and civil servants, brought together to advise or harass the King. The Commons are already acquiring a limited importance of their own. In high politics it may be that the members of the Lower House are only pawns in the game of rival parties at Court, but on their own account they voice the economic policy of the new middle classes in town and village, often selfish enough; they express the nation's anger at the misconduct of the war by land and sea, and the perpetual demand for better order and stronger justice at home, not to be had till Tudor times.

Thus the age of Chaucer speaks to us with many voices not unintelligible to the modern ear. Indeed we may be tempted to think that we 'understanden' more than in fact we do. For these ancestors of ours, in one half of their thoughts and acts, were still guided by a complex of intellectual, ethical, and social assumptions of which only medieval scholars can today comprehend the true purport.

The most important of the changes proceeding during the lifetime of Chaucer (1340–1400) was the break-up of the feudal manor. Farm leases and money wages were increasingly taking the place of cultivation of the lord's demesne by servile labour, so beginning the gradual transformation of the English village

2. 'The archer in the forefront of his country's battle'

from a community of semi-bondsmen to an individualist society in which all were at least legally free, and in which the cash nexus had replaced customary rights. This great change broke the mould of the static feudal world and liberated mobile forces of capital, labour, and personal enterprise, which in the course of time made a richer and more varied life in town and village, and opened out new possibilities to trade and manufacture as well as to agriculture.

In order to understand the meaning of this change, it is necessary to give a brief account of the older system that was gradually displaced.

The most characteristic, though by no means the only, method of cultivation in medieval England was the 'open field'.[1] It was established throughout the Midlands from the Isle of Wight to the Yorkshire Wolds. It implied a village community, working huge unenclosed fields on a principle of strip allotments. Each farmer had a certain number of arable strips, of half an acre or one acre each. His long, narrow strips did not lie next to one another in a compact farm, which would have involved the expense of hedging; they were scattered over the 'open field' between those of his neighbours.

The outline of many of these 'strips', ploughed by the farmers of Saxon, medieval, and Tudor–Stuart times can still clearly be seen. The 'ridge and furrow' of pasture-fields that once were arable is one of the commonest features of the English landscape today. The long, raised, round-backed 'ridges' or 'lands', were divided from one another by drains or 'furrows', made by the turn of the plough in order to carry off the water.[2] Often, though not always, the curved 'ridge' or 'land', thus clearly visible today, represents a 'strip' that was held and worked long ago by a peasant farmer, who also held and

1. See C. S. Orwin, *The Open Fields* (1938), for the best account of the system.

2. The first sentences of Dorothy Wordsworth's *Journal*, written after a night of rain, illustrate the nature and appearance of this system of surface drainage, once almost universal in English ploughlands:

'Alfoxden, 20 Jan., 1798. The green paths down the hillsides are channels for streams. *The young wheat is streaked by silver lines of water running between the ridges.*'

3. The open-field system, Laxton village, Nottinghamshire

4. 'The ridge and furrow of pasture fields that once were arable';
Crimscote, near Whitchurch, Warwickshire

worked many other strips in other parts of the 'open field'. The strips were not, in most cases, divided from one another by grass balks, but only by the open drain made by the plough [3, 4].

The strips or 'lands' were not severally enclosed. The whole vast 'open field' was surrounded, when necessary, not by permanent hedges but by movable hurdles. There might be two, three, or more of these great arable 'fields' belonging to the village and subdivided among the farmers; one of the fields lay fallow while the others were under crop.

The meadowlands for hay were cultivated on a similar principle. Both meadowland and arable, after hay and corn had been cut, were thrown open for common pasture, the grazing rights being ascribed to each man by stints and regulations settled by the village community as a whole, to do justice to each of its members.

This system of cultivation, originated by the first Anglo-Saxon settlers, lasted down to the time of the modern enclosures. It was economically sound as long as the object of each farmer was to raise food for his family rather than for the market. It combined the advantages of individual labour and public control; it saved the expense of fencing; it gave each farmer a fair share in the better and worse land; it bound the villagers together as a community, and gave to the humblest his own land and his voice in the agricultural policy to be followed for the year by the whole village.

On this democracy of peasant cultivators was heavily superimposed the feudal power and legal rights of the lord of the manor. The peasant cultivators, in relation to each other were a self-governing community, but in relation to the lord of the manor they were serfs. They had not the legal right to leave their holdings: they were *ascripti glebae*, 'bound to the soil'. They must grind their corn at the lord's mill [6]. They could not give their children in marriage without his consent. Above all they owed him field service on certain days of the year, when they must labour not on their own land but on his, under the orders of his bailiff [5]. In some villages many of the strips in the great field belonged to the lord; but he also had in most cases a compact demesne land of his own.

This system of servile tenure with the fixed 'workdays' of service on the lord's demesne held good all over England, not only in the regions of open-field strip cultivation, but in the south-east, the west, and the north, lands of old enclosure where other systems of cultivation were practised. The Norman lawyers had made the feudal law of the manor more or less uniform for all England. In Norman and early Plantagenet times the typical rural village was a society, constituted by the lord of the manor or his agents on the one side and by his peasant serfs on the other. The freeman were few and far

5. Working under the lord's bailiff

6. Taking corn to be ground at the lord's mill

between, fewer than they had been in Anglo-Saxon times, particularly in the Danelaw.

But, for a true picture of medieval agriculture in England, we must never forget sheep-farming and the shepherd's life. Our island produced the best wool in Europe, and had for centuries supplied the Flemish and Italian looms with material with which they could not dispense for luxury production, and which they could get nowhere else. The woolsack, the symbolic seat of England's Chancellor, was the true wealth of the King and of his subjects, rich and poor, cleric and lay, supplying them with coin over and above the food they wrung from the soil and themselves consumed. Not only the distinctively pastoral regions, the great Yorkshire dales and the Cotswold hills and Sussex downs and the green oozy islands of the fens, but ordinary arable farms had sheep in abundance. Not only the great sheep-farming barons, bishops, and abbots – with their flocks counted by thousands and tens of thousands, tended by professional shepherds – but the peasants of ordinary manors themselves dealt in wool, and often together owned more sheep than were fed on the lord's demesne. Indeed the proportion of English sheep reared by the peasants was increasing in the reign of Edward III as against the number reared by lay and ecclesiastical landlords [7, 8].[1]

The lifetime of Chaucer roughly corresponds with the years when the disruption of the old manorial system was in most rapid and painful progress. But the change was not complete till long after his death. and it had begun long before his birth. As early as the twelfth century the lords of a number of manors had adopted a custom of commuting, for money rents, the forced services due on their demesne lands. The serfs did not thereby become freemen in the eye of the law, they were still subject to other servile dues, and even their liability to work for certain days on their lord's land might be revived if he chose to renew his claim. Meanwhile it stood commuted from year to year. For experience had taught the bailiff that the demesne was better cultivated by hired men working all the year round, than by the grudging service of farmers called

1. See Eileen Power, *Medieval English Wool Trade*, 1941, chap. 11.

28

off from labour on their own strips, only on such 'workdays' as the custom of the manor assigned to the lord. In some cases the villeins themselves actually preferred the old system of personal service.

The commutation of field services had thus made some headway before the twelfth century closed. But in the following century the process was very frequently reversed. 'Workdays', for which money payments had been substituted in the age of Becket, were being again demanded in the age of Simon de Montfort, and in some cases new burdens were imposed. A

rvm c xvii kl' iunlis

7. The shepherd's life

8. Peasants keep sheep

general tightening up and defining of the lords' claims characterized the thirteenth century, particularly on certain great
ecclesiastical estates where commutation had formerly been
creeping in.

One cause of this 'feudal reaction' was the rapid increase of
population and the consequent land-hunger of the thirteenth
century. As the families of the villeins multiplied, the number
of strips in the open field assigned to a single farmer grew less.
The pressure of population on the means of subsistence, and the
competition for land to farm, enabled the lord's bailiff to drive
harder bargains with the villeins, and to re-enforce or enforce
more strictly the demand for field work on the home farm as
the condition for tenure of other lands.

When therefore the fourteenth century began, the lords of
the manors were in a strong position. But then the tide turned
once more. The increase of population had slowed down in the
reign of Edward II and it was again becoming usual to commute field services for money rents, when the disaster of the
Black Death (1348-9) came to speed the change.

When a third or possibly a half of the inhabitants of the
Kingdom died of plague in less than two years, what was the
effect on the social and economic position in the average
English village? Obviously the survivors among the peasantry
had the whip-hand of the lord and his bailiff. Instead of the
recent hunger for land there was a shortage of men to till it.
The value of farms fell and the price of labour went up at a
bound. The lord of the manor could no longer cultivate his
demesne land with the reduced number of serfs, while many
of the strip-holdings in the open fields were thrown back on
his hands, because the families that farmed them had died of
plague.

But the lord's difficulty was the peasant's opportunity. The
number of strips in the open field held by a single farmer were
increased by the amalgamation of derelict holdings; and the
villein cultivators of these larger units became in effect middle-
class yeomen employing hired labour. Naturally they rebelled
all the more against their own servile status and against the
demands of the bailiff that they should still perform their
'workdays' in person on the lord's demesne. Meanwhile free

labourers who had no land were able, in the general scarcity of hands, to demand much higher wages than before, whether from the bailiff of the demesne or from the farmers of the open field.

Some lords still relied on the compulsory labour of the serfs to cultivate the home farm, but the decreased numbers and the increasing recalcitrance of the villagers from whom such services were due clogged the wheels of the old system. Often, when the bailiff pressed a villein to perform his field work, he 'fled' to better himself on the other side of the forest, where every town and every village was so short of labour after the Black Death that high wages were given to immigrants, and no questions asked as to whence they came. A serf, 'bound to the soil' of a manor by law, might detach himself in physical reality, unless indeed he was encumbered by a wife and children whose migration was more difficult. Such 'flights' of single villeins, usually the young and energetic men, left on the lord's hands the holding in the open field that the fugitive had deserted, and often there was no one willing to take it except for a low money rent.

More and more, therefore, as Chaucer was growing to manhood, the lords abandoned the attempt to cultivate their demesne lands by the old method, and consented to commute field services for cash. Since there was more coin per head of the reduced population, it was easier for the serf to save or borrow enough shillings to buy his freedom and to pay money rent for his farm. And many of the peasants kept sheep, by the sale of whose wool they obtained coin to buy their freedom.

With the money received in lieu of field service, the lords could offer wages to free labourers. But they could seldom offer enough, because the price of labour was now so high. Many landlords therefore ceased to cultivate the demesne themselves, and let it on lease to a new class of yeoman farmer. These farmers often took over the lord's cattle on a stock-and-land lease. Sometimes they paid money rents, but often it was agreed that they should pay in kind, supplying the household of the manor with its food and drink. The lord's 'family' had always been fed from the produce of the home farm and, now that it was let, the old kindly connexion was continued with mutual convenience. On some manors in pastoral districts

9. Sowing grain

where the peasants grew rich by selling wool, the bondage
tenants took a lease of the whole of the lord's demesne and
divided it among themselves.

In a number of different ways, therefore, new classes of sub-
stantial yeomen came into existence. Some of them farmed the
lord's demesne, others the new lands lately enclosed from the
waste, others took over strips in the old open field [9]. Some
dealt in corn, others in sheep and wool, others in a mixed
husbandry. The increase in their numbers and prosperity set
the tone of the new England for centuries to come. The motif
of the English yeoman – h s independence, his hearty good
nature, his skill in archery [10] – fills the ballads from the time
of the Hundred Years War to the Stuart era.[1]

The wide gap between lord and villein that had characterized
the society of the feudal manor is being filled up. Indeed the
villein serf is in process of extinction. He is becoming a yeoman
farmer, or else a landless labourer. And between these two
classes enmity is now set. The peasantry are divided among
themselves as employers and employed, and an early phase of
their strife is seen in the famous 'Statutes of Labourers'.

1. The word 'yeoman' meant any sort of countryman of the
middling classes, usually a farmer, but sometimes a servant or an
armed retainer (like the Knight's and the Canon's yeomen in the
Canterbury Tales). In the earlier ballads Robin Hood is not a disguised
earl but a yeman '. The idea that a yeoman must be a freeholder
owning his own land is very late indeed.

10. Practising at the butts

These Parliamentary laws to keep down wages were passed at the petition of the Commons, at the instance of the smaller gentry and tenant farmers – 'husbands and land-tenants' as the Statutes called them. The policy was dictated by the new agricultural middle class rather than by the old-fashioned feudal magnates, though the great landlords supported the demand of their tenants, because high wages indirectly endangered the payment of rents. But the direct quarrel lay between two classes of peasants, the small farmer and the landless labourer whom he hired: their fathers might have worked their strips of land side by side in the village field and laboured together as serfs on the lord's demesne, but the sons' interests were opposed.

These Parliamentary laws in restraint of wages mark the gradual change from a society based on local customs of personal service to a money economy that is nation wide. Each medieval manor had been governed by its own custom, which had now in many cases broken down, and here we have an early attempt of Parliament to substitute national control. The avowed purpose of the Statutes of Labourers is to prevent the rise of wages, and to a lesser degree of prices also. Special justices are appointed to enforce the Parliamentary rates, and to punish those who demand more.

So the battle of the landless labourers against the farmers backed by the Parliamentary justices went on, from the time of the Black Death to the rising of 1381 and after. Strikes, riots, and the formation of local unions were met by prosecution and imprisonment. But on the whole the victory lay with the wage-earner, because of the shortage of labour caused by the great pestilence and by its continual local recurrence. Prices indeed rose, but wages rose faster still. During this period the landless labourer stood in the fortunate position described by Piers Plowman:

> Labourers that have no land to live on but their hands
> Deigned not dine a-day on worts a night old.
> May no penny-ale pay, nor no piece of bacon,
> But if it be fresh flesh or fish fried or baked
> And chaude or plus chaude [hot and hotter]
>   for chill of their maw
> And but if he be highly hired else will he grieve
> And that he was workman wrought wail the time
> [And bewail the time when he was born a working man.]
> And then curseth he the King and all his council after
> Such laws to loke [enforce] labourers to grieve.[1]

So let us leave the landless labourer, eating, occasionally at least, his dinner of hot meat, or growling seditiously over his cold bacon and stale cabbage, and turn back to the small peasant cultivator, the farmer of the open-field strips. How was it going with his fight for freedom – while Chaucer was reaching plump and prosperous middle age at the Court of the boy King Richard?

On some manors the change in the relation between landlord and tenant had taken place without a struggle, in accordance with the clearly perceived interest of both parties to replace villein services by money rents. But even on manors where field service had thus been commuted, the lords often continued to claim other servile dues: such were the *merchet*, the fine paid for marriage; the *heriot*, the seizure of the family's best beast on the death of a tenant; the compulsory use of the lord's mill for grinding the family corn at a monopoly price – and many more such galling instances of servitude. The half-freed farmers would be content with nothing less than com-

1. B. VI, pp. 308–19.

plete emancipation, and the status of freemen before the law with all the rights of the *liber homo* of Magna Carta. Moreover, on many estates the attempt was still being made to enforce the field work of the villein on the demesne lands, rendering strife yet more acute.

The battle for freedom, differing in its precise character from manor to manor and from farm to farm, led to sporadic acts of violence that prepared the way for the rising of 1381. The preamble of a statute passed by the Parliament of 1377 is significant. The lords of manors, 'as well men of Holy Church as other', complain that the villeins on their estates

affirm them to be quit and utterly discharged of all manner of serfage, due as well of their body as of their tenures, and will not suffer any distress or other justice to be made upon them; but do menace the ministers of their lords of life and member, and, which more is, gather themselves in great routs and agree by such confederacy that every one shall aid other to resist their lords with strong hand.[1]

If such had for years been the state of the countryside, we can better understand the astonishing events of 1381. In the villages within a hundred miles of London, and in many regions yet more distant to west and north, unions of labourers to resist the Parliamentary laws fixing wages, and unions of villein farmers to resist the custom of the manor, had taught whole communities to defy the governing class by passive and active resistance. Nor was social discontent confined to the village. In the market towns overshadowed by great abbeys, like St Albans and Bury St Edmunds, not only the serfs but the burghers were at constant strife with the monks who refused the municipal liberties which successive kings had readily sold to towns fortunate enough to have grown up on royal land.

The English rebels were not, like the *jacquerie* of France, starving men driven to violence by despair. In wealth and independence their position was improving fast, but not fast enough to satisfy their new aspirations. And many of them had the self-respect and discipline of soldiers, having been armed and drilled in the militia. Not a few of the famous

1. *Statutes of the Realm*, 11, p. 2.

11. 'Many of the English rebels had the self-respect and discipline of soldiers'

English longbowmen were found in the rebel ranks. And in the forests lurked formidable allies of the movement, Robin Hood bands of outlaws, peasants whom upper-class justice had driven to the greenwood, professional poachers, broken men, criminals, and discharged soldiers of the French war.

These various formidable elements of social revolt had been inflamed by a propaganda of Christian Democracy, demanding in God's name freedom and justice for the poor. Such was the preaching of John Ball and of many itinerant priests and friars [11]. And the parish priest, being usually of much the same class as the villein farmer, often sympathized with his desire for freedom. The idealism of the movement was Christian, in most cases not unorthodox, though some of Wyclif's Lollard preachers were involved. But whether orthodox or heretic, the rebels had lost all respect for the privileges of the wealthy Churchmen, 'the Caesarean clergy' allied to the upper class in resistance to the demands of the poor. The rich monasteries, prelates, or laymen, who took the tithe of the parish and starved the parson, were hateful alike to the priest and his parishioners.

In the south-eastern half of England, the chief area of the revolt, the monasteries were specially unpopular, and suffered much from the violence of the rebels. The Prior of Bury St Edmunds was murdered by his own serfs. In London, Wat Tyler's men beheaded the Archbishop of Canterbury on Tower Hill, because as Chancellor of the realm he represented the unpopular government. In revenge, the fighting Bishop of Norwich led in person the army that suppressed the rising in East Anglia. Thus the equalitarian and the conservative elements, always present together in the Christian Church, were for a while at open war with one another.

The rising originated from an unpopular poll-tax. Its oppressive and corrupt administration caused local revolts in Essex and Kent, which became the signal for a national rebellion in no less than twenty-eight counties. The word was

12. Wat Tyler's men beheading the Archbishop of Canterbury on Tower Hill

sent round by the popular leaders that 'John Ball hath rungen your bell'. Headed sometimes by the parish priest, sometimes by old archers, in a few cases by sympathetic gentry, the half-armed villagers and townsfolk rose. They invaded the manor-houses and abbeys, extorted the rights they claimed, and burnt obnoxious charters and manor rolls. Some murders were committed, and the gentry fled from their homes to hide in the thickets of the woods, whence the outlaws had just emerged.

Then took place the most remarkable incident of our long social history – the capture of London. Many of the village bands had been advised to march on the capital, where the popular leaders had allies. The London mob and a party among the aldermen opened the gates to the rustic armies. The panic of the governing class was such that the impregnable royal fortress of the Tower was surrendered to the rebels, much as the Bastille was surrendered in 1789. Unpopular characters were murdered, including the mild Archbishop Sudbury, whose head was placed over London Bridge [12]. Lawyers were specially obnoxious. And a massacre of foreign artisans was perpetrated by their trade rivals.[1]

The cause of law and order had been lost by the poltroonery of the Government; it was revindicated, partly by courage and partly by fraud. The boy King Richard II, whom the rebels had everywhere declared to be on their side, met their London army at Mile End and granted commutation of all servile dues for a rent of four pence an acre, and a free pardon for all the rebels. Thirty clerks were set to work drawing up charters of liberation and of pardon for the men of each village and manor, as well as more generally for every shire. After this great concession, which satisfied the majority of the rebels, it became possible to deal sternly with the more recalcitrant. Wat Tyler was slain at Smithfield in the presence of the mob he led [13]. After that bold stroke by Mayor Walworth, the

1. The only reference in the *Canterbury Tales* to the events of 1381 occurs in *The Nun's Priest's Tale* when the farm hands are chasing the fox:

> Certés Jack Straw and his meinie
> Ne maden never shoutes half so shrille
> When that they wolden any Fleming kille
> As thilke day was made upon the fox.

13. Wat Tyler slain at Smithfield in the presence of the mob he led

upper class recovered its courage, called out its men-at-arms, put down the rising in London and in the provinces, and punished it with cruel severity. The charters of liberation, which had served their turn, were repealed by Parliament as having been extorted under duress.

The rebellion had been a great incident, and its history throws a flood of light on the English folk of that day. Historians cannot decide whether it helped or retarded the movement for the abolition of serfdom, which continued at much the same pace after 1381 as before. But the spirit that had prompted the rising was one of the chief reasons why serfdom died out in England, as it did not die out on the Continent of Europe.

Personal freedom became universal at an early date in our country, and this probably is one reason for the ideological attachment of Englishmen to the very name of 'freedom'. But many of the serfs won this freedom at the price of divorce from the soil; and the ever increasing wealth of the country was accompanied by greater inequalities of income. The feudal manor under its lord had been a community of serfs, all poor, but nearly all with rights of their own in the land to which they were bound; the land was tied to them as well as they to the land. The modern village under the squire was a society of wealthy farmers, village craftsmen, and a proletariat of free but landless labourers constantly drifting off to the towns. The change from the one form of society to the other was long drawn out through centuries, from the twelfth to the nineteenth.

Typical of the new England of Chaucer's day was the yeoman farmer, Clement Paston, whose descendants became great landowners and politicians in East Anglia in the following century. Of him it was told that –

He was a good plain husband[man], and lived upon his land that he had in Paston, and kept thereon a plough all times in the year, and sometimes in barleysell two ploughs. The said Clement yede [went] at one plough both winter and summer, and he rode to mill on the bare horseback with his corn under him, and brought home meal again under him; and also drove his cart with divers corns to Wynterton to sell, as a good husband[man] ought to do. Also, he had in Paston a five score or a six score acres of land at the most [about four times a normal villein holding], and much thereof bondland to Gemyngham Hall, with a little poor water-mill running by the river there. Other livelode nor manors had he none, nor in none other place [6, 14–16].

Himself free, he married 'a bondwoman'. He saved enough money to send their son to school and thence to the law, and so founded the fortunes of the famous Norfolk family that in two generations acquired many manors in many another 'place' – and left to posterity the *Paston Letters*.

The story of the rising of 1381 reminds us how ill policed was the England of that day and how weak the arm of the law. Murder, rape, beating, and robbery by violence were everyday incidents. Lord, miller, and peasant must each guard his own family, property, and life. The King's peace had never been

14. Ploughing with oxen

15. The water-mill (with eel-traps set in the mill stream)

16. Carrying the corn uphill

very strong, but it had probably been stronger in the reign of Edward I and possibly even under Henry II. The Hundred Years War enriched individuals with plunder and ransoms from France, and swelled the luxury of court and castle, but was a curse to the country as a whole. It increased disorder and violence, by raising the fighting nobility and their retainers above the control of the Crown.

The King was powerless to act against the great nobles, because his military resources were the resources commanded by the nobles themselves. His army consisted, not of his own Life Guards and regiments of the line, but of numerous small bodies of archers and men-at-arms enlisted and paid by earls and barons, knights and professional soldiers of fortune, who hired out their services to the Government for a greater or less time. Such troops might do well for the French war, and might rally round the throne on an occasion like the Peasants' Rising, when all the upper classes were threatened by a common danger. But they could scarcely be used to suppress themselves, or to arrest the employers whose badges they wore on their coats, and whose pay jingled in their pockets. Once indeed, in 1378, the Commons insisted that a special commission should be sent into the country to restore order. But the new body was necessarily composed of great lords and their retainers, who were soon found to be even more intolerable than the lawbreakers whom they were sent to suppress. The Commons next year asked that they might be recalled, as the King's subjects were being brought into 'serfage to the said Seigneurs and commissioners and their retinues'.

A very similar story is told in *Piers Plowman*, where 'Peace' comes to Parliament with a petition against 'Wrong', who, in his capacity of King's officer, has broken into the farm, ravished the women, carried off the horses, taken wheat from the granary, and left in payment a tally on the King's exchequer. 'Peace' complains that he has been unable to get the law of him, for 'he maintaineth his men to murder mine own'. Such were the King's officers as known in the country districts. They were really ambitious lords using the King's name to acquire wealth for themselves. These evils were partly the result of the bankruptcy of the government. The King could not change the military system, because he could not hire men to take the place of the nobles' retainers. He had to accept the aid of the lords for the French wars very much on their own terms.

Yet the peasant profited as much as he lost by the absence of police. The villein farmer striving for freedom, the free workman in constant revolt against the Statute of Labourers, were neither of them in such real subjection to their 'betters' as the agricultural labourer in the well-policed countryside of the nineteenth century, when the poor had been deprived of bow and club, and had not yet been armed with the vote. In the fourteenth century, when every man was expected to 'take his own part' with stick or fist, with arrow or knife, a union of sturdy villagers was less easily overawed.

The military system by which England fought the Hundred Years War strengthened the power not of the King himself but of more than one class of his subjects. While the armies that invaded France were raised by the King contracting with lords and gentry for the service of their retainers, home defence was provided for by a militia compulsorily raised among the common people. And this conscript militia was so well armed and trained that the Scots often rued their temerity in invading the land while the King and nobles were away in France. The good yeoman archer 'whose limbs were made in England' was not a retrospective fancy of Shakespeare, but an unpleasant reality for French and Scots, and a formidable consideration for bailiffs and justices trying to enforce servile dues or statutory rates of wages in the name of law, which no one, high or low, regarded with any great respect [17, 18].[1]

1. The secret of that greater efficacy of which English archers had the monopoly in Europe lay in the fact that 'the Englishman did not keep his left hand steady, and draw his bow with his right; but the keeping his right at rest upon the nerve, he pressed the whole weight of his body into the horns of his bow. Hence probably arose the phrase "bending a bow", and the French of "drawing" one.' (W. Gilpin in *Remarks on Forest Scenery*, 1791.)

This is what Hugh Latimer meant when he described how he was early taught 'not to draw with strength of arms as divers other nations do, but with the strength of the body'. It was an art not easily learned.

17 and 18. 'Every man was expected to "take his own part" with stick

In most of the counties of England the King's writ ran, though it was often evaded or defied. Murderers and thieves, when not in the service of some great lord, were often obliged to fly to the greenwood, or to take sanctuary and then forswear the realm. Sometimes they were actually arrested and brought into court. Even then they often slipped through the meshes of law by pleading their 'clergy' or by some other lawyer's trick. But, at worst, a great many thieves and a few murderers were hanged by the King's justice every year. The engine of law worked in the greater part of England, though cumbrously, corruptly, and at random.

But in the counties bordering on Scotland the King's writ can scarcely be said to have run at all. War seldom ceased, and cattle-raiding never. On those roadless fells, society consisted of mounted clans of farmer-warriors, at feud among themselves and at war with the Scots. No man looked to the King's officers to protect or avenge him. In the land of the Border ballads all men were warriors and most women were heroines.

To Chaucer it was an unknown, distant, barbarous land – much further off than France – 'far in the North, I cannot tellen where'. There the Percies and other border chiefs were building magnificent castles to resist the siege of the King of Scotland's armies – Alnwick, Warkworth, Dunstanburgh, Chipchase, Belsay, and many more. The lesser gentry had their square 'peel towers', smaller copies of the castles of the great; there were no manor-houses, a product of relative peace. The peasants lived in wooden shanties that the raiders burnt

44

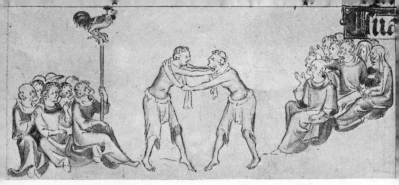

or fist, with arrow or knife'

as a matter of course, while the inhabitants and their cattle hid
in the woods or sheltered in the peels [19–21].

This state of things outlasted the Tudors who gave such
firm peace to the rest of England. Only after the union of the
Crowns on the head of James Stuart had made an end of
Border War (1603) did peaceful manor-houses begin to rise
beside the castles and peel towers of the north.

One result of this long continuance of warlike habits, amid a
sparse population, was that a greater familiarity between high
and low prevailed in those wild regions and lasted into modern
times. The moorland shepherd and the 'hind', as the northern
farm hand was called, never became as subject to 'squire and
farmer' as the pauper labourer of the south in days to come.
There was always a breath of freedom blowing off the moors.

While the north was still armed and fortified for war, and
while the Marcher lords still relied on their castles to hold
down the Welsh, in the more civilized parts of England it was
no longer usual for lords and gentlemen to build fortress-
homes meant to withstand the siege of a regular army. While
the Black Prince was ravaging France, war was no longer a
normal incident in the English countryside. But local violence
was always to be feared, whether from the retainers of a bad
neighbour, the rebellious peasants of the village, or outlaws
from the greenwood.

Modified precautions were therefore taken in the domestic
architecture of the day. The manor-houses that rose through-

45

19. Alnwick Castle, Northumberland

20. Peel tower – Smailholm Tower, Roxburghshire (note the girdling wall for enclosing retainers' huts and cattle)

21. The fortified tower of Great Salkeld Church, Cumberland

out the southern and midland counties were seldom more than two storeys high and they were not completely castellated; but they presented narrow shot-hole windows on the sides that overlooked the moat, across which entry was made by the drawbridge. The inner and safer aspect that looked on to an enclosed courtyard had larger windows and more domesticated architecture. The courtyard was surrounded by suites of rooms; the demands of luxurious living had recently added more accommodation to the high hall, parlour, and kitchen which had met the needs of a simpler age. Holes in the roof no longer sufficed to conduct the smoke of the hearth away from throats and eyes; noble fireplaces were now built in the dwelling rooms and great chimneys in the thickness of the walls. But the farm and the cottage were still without chimneys. Near the manor-house lay the formal garden or lady's pleasaunce, the traditional place for flirtation according to the poetry of the 'laws of love' [22, 23].

In hilly country a moat filled with water was less usual and the rise of ground took its place in the scheme of defence.

es seuent lanchier
e cors damagier
le trait premier

A pres ceste raison
p or ce que il uolo
i beaudrains fu h

22. A fireplace

Haddon Hall in Derbyshire is a perfect example of a half-fortified English manor-house, built round two courtyards and adapted by constant enlargements to the use of many succeeding generations [24]. In the west, fine houses were sometimes built of wood and plaster instead of stone, with a lessening regard for considerations of defence. Brick was very rare in England from the time of the departure of the Romans until the fifteenth century, when it came into general use in East Anglia and other regions where local stone was scarce, and where the timber of the forests was beginning to run short.

In Chaucer's day, life was already somewhat safer and a good deal more comfortable than in the warlike era when the most wealthy families had been crowded into the darkness of grim, square, Norman keeps. In the thirteenth century, Kenilworth Keep had resisted the force of the Kingdom for six months, but the cannon of the Hundred Years War would soon have breached its antique strength. Nor was it any longer regarded as tolerable quarters for a great man's court. John of Gaunt therefore built at its foot a palace with a banqueting hall, into which light flooded through wide windows of delicate tracery. But he took care to protect his new home, at each end, with a tower suitable to carry cannon.

While the square keeps of the Norman warriors were being deserted as no longer habitable, some of the finer Plantagenet castles were being enlarged and adapted to the uses of a new age. Not a few of them continued as royal or private palaces down to the time when Milton's *Comus* was acted in Ludlow Castle. Finally Cromwell's men stormed and dismantled a large proportion of the castles which had till then served as homes of the great.

The farms and cottages of the poor were built of logs or planks, or of uprights and beams supporting rubble and clay. The floors were usually bare earth, and the roof of thatch. But since these humble homes have disappeared, we know very little about them. Something has already been said about their

23. The formal garden or lady's pleasaunce

inhabitants, during this period of social change and strife. But nothing is more difficult to assess than the real degree of the peasants' poverty or well-being, which differed greatly not only from place to place but from year to year. Many of them by feeding sheep acquired considerable wealth by the sale of the wool; the great English wool mart was supplied largely by the peasants. Their bread and ale depended on the uncertain harvest of the common field, and in bad seasons there was local shortage or famine. But meat, cheese, and vegetables made up an equally important part of their diet. Many peasants kept poultry and ate the eggs. Most had a plot of land with their cottage, where peas, beans, or more primitive 'worts' were grown, and where sometimes a cow or pig was kept. The farmers of the open field, whether serf or free, had each his

24. Haddon Hall, Derbyshire (note the two courtyards of this half-fortified manor-house)

oxen on the village stubble and pasture; the poor beasts, half the size of modern cattle, were lean with scant fare and tough with years of tugging at the plough; but some were slaughtered every Martinmas to be salted for the winter's food, or were killed fresh for Christmas feasting [25-32].

Bacon was a more common dish on the cottage table; but the number of pigs in the village herd depended on the extent and character of the 'waste'. On some manors the heaths and woods had shrunk to small proportions before the encroachments of 'assart' farms enclosed for agriculture. In others, particularly in west and north, the waste was essential to the life of many families. Lonely squatters, with or without leave, built their huts and fed their beasts on some outlying bit of land. And every lawful villager required timber from the trees on the

25. Spinning and carding wool

26. Keeping poultry

27. Feeding swine

28. Cattle 'lean with scant fare'

29. 'The uncertain harvest of the common field'

30. Catching fish

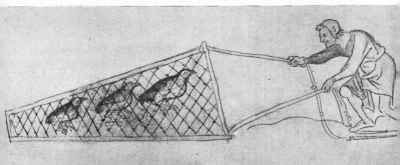

31. Netting partridges

32. Snaring rabbits

53

waste, to build his cottage, to warm his hearth and cook his food, to make his carts, ploughs, farm tools, and household furniture. The rights of the customary tenants differed from manor to manor, but often they had the privilege of cutting wood for building and carpentry, and of taking sticks for fuel by 'hook and crook', that is, by pulling branches from standing trees. The waste, too, meant pigpannage and extra pasture for cattle and sheep, the latter often the most valuable item in a peasant's budget by the sale of the wool. In these respects the comfort and wealth of the villager diminished as the cornfields encroached on wild nature. There was gain with loss and loss with store.

But there is other meat besides beef and mutton, poultry and bacon. The waste and the woodland swarmed with game. In the King's forests, an ever diminishing area, and in the warrens and enclosures of lords and gentry, which were always on the increase, the deer and lesser game were guarded by severe laws, and still more effectively by keepers who administered club law of their own without bothering the King's courts. Poaching was not only the livelihood of outlaws, but the passion of men of all classes – gentry, clerks of Holy Church, besides farmers and workmen seeking a pheasant or hare for the pot.[1]

In 1389 the Commons complained in Parliament that 'artificers and labourers, and servants and grooms keep greyhounds and other dogs, and on the holy days, when good Christian people be at Church, hearing divine service, they go hunting in parks, warrens, and coneyries of lords and others, to the very great destruction of the same'. Evil indeed is the heart of man! Henceforth let no layman with less than forty shillings a year in land, and no priest or clerk with less than ten pounds income a year, be so bold as to keep sporting nets or dogs. So the Statute decreed; how far it was observed may well be doubted.[2] There were, moreover, great regions of moor, fen,

---

1. The proverbial efficiency of 'the poacher turned gamekeeper' is as old as Chaucer:

> A thief of venison, that hath forlaft
> His likerousness and all his olde craft.
> Can kepe a forest best of any man. (*Doctor's Tale*)

2. *Statutes of the Realm*, ii, p. 65.

and woodland where game was not strictly preserved and could be taken with little or no risk of challenge.

Rabbits, then called 'coneys', were a plague in many parts of medieval England, and were snared and dug out by all classes, except in private warrens [32]. To take and eat small birds like thrushes and larks was then as usual in our island as it still is on the Continent; they were limed and netted in great numbers both by the peasants and by the sporting gentry [32]. But most of all did it rejoice the farmer's heart to slay secretly for his own pot one of the legion of privileged birds from the dovecot of the manor-house, whose function in life was to grow plump on the peasants' corn till they were fit for the lord's table.[1] Then there were trout in the streams and meres, and great pike in the 'stews' (ponds) of manor-house and abbey. Of Chaucer's Franklin we read –

> It snowed in his house of meat and drinke
> Of alle dainties that men coulde thinke.
> After the sundry seasons of the year,
> So changed he his meat and his supper.
> Full many a fat partridge had he in mewe [cage]
> And many a bream and many a luce in stewe
> [pike in fishpond] [30, 31, 34–6].

The gentry spent much of their lives hunting the deer with horse and hound, or flying hawks at pheasant, partridge, and heron, or lying out at night to net the fox and the badger [37–41]. Such field sports, and tilting in tournaments before the gallery of ladies, were the lighter sides of their life; the more serious were war abroad, and at home law-suits, national politics, and local administration.[2] The improvement of agricultural methods did not interest them as much as their

1. In the fifteenth century, the Fellows of King's College, Cambridge, ate or sold from two to three thousand doves a year from the great dovecot of their Grantchester estate.

2. The 'knights of the shire' (county members in the House of Commons) were busy in local administration. Miss Wood-Legh has ascertained that of 1,636 persons who were knights of the shire in the fifty-odd Parliaments of Edward III, 125 served as escheators, 371 as collectors at 'tenths and fifteenths' (taxes), 381 as sheriffs, and 641 as Justices of the Peace. Chaucer's Franklin is an example. (*Review of English Studies*, April 1928)

33. Netting song-birds

descendants. The historian of English farming has said: 'Feudal barons are rarely represented as fumbling in the recesses of their armour for samples of corn.'[1] But the break-up of the feudal manor, and the new opportunities it afforded of producing for the market, opened the way to agricultural improvement and thereby encouraged the landlord class to take a greater interest in farming methods. Indeed, Lord Berkeley, though very exceptional, was a great improver of his land, a fourteenth-century Coke of Norfolk.

By self-flattering fallacy, some of our city-bred folk today suppose that their ancestors, because they were accustomed to country sights and sounds on workdays as well as week-ends, cared nothing for the loveliness around them. No doubt many of them raised their eyes to nature's beauty as little as the Philistines of today. But the poetry of the age of Chaucer and Langland shows that they were by no means all so indifferent.

Here, in an alliterative poem of the mid fourteenth century, is a poacher's account of dawn in the woods as he waits for the deer:

> In the monethe of Maye when mirthes bene fele,
> And the sesone of somere when softe bene the wedres,
> Als I went to the wodde my werdes to dreghe,
> In-to the schawes my-selfe a schotte me to gete
> At ane hert or ane hynde, happen as it myghte:
> And as Dryghtyn the day droue from the heuen,
> Als I habade one a banke be a bryme syde,
> There the gryse was grene growen with floures –
> The primrose, the pervynke, and the piliole the riche –
> The dewe appon dayses donkede full faire.
> Burgons and blossoms and braunches full swete,
> And the mery mystes full myldely gane falle:
> The cukkowe, the cowschote, kene were they bothen,
> And the throstills full throly threpen in the bankes,
> And iche foule in that frythe faynere than other
> That the derke was done and the daye lightenede:
> Hertys and hyndes one hillys thay gouen,
> The foxe and the filmarte thay flede to the erthe,
> The hare hurkles by hawes, and harde thedir dryves,
> And ferkes faste to hir fourme and fatills hir to sitt.

1. Ernle, p. 31.

34 and 35. 'It snowed in his house of meat and drinke'

36. The lord of the manor's table

37 and 38. Hunting

39. Hawking

At last the hart appears, with tall antlers. The poet-poacher watches him, cross-bow in hand:

> And he statayde and stelkett and starede full brode,
> Bot at the laste he loutted doun and laugt till his mete
> And I hallede to the hokes and the herte smote,
> And happened that I hitt hym be-hynde the
>   lefte sholdire. . . .
> Dede as a dorenayle doun was he fallen.[1]

The poet then hides the body lest the gamekeepers should find it.

In men's dress, as well as in so much else, the beginning of

1. *The Parlement of the Three Ages*, ed. Gollancz, 1915. The

40. 'Tilting in tournaments before the gallery'

the change from medieval to modern might be ascribed to the age of Chaucer. He himself, like Dante, is known to us clad in the dignified long gown and plain hood – the distinctively medieval dress that the Franciscan brotherhood still preserves in our midst in its simplest form. But Chaucer's fashionable contemporaries, especially the younger sort, abandoned the decent gown for a short coat or jacket and displayed the symmetry of their legs in tight-fitting 'hosen'. The new mode resembled in fundamental form the 'coat and trousers' of the modern male biped, but by no means in our drab detail and monotony of dullness. In Richard II's court, coats and 'hosen' blazed with colour. One leg might be draped in red, the other in blue. Men 'wore their estates on their backs', and flashed in jewels and costly stuffs no less than their wives. Following the fashion of an extravagant court, gilded youth was every-where 'expressed in fancy'. Sleeves 'slod upon the earth'; shoes with long toe-points chained to the waist prevented the wearer from kneeling to say his prayers [42–6].

The long gown did not, however, go out of use among the more sober part of mankind till Tudor times. And sometimes

---

following is the translation of these lines given in H. S. Bennett's *Life on the English Manor*, p. 271:

'In May, when there are many things to enjoy, and in the summer season when airs are soft, I went to the wood to take my luck, and in among the shaws to get a shot at hart or hind, as it should happen. And, as the Lord drove the day through the heavens, I stayed on a bank beside a brook where the grass was green and starred with flowers – primroses, periwinkles, and the rich pennyroyal. The dew dappled the daisies most beautifully, and also the buds, blossoms, and branches, while around me the soft mists began to fall. Both the cuckoo and pigeon were singing loudly, and the throstles in the banksides eagerly poured out their songs, and every bird in the wood seemed more delighted than his neighbour that darkness was done and the daylight returned. Harts and hinds betake themselves to the hills; the fox and polecat seek their earths; the hare squats by the hedges, hurries and hastens thither to her forme and prepares to lurk there.

The hart paused, went on cautiously, staring here and there, but at last he bent down and began on his feed. Then I hauled to the hook [i.e. the trigger of the cross-bow] and smote the hart. It so happened that I hit him behind the left shoulder . . . he had fallen down, dead as a door nail.

41. 'Cloth of Arras', one of the Hardwick Hunting Tapestries (deer-hunting and hawking)

42. 'In Richard II's court, coats and "hosen" blazed with colour'

43. Chaucer in 'long gown and plain hood'

44. The 'magnificence and outlay' of the feudal lord

45. The Parliament at Westminster

the gown itself became an extravagance; men of high rank wore rich gowns trailing behind them on the ground as if they were women. Both men and women of fashion wore enormous head-dresses of fantastic shape, like horns, turbans, or towers.

With much absurd and ephemeral luxury came in much solid comfort and new habits of life that have survived. Now for the first time in our country, gentlemen's families retired from the great hall where they used to feed in patriarchal community with their household, and ate their more fashionable meals in private. The tribute and plunder of France that had been poured into England during the early and more successful part of the Hundred Years War revolutionized the primitive economy of the English feudal household, just as, among the ancient Romans, the tribute and plunder of the Mediterranean overturned the austere simplicity of Camillus and Cato. French nobles, taken in war, waited sometimes for years till their ransoms could be wrung from their peasants, and meanwhile they lived as honoured guests in the country houses of their English captors; they hunted with the men, made love to the ladies, and taught English provincial simplicity that every gentleman must have this fashion in his clothes or that dish on his table.

Under such tutors luxury increased, and with it commerce grew and refinement spread by the very means which the moralists denounced. The merchants of the town rejoiced to supply the noblemen's courts with every new fashion and requirement, in dress, furniture, or food. By their own magnificence and outlay the feudal lords were helping the rise of the mercantile classes who were one day to take their place. Most of our town manufactures and overseas commerce, and almost all European trade with the East were conducted to supply the luxuries of castle and manor-house, and not, as in modern times, the needs of the mass of the population. English towns and English trade would have made little headway in those days if they had catered only for the farm and the cottage, which produced their own food, while almost all their clothing, furniture, and farm implements were home-made either by the peasant family itself or by the craftsmen of the village.

46. Chaucer reading his poems to a noble company

CHAUCER'S ENGLAND

TOWN AND CHURCH

In the fourteenth century the English town was still a rural and agricultural community, as well as a centre of industry and commerce. It had its stone wall or earth mound to protect it, distinguishing it from an open village. But outside lay the 'town field' unenclosed by hedges, where each citizen-farmer cultivated his own strips of cornland; and each grazed his cattle or sheep on the common pasture of the town, which usually lay along the riverside as at Oxford and Cambridge.[1] In 1388 it was laid down by Parliamentary Statute that in harvest time journeymen and apprentices should be called on to lay aside their crafts and should be compelled 'to cut gather and bring in the corn'; mayors, bailiffs, and constables of towns were to see this done.[2] In Norwich, the second city of the Kingdom, the weavers, till long after this period, were conscripted every year to fetch home the harvest. Even London was no exception to the rule of a half-rustic life. There was none of the rigid division between rural and urban which has prevailed since the Industrial Revolution. No Englishman then was ignorant of all country things, as the great majority of Englishmen are today [47–50].

The town was more insanitary than the village and was often visited by plague. But it was not, as in later centuries, crowded thick with slums. Its houses still stood pleasantly amid gardens,

1. Cambridge was protected not by walls but by water, the river on the west, the King's ditch on the east.
2. *Statutes of the Realm*, 11, 56.

47. Constantinople drawn as an English medieval walled city with inn signs

48. The houses of the town 'still stood pleasantly amid gardens . . .'

49. Oxford in the late seventeenth century

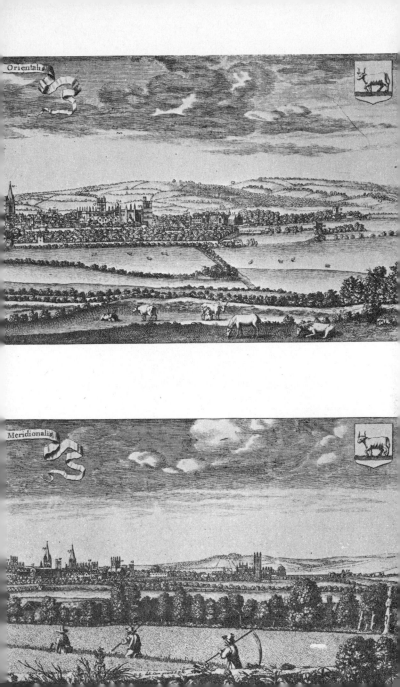

50. Cambridge in the late seventeenth century

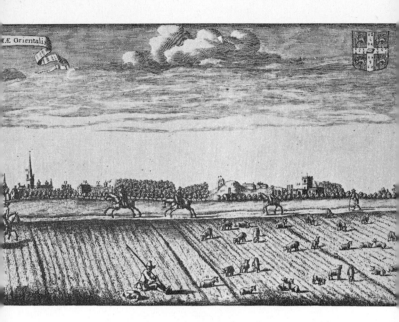

'Open fields and enclosures were found together from the Middle Ages to the nineteenth century'

orchards, paddocks, and farmyards. For the number of inhabitants was still very small – two or three thousand for a town of fair size.

The life of the burgher combined the advantages of town and countryside. The all-pervading atmosphere of natural beauty unconsciously affected the language and thoughts of all. Chaucer was a Londoner, but, in describing a beautiful and sprightly young woman, he employs four metaphors, one taken from the Tower mint, the other three from familiar, vulgar sights, sounds, and smells of the rustic farm:

> Full brighter was the shining of her hewe
> Than in the Tower the noble yforged newe.
> But of her song, it was as loud and yerne [brisk]
> As any swallow sitting on a berne [barn].
> Thereto she could skip and make game
> As any kid or calf following his dame.
> Her mouth was sweet as brachet or the meeth
> [honeyed ale or mead]
> Or hoard of apples laid in hay or heeth.

How simple, strong, yet exquisite it is – a lost quality, because the influences of daily life that made it are lost, or at least are overmastered by others more ugly and mechanical. It was equally characteristic of the age of Chaucer that the young woman so beautifully described was no better than she should have been![1]

But these little towns, half rural though they were, had burgher pride of the most exclusive kind. Their constant preoccupation was to keep and extend the privileges of self-government and the monopoly of local trade, which they had bought from king or lord, abbot or bishop. To defend the merchants of their own town in their dangerous journeys, and to gather in their debts owing in other towns, municipal action was quasi-diplomatic; Norwich talked to Southampton as England to France. Commercial treaties between towns were common. As to London, its power of self-government, which included jurisdiction over wide territories up and down the river, might have been the envy of many German 'free cities'. Woe to the King's officer, or to one of John of Gaunt's

1. *The Miller's Tale.*

'meinie', who infringed the right of a London citizen or challenged the jurisdiction of the Mayor.

Yet, great as was the power of London and considerable as were the 'liberties' of other towns, they were loyal members of a State whose Parliament legislated, partly by their advice, on their economic concerns in so far as they were national; and in the fourteenth century trade was becoming more and more national without ceasing to be municipal. The history of all English towns was swallowed up in the history of England which they helped to make; while in Germany, not then a nation, the history of Nuremberg and of the Hanse Towns form separate chapters in the annals of Europe.

But even in England and even during the Hundred Years War, national sentiment and loyalty to the Kingdom at large made no such daily and urgent claims as did the civic patriotism that a man felt for his own town. The first duty of the burgher was to play his part in the city militia, to defend the walls and if possible the fields of the town against French or Scottish raiders, bands of outlaws, or the retainers of great men at feud with the privileges of the borough. The principle of 'conscription' raised no difficulty in the mind of the medieval Englishman. How indeed could he expect other people to defend him and his fellows from dangers constantly at his door? For purposes of war and police, and for town-works of all sorts like digging a town ditch or drain, repairing the town bridge, helping in the harvest of the town fields, very occasionally cleaning or mending the street in front of his own house, a man might be called on for personal service by the civic authorities. Such work in the common cause was not regarded as 'servile', like work on the lord's demesne. No one then thought that 'liberty' consisted in avoiding military or other obligations on the performance of which the cherished 'liberties' of his town and of his fellow burghers ultimately depended. Self-help and self-government were for long centuries taught to the English in the school of town life, and to a less degree in the shire-court and in the manor-court of the village. There were no rights without duties.

Political strife ran strong and fierce in the streets of every town of England, not the strife of national parties, but the politics of the craft and of the town which touched the burgher in his daily life. The struggle for power was constantly being waged in disputes of the crafts with the corporation; of the big merchants with the small manufacturing masters; of the masters with their men; of the whole body of citizens with outsiders trying to settle and trade in the town; of all the inhabitants of the borough with the King's Sheriff, the lord's or bishop's bailiff, or the monks of the Abbey the worst enemies of all. In a hundred ever changing forms such disputes went on for centuries, with different fortunes in a hundred different towns, from great London, itself a State within the State, to the smallest would-be borough that was struggling to rise above the position of a feudal village ruled by the lord's bailiff and manor-court. In all these civic battles, external and internal, each party used every appropriate weapon of legal proceedings, open riot, and economic pressure.

In London, 'sea' coal, so called because it was brought by ship from Tyneside, was being more and more used in place of wood and charcoal, causing 'clergy and nobility resorting to the city of London' to complain of danger of contagion from 'the stench of burning sea-coal'.[1] For fear of fire, thatch was gradually giving way to red tiles on London roofs. The walls of the houses were still of mud and timber, though the number of fine stone mansions built by great lords or wealthy citizens was on the increase, like John of Gaunt's Savoy on the way between London and Westminster. But the chief architectural glory of the capital was its hundred churches [51]. The streets were ill paved and had no side walks; the crown of the causeway sloped down on both sides to the 'kennels', into which the filth ran; weaker passengers, shoved down off the centre of the road, 'went to the wall' and splashed through the mud. Too little checked by municipal authority, householders and tradesmen threw their garbage, litter, and offal into the street from doors and windows, without regard to amenity or sanitation.

Two miles from London lay Westminster, clustering round

1. There was a prejudice against coal as domestic fuel until the shortage of wood brought it increasingly into use. In the country at large it was, till Tudor times, chiefly used by smiths and lime burners.

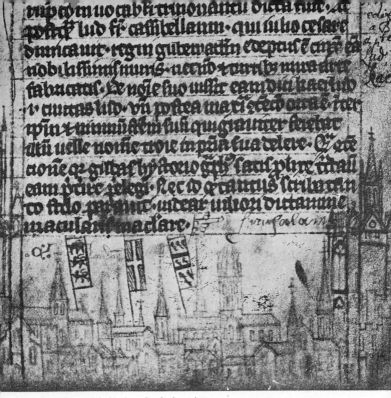

51. London with its hundred churches

its abbey, and its hall which Rufus had built and which
Richard II was adorning with rafters of oak. Westminster had
become the recognized centre of royal administration, law, and
Parliament [45], although it had no commerce and no municipal privileges of its own, and was only a village at great
London's gate. There was no royal foothold inside the English
capital corresponding to the Louvre in Paris. When the King
came up to town, he lived sometimes at Westminster on one
side of London, sometimes in the Tower on the other. But the
City that lay between was not his ground, and Richard II was
no more able than Charles I to dictate to its militia, its magistrates, and its mob. The medieval balance and harmony of
powers, from which modern English liberty has sprung, is

clearly illustrated in the relation of the Plantagenet kings to their capital.

The richest citizens of London were now on a par with the great territorial nobles, not only because they had at their command the City militia and a large proportion of the shipping of England, but because they lent money to government. In 1290 Edward I had expelled the Jews from England, so putting an end to the older method of raising royal loans. This expulsion of the Jews is one reason why anti-semitism is today less strong in England than in many countries of Europe: our forefathers were compelled by the action of Edward I to undertake their own financial and intellectual life unaided by Jewry, so that when in Cromwell's time the Jews were allowed to return, the English had learnt to stand alone, and could meet without jealousy that gifted race on equal terms.[1]

And so, in the absence of the Jews, Edward III borrowed money for his wars from Florentine bankers, who also supplied the needs of his barons. In the Second Day of Boccaccio's *Decameron* we read how three Florentines 'coming to London, took a little house, and lived as frugally as possible, letting out money on interest'. When they had made enough money they returned to Florence, but 'keeping on their banking trade in England, they sent a nephew thither, named Alessandro, to manage their business. . . . He let out money to the barons upon their castles and other estates, which turned to good account.'

But the King also borrowed from his own subjects, the 'great City men' as we may already call them, and from the wealthy merchants of other towns, like Sir William de la Pole of Hull, the first English business man to become the founder of a great noble house. The relation of the Crown to these new creditors

1. The expulsion of the Jews had been preceded by a decline in their wealth and power of lending; otherwise they would not have been expelled. English and foreign Christians had already been taking their place as moneylenders to the King and to his subjects. Industry and agriculture were changing and expanding all through the later Middle Ages and required the borrowing of capital by King, lord of manor, farmer, villein, and trader. The laws against usury prohibited interest instead of limiting it; the result was that very high interest, often 50 per cent, was asked and given, as the transaction was illegal. (Lipson, *An Economic History of England*, i, pp. 616–20.)

was very different from its previous relation to the Jews, who had been mere sponges in the King's hand to suck up his subjects' wealth, helpless clients whom he alone protected from popular malice and massacre. But the English merchants who lent money to government for the Hundred Years War could give or withhold their aid as they chose, and they took advantage of the need the King had of them to bargain for commercial or other advantages for themselves or their families, for their city, their craft, or their trade.

It was in these circumstances that the network of Edward III's financial, home, and foreign policy was elaborated. The Hundred Years War was not merely an adventure for military plunder and dynastic ambition; it was also an attempt to keep open the market for our wool and cloth trade in Flanders and in France. The alliance with Van Artevelde and the Flemish burghers against France was at once diplomatic and commercial.

English national policy was continually changing under the pressure of the King's necessities, and of rival interests among his own subjects and among his allies oversea. Experiments in protection and free trade, neither yet an established doctrine, were made in bewildering alternation. The 'mercantilist' era of a fixed protectionist policy had not yet come, but the country was already groping towards it. Navigation laws to exclude foreign vessels from trading in English ports were passed as early as the reign of Richard II, but could not be enforced, because our merchant shipping was not large enough, until Stuart times, to cope alone with the ever increasing volume of our trade. English merchants did much of their overseas trade in foreign bottoms.

But the English marine was at last beginning to be formidable. Edward III used it to clear the Channel of foreign pirates, and succeeded for a number of years. The fleet that defeated the French at Sluys (1340) was not a royal navy: it was composed of the merchant ships of many different towns, temporarily conscripted to fight under a royal admiral. Cannon had as yet no place in warfare at sea. Still, as at Salamis, ships rammed and grappled each other, and the fight was conducted with swords, spears, and arrows, like a battle on land [52].

The 'Staple', where English goods for export had to be

52. A sea fight in the Channel

collected, taxed, and sold, was necessary for levying the
customs duties on which the King's finances depended, and it
was thought also to be of service in protecting English
merchants against the fraud and violence of international
commerce in that age. But 'the Company of the Staple'
obtained a partial monopoly in export that was not at all
agreeable to many wool growers and to many rival merchants
[53]. Numerous and divergent interests, agricultural, industrial, and mercantile, held conflicting views about the Staple,
and particularly about its proper location. At one time it was
fixed in certain English towns, then in Flanders, finally in

Calais, which English arms won and held as the port of entry into France. 'When the wool reached Calais, it was the common practice for the foreign buyer to pay a certain sum in cash and give bills for the rest. The discounting of bills by *assigning* or transferring them was also usual, so that the trade custom of circulating bills from one creditor to another is at least five hundred years old'.[1]

Most of the English goods exported through the Staple at Calais consisted of raw wool; but woollen cloth was constantly gaining ground, till in Tudor times the export of cloth killed the export of raw wool. But in Chaucer's day and for long after, the men who lent most money to the King were the Staplers who exported wool to feed the foreign looms; and the customs levied at the Staple on exported wool were the great source of royal revenue.[2]

1. Lipson, I, p. 549, ed. 1937.
2. Both wool and cloth were collected, taxed, and sold at the Staple. But the 'Staple Company', the 'Staplers' *par excellence*, dealt in wool, not in cloth, and their gradual decline was due to the increase of the export of cloth by the Merchant Adventurers. In the early fourteenth century wool exports were 30,000 sacks a year and cloth exports about 5,000 cloths. In the middle of the sixteenth century the wool exports were 4,000 sacks and the cloth exports well over 100,000 cloths. See E. E. Rich, *The Ordinance Book of the Merchants of the Staple*, 1937.
On the early history of the Staple, see Eileen Power, op. cit.

53. The Master of the Staple in audience of Duke Albert

These London–Calais merchants, with whom the King had to bargain for loans and levies as if with a fourth estate of the realm, had extensive business and personal connexions with wool-growing districts like the Cotswolds, where they and their rivals the clothiers bought estates and founded many of the great county families of western England. In 1401 was laid to rest in Chipping Campden the body of William Grevel, 'late citizen of London and flower of the wool merchants of England', and his stone house is still an ornament of the most beautiful village street now left in the island: for Chipping Campden was not an ordinary Gloucestershire village but a collecting centre for England's greatest trade [54, 55].

It is, in fact, to the age of Chaucer that Professor Postan points as the 'great breeding season of English capitalism; in the early phases of the Hundred Years War, the time when the exigencies of royal finance, new experiments in taxation, speculative ventures with wool, the collapse of Italian finance, and the beginning of the new cloth industry, all combined to bring into existence a new race of war financiers and commercial speculators, army purveyors and wool monopolists'.[1]

If the capitalist as financier and public creditor was found chiefly in the wool trade, the beginnings of the capitalist as organizer of industry were found during the same period in the cloth manufacture.

While raw wool was still the chief article of export, domestic needs were supplied for the most part by cloth made in England. In the times of Ancient Britons, Romans, and Saxons and ever since, the spare moments of the housewife, her maids, and daughters had been devoted to spinning – the supposed occupation of our mother Eve. And equally from the earliest times the more difficult art of weaving had been practised by men specially trained as websters, sitting all day each at the loom in his own cottage, to provide the coarse clothes of the local peasantry. In the twelfth and thirteenth centuries a better class of manufacture was conducted by weavers' guilds in many towns, including London, Lincoln, Oxford, and Nottingham. In Henry III's reign, Stamford cloth was well

1. *Economic History Review*, May 1939, p. 165.

54. William Grevel's House, Chipping Campden, Gloucestershire

55. High Street, Chipping Campden, from the market house arches

known in Venice, while Yorkshire, both east and west, was already famous for its woollens.

In the thirteenth and early fourteenth centuries the production of standardized cloth for the market began to deteriorate in English towns, where the number of weavers seriously declined. The fact was that the manufacture had begun to move into the country districts, particularly to those of the west where running water was obtainable to work fulling-mills. One of the many processes necessary in cloth-making, that which was conducted by the fuller, had in all previous ages been done by human labour with hand, foot, or club; but it was now beginning to be done by water-power. Already therefore when the fourteenth century opened, the Cotswold and Pennine valleys and the Lake District had begun to compete seriously with eastern England in the manufacture of cloth. And the country was already vying with the town as the seat of the industry. It was an early case of technical invention having important social results.[1]

Government action in the reigns of Edward II and III further stimulated our greatest industry. The importation of cloth from abroad was prohibited. Skilled artificers with trade secrets were invited over, particularly into London and East Anglia, and were protected by the Government against native jealousy; special privileges were at the same time extended to English clothiers. During the lifetime of Chaucer the production of broadcloth in England was trebled, and the export of broadcloth was increased ninefold. The enormous advantage that England had over other countries as a feeder of sheep and a producer of the best wool gave her the opportunity gradually to win the command of the world's cloth market, as she had long commanded the European market for raw wool [56–9].

The growth of the cloth trade was destined to go on for generations to come, creating new classes in town and country, adding to the luxury of the manor-house and relieving the poverty of the cottage, altering the methods and increasing the rewards of agriculture, supplying our ships with their cargoes, spreading our commerce first over all Europe and then over all

1. *Economic History Review*, 1941, Miss Carus Wilson's article, 'An industrial Revolution of the 13th Century'.

56. Flemish weavers' cottages, Lavenham, Suffolk

57. The Merchant Adventurers' Hall at York

THE CLOTH TRADE
58. Weaving

59. Dyeing

the world, dictating the policy of our statesmen and providing the programmes of our parties, causing alliances, treaties, and wars. The cloth trade held its place as incomparably the most important English industry, till the far distant day when coal was wedded to iron. For centuries it occupied men's daily thoughts in town and village, second only to agriculture; our literature and common speech acquired many phrases and metaphors borrowed from the manufacture of cloth – 'thread of discourse', 'spin a yarn', 'unravel a mystery', 'web of life', 'fine-drawn', 'homespun', 'tease' – while all unmarried women were put down as 'spinsters'.

Already in the fourteenth century it was evident that the rapid expansion of the cloth trade required a new economic organization. The manufacture of raw wool into the best cloth called not for one craft alone but for many – carding, spinning, weaving, fulling, dyeing, cloth-finishing. Therefore a large expansion of the cloth industry for the market at home and abroad could not be organized by the craft guilds which had done so much to improve weaving in former centuries. The entrepreneur, with a more than local outlook and with money at his command, was required to collect the raw material, the half-manufactured and the finished article, and pass them on from craftsman to craftsman and from place to place, from village to town, from town to port, and finally to bring a standardized article to the best market. For all this capital was needed.

Capitalism as the organizer of industry is first clearly visible in the cloth trade. Already in the lifetime of Chaucer, the capitalist clothier could be found, employing many different people in many different places. He was a social type more modern than medieval, and quite different from the master craftsman labouring at the bench with his apprentices and journeymen.[1] The ultimate future lay with the capitalist

1. Until the coming of elaborate machinery in the eighteenth century, capitalism did not mean factories. Except for the water-worked fulling-mills, the capitalist employed the various workmen in their own homes, and they owned their own tools and plant. This is the 'domestic' system of industry. The capitalist had indeed to provide warehouses to store the goods.

60. Building

employer, in the far distant days of the Industrial Revolution. But the cloth manufacture had brought him into existence four hundred years before he swallowed industry whole. Shipping, the coal trade, and the building trade [60, 61] were also conducted in part on a capitalist basis at this early date.

But, for centuries to come, most industries were still conducted by the old-fashioned master craftsman, with a few apprentices and journeymen sleeping and working under his roof, subject to the general supervision of the craft guild. Here too trouble was brewing between the master craftsmen and the journeymen whom they employed, corresponding to the trouble between the farmers and the free labourers. The journeyman in the shop felt the same movement of aspiration and unrest as the labourer in the field. He too struck for higher wages when the Black Death made labour scarce, and the Statute of Labourers was in part directed against his claims [62].

But there was more in it than a struggle for wages. The unrest in the towns had deeper causes. Owing to the expansion of trade and the increase of its rewards, the harmony of the medieval craft guild was being disturbed by social and economic cleavage between master and man, which had not been felt in the simpler day of small things.

In the earlier stages of the craft guild, masters, apprentices, and journeymen were more or less of one class. They were all 'small men' together, brother labourers in the shop, sharing the same meals. Though poor by any modern standard, they

61. The Tower of Babel, illustrating the medieval builder's craft and implements

62. A guild master with craftsmen

were a proud fraternity the skilled men of the trade. Their guild
represented their common interest and, subject to the general
control of the municipality, it managed the affairs of the craft
within the town, fixing prices, wages, and conditions of work
to the general satisfaction of masters and men. The apprentices
at the expiry of their indentures became either masters or
journeymen, and most journeymen sooner or later became
small masters. The master craftsman worked with his men. He
often beat his apprentices and sometimes beat his journeyman,
for blows were common currency in those days. But there was
no marked division of social standard and way of life. Outside
the guilds, indeed, there had always been a pool of unskilled

labour in the town, ill paid and uncared for. But in the guilds themselves there had been much harmony and content.

In the age of Chaucer these things were changing. The expansion of industry and trade were bringing variety of function and an increasing difference of monetary reward. The master was becoming less the brother craftsman and more the entrepreneur, engaged in organizing the business and selling the goods. Some apprentices became masters, especially if they 'married their master's daughter'. But most apprentices could only look to become journeymen, and few journeymen could any longer look to become masters. In proportion to the increasing numbers engaged in the trade, the number of masters was less than of old. The harmony of the craft guild had depended on the identity of interest of its members, and on a certain sense of social equality among them. But this was growing less every year. The distinction between 'employer and employed' was becoming more marked. There was also an increasing difference between the rich trading master and the poor manufacturing master, who worked with a couple of journeymen to make the goods that the great man sold.

And so we find in the towns of the fourteenth century not only occasional strikes for higher wages inside the guild, but in some cases the formation of permanent 'yeomen guilds', to champion the interest of the employees and perform the fighting functions of a modern trade union. In some trades and in some towns these yeomen guilds also included small master crafts-men. For they too were opposed to the richer masters, who were ceasing to be craftsmen at all and were concerned only in selling the goods. The trader and the manual worker were in some trades beginning to be separated, and the trader was assuming control of the industry, by his command of the craft guild or the livery company. The manual worker, whether journeyman or small master, was losing most of his economic independence and was acquiring an inferior status. The government of the towns was in the hands of the big merchants. But the modern trade-union spirit was already active.[1]

1. The gangs of workmen who built the glorious cathedrals and lovely churches and manor-houses of the later Middle Ages were organized not as a guild but on a capitalist basis. Trade unionism was

These economic and social changes, begun in the fourteenth century, were going on all through the succeeding epoch. But there was no uniformity, and generalization is necessarily inaccurate. The history of each craft and of each town differs from every other. But such was the general direction of growth in industry and commerce during the Hundred Years War and the Wars of the Roses.

Great changes, therefore, were taking place in Chaucer's day in the structure of society. Servitude was disappearing from the manor and new classes were arising to take charge of farming and of trade. Modern institutions were being grafted on to the medieval, in both village and town. But in the other great department of human affairs – the religious and ecclesiastical, which then covered half of human life and its relationships – institutional change was prevented by the rigid conservatism of the Church authorities, although here too thought and opinion were moving fast.

Change indeed was long overdue. The 'corruption' of the clergy was being denounced not merely by Lollard heretics but by the orthodox and the worldly, by Langland, Gower, and Chaucer no less than by Wyclif. 'Corrupt' the Church certainly was, but that was not the whole of the matter: she had been 'corrupt' yet perfectly safe for centuries past, and was no more 'corrupt' in the time of Chaucer than was royal justice or the conduct of the lords and their retainers. Most institutions in the Middle Ages were 'corrupt' by modern standards. But whereas the laity were moving with the times, the Church was standing still. Entrenched behind her immu-

---

therefore strong among the 'free masons' – a very different folk from modern 'freemasons'. Wyclif thus describes their trade-union policy, which seems to have been already highly developed:

'Also men of sutel craft, as fre masons and othere . . . conspiren togidere that no man of here [their] craft schal take lesse on a day than thei setten [agree] . . . and that noon of hem schal make sade trewe work to lette othere mennus wynnyng at the craft [namely that none of them shall do steady true work which might hinder the earnings of other men of his craft] and that non of hem schal do ought but only hewe stone, though he migght profit his maister twenty pound bi o daies werk by leggyng on a wal [laying stones on a wall] without harm or penyng [paining] to himself.' (Wyclif, *Select English Works*, iii, p. 333, and *Statutes of the Realm*, iii, p. 227.)

table privileges and her inalienable and ever increasing wealth, her leaders took no steps to pacify the clamour of moral disapprobation and the growls of envious greed that rose on every side against her and her possessions. The laity were not only more critical but were far better educated and therefore more formidable than in the days of Anselm and Becket, when the clergy had enjoyed a fairly close monopoly of trained intelligence. The Church, however, refused to do anything to satisfy the general discontent, and during the fifteenth century the storm subsided. But the respite was not lasting, and the refusal of all reform under the Plantagenets led under the Tudors to revolution.

Many of the clergy themselves were critics of the Church as outspoken as the laity. The scholars of Oxford and not a few of the priests serving parishes whose tithes went to rich monks and foreign prelates were reformers and even rebels. Moreover the accused parties themselves denounced one another with the intemperance of language habitual in medieval controversy. The friars attacked the bishops and secular clergy, who repaid their abuse with interest. In Chaucer's *Tales* it is the friar and the summoner who expose each other's tricks, to make mirth for the company of laymen. From every quarter, within and without the Church, the air resounded with attacks on the various orders of clergy [63, 64].

Yet nothing was done. The Church, unlike the manor and the guild, could not be transformed by the natural working of economic change or by the mere pressure of opinion. Definite measures of administrative and legislative reform were required, and there was no machinery to effect them, except such as rested in the hands of the Pope and the bishops. But the Pope, who in former ages had done so much, now did less than nothing to improve the condition of the Church in England. He used his powers to foster abuses that brought wealth to the Roman Court – simony, non-residence, plurality, the sale of indulgences, all of which offended the roused conscience of a censorious age.

Yet even without the support of the Pope, the English bishops might have done at least something. And the bishops in the age of Chaucer were, with scarcely an exception, able, hard-working, highly respectable men. Why then did they not at least attempt to make some reform in the Church ?

63. Fox masquerading as bishop

The main reason was their preoccupation with secular interests. Though paid out of the revenues of the Church, the bishops gave their lives to the service of the State. In spite of Parliamentary laws, the best places in the Church were disposed of by collusive agreement between Pope and King. The Pope thrust foreign favourites into many rich benefices, but as part of the bargain he usually left the appointment of bishops in royal hands. So the King paid his Ministers and civil servants not out of the public taxes but out of the episcopal revenues. Among the twenty-five persons who were bishops in England and Wales between 1376 and 1386, thirteen held high secular office under the Crown, and several others played an important part in politics. Sometimes they were sent abroad as ambassadors to foreign powers. Others had risen by secular services rendered to the King's sons; the Bishop of Bath and Wells had been Chancellor of Gascony for the Black Prince, the Bishop of Salisbury had been Chancellor of Lancaster for John of Gaunt. The Chancellor of the Realm was usually a bishop like the Primate Sudbury and William of Wykeham.

In the days of the Norman kings, the close connexion between the bench of bishops and the royal ministry had supplied a barbarous land with able and learned bureaucrats, who derived from their episcopal authority a prestige which enabled them to cope as the King's servants with an ignorant and brutal baronage. But the need for a system once so valuable to the country was growing less with every generation. The laity, of whom Chaucer was one, were many of them now qualified to be the King's civil servants. The monopolization

64. Monk in the stocks

of secretarial work by the clergy, and of the principal offices of State by the bishops, was beginning to arouse a reasonable jealousy. There were now ready to hand intelligent and highly trained lawyers, like Knyvet, and gentlemen, like Richard Scrope, well capable of conducting the highest business of the State. It was men of this type who, under the Tudor monarchs, replaced both prelates and nobles as the instruments of royal government. Already under the later Plantagenets the first signs of such a change were visible. Owing to a petition of the House of Commons of 1371 against the employment of clergy in the royal service, laymen for some years alternated with clerics as chancellors and treasurers of the realm.

Occupied as they were by the cares of secular office, the bishops paid little attention to the deplorable state of their dioceses. If rectories were empty or filled with scandalous persons or under-paid substitutes, it had always been so. If the Pope pushed the sale of indulgences and sham relics, the bishops could only regard it as a legitimate piece of business; without thinking more of the matter, they supplied the Pardoners with episcopal letters commending their wares to the public.

One branch of their duties, the proper control of the Spiritual Courts, the bishops neglected with unfortunate results. As regards the business of wills and marriages, then conducted by the Church, the ecclesiastical tribunals were no more corrupt or inefficient than the lay judges and lawyers of that time. But the more specifically religious function of the bishop's court, which he usually left to the archdeacon, was causing grave scandal in Chaucer's day, as his *Friar's Tale* illustrates. Punishment for sins not cognizable by the lay courts, particularly sexual incontinence, was then undertaken by the Church. But in fact the habit of commuting penance for money payment had become general. And from that official practice the step was short to blackmail of sinners in their homes by the officers of the bishop's court, particularly the 'summoners', who had a most evil reputation:

> 'Art thou a bailiff?' 'Yea', quod he
> He dorste not for veray filth and shame
> Say that he was a Sompnour, for the name.[1]

But the bishops, though they neglected many of their duties, were so far interested in ecclesiastical affairs as to fight for Church privileges and endowments against all comers, and hunt down the heretics when heresy, now for the first time, seriously raised its head in England with Wyclif's denial of transubstantiation in the sacrifice of the mass (1380).

Many parishes, no doubt, were faithfully and sufficiently served by men like Chaucer's 'poor parson', the only type of churchman for whom the poet seems to have felt affection and respect. But a large proportion of the livings in lay gift were presented to people not in priests' orders at all, or to mere laymen. And far too often the church belonged to a monastery or to a wealthy absentee pluralist, and was served by some underpaid and ignorant 'mass-priest', who scarcely understood the Latin words he mumbled any better than his audience. Other parsons, who might have done their duty well, wandered off from their charges to London, Oxford, or some great man's house, in search of a more free and exciting life and additional stipends. The parish priest was seldom the rector, very often not even the vicar, but a chaplain or clerk miserably paid to do the duty neglected by the incumbent.

It followed that teaching and preaching often amounted to very little in an English village, so far as the resident priest was concerned, though mass was regularly performed. But this deficiency was to a large extent supplied by the preaching friar on his regular beat, by the travelling Pardoner with his wallet 'bretful of pardons come from Rome all hot', by Wyclif's

1. *The Friar's Tale.*

heretical missionaries, by John Ball's agitators of Christian Democracy. Whether we regard these interlopers as sowing tares in the wheat, or as enriching the Lord's harvest, they played a great part in the religious and intellectual life of the nation. They carried the latest thoughts, teaching, and news of the time to remote farms and hamlets, whose inhabitants never moved from the neighbourhood and could read no written word. These religious roundsmen, on foot and on horse-back, were always on the move along the winding muddy roads and green lanes of England; and to their peripatetic fellowship must be added the more secularly minded minstrels, tumblers, jugglers, beggars, and charlatans of every kind, and pilgrims pious and worldly alike. All these wayfarers acted the part of 'microbes', as their historian Jusserand[1] has said, infecting the stationary part of the population with the ideas of a new age and of a larger world. They too were preparing the change from medieval to modern [65–73].

But the parish priest reigned within the walls of his church and there he said the mass, attended on Sundays by the greater part of the village. It was the heart of medieval religion.

The peasant as he stood or knelt on the floor of the church each Sunday, could not follow the Latin words, but good thoughts found a way into his heart as he watched what he revered and heard the familiar yet still mysterious sounds. Around him blazed on the walls frescoes of scenes from the scriptures and the lives of saints; and over the rood-loft was the Last Judgement depicted in lively colours, paradise opening to receive the just, and on the other side flaming hell with devil executioners tormenting naked souls. Fear of hell was a most potent force, pitilessly exploited by all preachers and confessors, both to enrich the Church and to call sinners to repentance [74, 75]. The orthodox consigned the heretics and the heretics consigned the bishops to eternal flames, and all parties agreed there would scarce be room in hell 'of friars there is such throng!'.

The peasant knew some of the sayings of Christ, and incidents from his life and those of the saints, besides many Bible

1. J. J. Jusserand, *English Wayfaring Life in the Middle Ages* (*XIVth Century*).

65. The showman and his bear

66. A pilgrim

67. Grinders

68. A beggar woman

69. A tinker

70 and 71. Puppets

72 and 73. 'Minstrels . . . jugglers . . . charlatans of every kind'

74. 'Fear of hell was a most potent force'

stories such as Adam and Eve, Noah's flood, Solomon's wives
and wisdom, Jezebel's fate, Jephthah and his daughter 'the
which he loved passing well'. All these and much more, with
many strange embellishments, he learnt from 'pious chansons'
and from the friars' sensational and entertaining sermons. He
never saw the Bible in English, and if he had he could not have
read it. There was nothing in his own home analogous to family
prayers and Bible reading. But religion and the language of
religion surrounded his life. The crucifix was often before his
eyes, and the story of the Crucifixion in his mind.

Confession was a compulsory duty, normally made to the

parish priest, but very frequently to the intruding friar, who gave absolution more easily, often it may well be more intelligently, and often (so all said) more corruptly for money, for a good meal, or for other favours.

But there is a great deal more to be said about the friars than that. Like Rob Roy they were 'ower bad for blessing, and ower gude for banning'. The black friars of St Dominic and yet more the grey friars of the gentle St Francis had been the true evangelical force in England in the thirteenth century, and in the fourteenth they still shouldered most of the missionary work of the Church. They were still the great preachers and had created a demand for preaching. The illiterate folk of an age awakening to intelligence demanded more and yet more of the spoken word, and could seldom get enough of it from the parish priest.

And so the friars still set the pace in the age of Chaucer. It was in imitation as well as in rivalry that the Wyclifites laid such stress on preaching to the people. If Protestants in times to come attached more importance to the pulpit than to the altar, they were only carrying further a movement begun by the friars [76].

If the orthodox secular clergy denounced the friars for filling their sermons with idle and unedifying stories to attract the vulgar, it was partly because those sermons attacked the

75. Medieval wall painting of a Doom, Pickworth Church, Lincolnshire

76. The friars 'were still the great preachers''

sloth of bishops, monks, and clergy and the corruption of the archdeacon and his summoner. In the first part of Wyclif's career the friars were his allies against the 'possessionate clergy', and it was only when he propounded his heresy on transubstantiation that the mendicant orders became his most effective enemies. In theory the friars, unlike the monks, lived by begging alms, had no property of their own, and preached the doctrine of evangelical poverty so dear to St Francis. In practice they had now amassed wealth and treasure which they stored in their magnificent convents. Wyclif liked their theory and condemned their practice.

If we seek the origins of some of the distinctive traits of English Puritanism, of its asceticism, its war on sin, its sabbatarian rigour, its fear of hell, its attacks on the bishops and wealthy clergy, its crude denunciation of opponents, its vigorous and soul-stirring sermons, its tendency to unctuous sentiment, its lapses into hypocrisy, its equalitarian appeal to the poor and lowly, they are all to be found in the medieval Church, and particularly in the work of the friars. But not of the friars alone; clerk Langland was Bunyan's forerunner, and Wyclif would have found his ideal of priesthood realized by Latimer and Wesley. Those scholars who have most recently and most fully studied the sermons and other pious literature in prose and verse of the fourteenth century are most averse to 'the appropriation of medieval religion by any modern party or the repudiation of it by any other party. For the medieval Church is the mother of us all.'[1] As Chaucer himself said:

Ther n'is no newé guise that it n'as old.

On the other hand there were elements in later English Protestantism which were not medieval at all. Family worship and the religious dedication of family life and of business life are later Protestant accretions. They had no place in medieval ideals or practice. For medieval ideals derived from more purely ascetic and anti-mundane sources in primitive Christianity, to which practice indeed seldom conformed but which held the field in theory.

While the enemies of the friars complained that they did too much and intruded too busily where they had no rightful place, the monks of this age were accused of doing too little. The fire of religious enthusiasm and the light of learning burnt low within the walls of monasteries that once had supplied England with noble leadership. The King no longer sent for some saintly abbot, to implore him to take pity on the land and exchange the government of his House for the government of a great diocese. The cloister of Canterbury no longer rivalled the University of Paris in scholarship and philosophy: the higher thought and education of the country was now concentrated at Oxford, and there the chief intellectual influences were the friars and the secular clergy. Nor did the monks any longer, as in the days of the Barons' War, play a patriotic and formidable part in politics. Chronicles were still compiled in monasteries, but they merely carried on the literary tradition of a former age, while the worldling Froissart was setting up a new standard of history. In the thirteenth century, Matthew Paris of St Albans cloister had been a truly great historian, but the monastic chroniclers of Chaucer's day, even the best of them like Walsingham, had no power to grasp the relative importance of events, or to appreciate the significance of what was going on in the world outside the abbey close. The monk had little thought except for the interests of his House. His

1. B. L. Manning, *The People's Faith in the Time of Wyclif*, pp. 186–8 and *passim*; G. R. Owst, *Preaching in Medieval England*, pp. xii, 91–5 and *passim* (Cambridge Press).

whole life was passed within its precincts, except when he was sent out to gather in the rents of distant estates, or to accompany the abbot on a hunting expedition or an occasional visit to London. At home he spent his time with brethren whose interests and experience were as limited as his own. It is, then, not wonderful that the monks offered so stubborn a resistance to the claims of the townsfolk and peasantry, to whom the local privileges of the abbey had, under changed conditions, become galling and vexatious. In every way the world was moving on, but the monastic life was standing still. Only in Yorkshire and the north the monasteries were popular, and continued to be so up to the time of the Dissolution.

The monks in Chaucer's England were worldly and well-to-do, living lives of sauntering comfort in the monastery, or roaming the land dressed like laymen, to hunt game or look after their estates. They were not numerous – probably rather more than the 5,000 at which they were estimated at the time of their Dissolution in the reign of Henry VIII. But, having themselves abandoned the manual labour practised by their predecessors, they maintained armies of servants to carry on the daily routine of their great establishments, which often covered many acres of ground, as at Bury St Edmunds and Abingdon. The monks performed in person their obligations of prayers and masses for the living and the dead, their patrons and their founders. They gave daily alms in money and broken meats to the poor, and showed a lavish hospitality to travellers, many of whom were wealthy and exacting guests. The rich fed at the table of the abbot or prior, while humbler wayfarers were accommodated in the guest house of the monastery [77–9]. Founders' kin, influential nobles and gentry, claimed rights as guests, officers, and agents of the monasteries, consuming much of their wealth; and at the same time the monks, especially the abbots, spent plenty upon themselves.[1]

The monasteries had by this time accumulated vast endowments in land, tithes, appropriated churches, treasures, and clerical patronage – enough to cause them to be bitterly envied

1. Snape, *English Monastic Finances*, Cambridge Press, 1926; Savine, *English Monasteries on the Eve of the Dissolution*, Oxford Studies, ed. Vinogradoff, 1909.

77 and 78. Hospitality for pilgrims

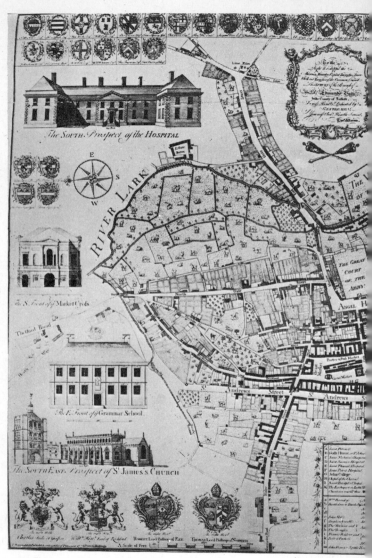

79. Bury St. Edmunds in 1776, showing the extent of the former abbey's grounds

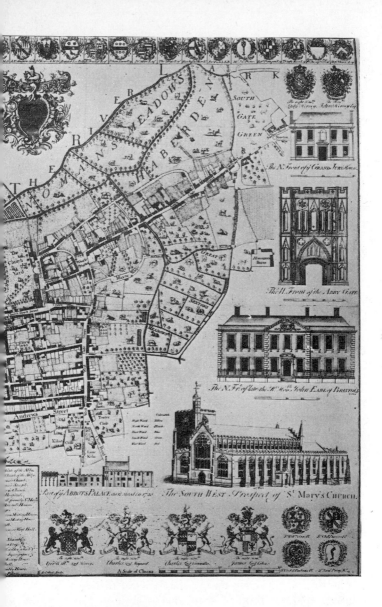

The N.th Front of ye GRAND JURY House.

The W.t Front of the Abby Gate.

The N.th Fr.t of late the R.t Hon.ble John Earle of Bristol's.

The SOUTH WEST Prospect of S.t Mary's Church.

Part of ye ABBOTS PALACE as it is remaining.

A Scale of Chains.

as idle drones, living at the expense of the impoverished kingdom. The Commons declared that a third of the wealth of England was in the hands of the Church, most of it belonging to the regular clergy. And yet the monks were constantly in financial straits, sometimes through their magnificent architectural zeal for enlarging and beautifying the abbey and its church, sometimes through sheer mismanagement. The abbot who, like Carlyle's Samson, had good business ability among his other qualities seems to have been rare in later times, though some of the cathedral priories, like Canterbury, continued to manage their finances and administer their far-scattered manorial estates well. The Black Death hit the monastic landlord as hard as the lay. The Italian and English moneylenders, who had succeeded the Jews, charged just as high interest, and the monks were reckoned an easy prey. The monasteries often speculated in a form of life annuity known as a 'corrody', whereby the abbey borrowed money in return for an undertaking to keep the creditor for the rest of his life – and often he lived disastrously long.

In earlier times the demesne lands of monastic manors, administered by the abbey's own officials direct, had often been admirable examples of estate management and agricultural improvement, not only in the sheep-runs of Yorkshire dales but in mixed arable and pasture regions of the south. But in the fourteenth and fifteenth centuries the demesne lands of the abbeys were increasingly let out on long leases to laymen, who either farmed them or sublet them to others. In this and other ways the lay control and enjoyment of monastic wealth began long before the final Dissolution.

There were occasional scandals in monasteries, and the orthodox Gower was as certain as Wyclif that the monks were unchaste. But if allowance is made for the low standards of all classes in that age and for the peculiar difficulties of the celibate clergy, there is no reason to think that the monasteries were wonderfully bad in that respect. Certainly the ascetic impulse of former ages had died away, and the monks were no longer famous for strict adhesion to their rule. The ordinary monk lived luxuriously by the standards of that age, dressed smartly, and was fond of good food. The former restrictions

on his meat diet had been relaxed. He was fond of field sports –
but so were other men. It was not the sinfulness but the
uselessness of the monk on which the world commented most.
The worst that Langland could say of him was that when
outside the cloister he appeared as –

> A rider, a roamer by streets
> A leader of lovedays [manor-court sittings] and a land buyer
> A pricker on a palfrey from manor to manor,
> An heap of hounds at his arse as he a lord were.[1]

And the poet looks forward to a day which indeed came in the
fullness of time –

> Then shall the abbot of Abingdon and all his issue for ever
> Have a knock of a King and incurable the wound.

Already it was to the kingly power that Church reformers,
baffled by Pope and bishops, were beginning to turn their
hopes. Parliament was already demanding a large disendowment of the Church, which had swallowed so much land from
countless generations of benefactors and gave not an acre back.
But the time had not yet quite come when the general conscience considered that lay power could dispose of the sacred
endowments of the Church. The omnicompetence of the King
in Parliament was not yet an established constitutional doctrine. The parallel authorities of Church and State, of Convocation and Parliament still represented the actual balance
of society.

In one great branch of service to mankind the Church in the
age of Chaucer was neither decadent nor even stagnant. The
continuous but ever moving tradition of ecclesiastical architecture still proceeded on its majestic way, filling England with

1. Langland's criticism of the monk's life was not, like much
modern criticism including Wyclif's, due to want of appreciation of
the retired, contemplative life of self-abnegation, but to Langland's
perception that the monks had ceased to realize that ideal. 'The
Middle Ages had no doubt that the Contemplative Mary had chosen
her part better than the Active Martha.' But the monks had ceased to
be Maries without becoming Marthas.

For the understanding of *Piers Plowman* I would recommend the
reader to the illuminating essays on the subject in Professor R. W.
Chambers's *Man's Unconquerable Mind*, 1939.

towering forests of masonry of which the beauty and grandeur have never been rivalled by either the Ancients or the Moderns. With a brief pause in building caused by the Black Death, the march of English architecture in cathedral, abbey, and parish church went forwards through the Decorated and the Flamboyant to the Perpendicular, the chief new feature being the elaboration of tracery, and the size of the great windows each with its framework of stone shafts [80–82]. Archdeacons on their visitations would condemn a little old Norman church, perfect in its own way, as 'too small and too dark'. In the newer churches the light no longer crept but flooded in, through the stained glass of incomparable beauty and richness of colour. No doubt the medieval Church became too wealthy, no doubt her rival chiefs and corporations suffered from the sins of pride and luxury and narrow *esprit de corps*; but if the Church had been as St Francis or as Wyclif wished, a poor, devoted evangelist, those cathedrals and minsters would never have been built in such supreme magnificence, to stand, century after century, silently praising God, giving to one generation of men after another the purest and highest delight of worship that can be kindled through the eye.

The section of the medieval Church that was under least discipline and had only too little 'corporate sense' was the army of unbeneficed priests, deacons, and clerks in holy orders who were scattered about the country, in every variety of employment, often under no control beyond that of their lay employers. In most cases they fulfilled functions performed in the modern world by laymen. They were the 'clerks' (in both senses of the word) who wrote papers and kept accounts for men of affairs, whether merchants, landowners, or officials. Others fulfilled sacred functions, as private chaplains in castle or manor-house, or as 'chantry priests', paid by laymen to say masses for the souls of departed relations. Many drifted about from one job to another, forming lazy and criminal habits that made them in the end 'unemployable' for any good purpose.

The 'clerks' in business houses and legal or State offices were performing functions necessary for society, and were neither better nor worse men than their neighbours. But in

80. 'Towering forests of masonry'; Exeter Cathedral, the nave looking west

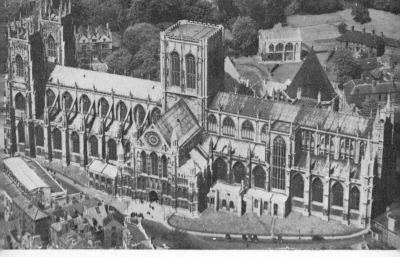

81. York Minster

view of the fact that they were under such slight ecclesiastical discipline it was perhaps unfortunate that they were 'clergy' at all. Except those in minor orders, clerks were expected not to marry,[1] and many of them would have been better with a wife and a settled home. In the literature of the time the 'clerk' is often the hero of an amorous intrigue. Moreover, when they committed crimes of theft or murder they could plead benefit of clergy and so escape from the severe justice of the King to the lighter penances of the Spiritual Court. No wonder that 'criminous clerks' often earned an ill name for themselves and for the Church to which they were so loosely attached.

There was already considerable provision for the education of clerks in reading, writing, and Latin. Three or four hundred grammar schools, most of them indeed very small establishments, were scattered through the length of England. They were usually under the control of monasteries or cathedrals,

1. In fact a number of clergymen, including parsons of parishes, were married. Such marriages were irregular and voidable, but not void until challenged. Others lived in concubinage of a more or less permanent kind. Many English clergy had always resented the rule of clerical celibacy gradually forced on the island after the Norman Conquest. The struggle against it continued till the Reformation gave victory to the rebels.

82. The elaboration of tracery in the great windows: Winchester Cathedral, the nave, looking west

hospitals, guilds, or chantries; the masters whom these authorities appointed were secular clergy. Clever boys of humble origin rose through such schools to be clerks and priests, for the Church was still the career of ambition most easily open to the poor. But no attempt was made to teach reading and writing to the mass of the people until the eighteenth century brought the charity schools.

In 1382 William of Wykeham [83], desiring better education for the secular clergy, founded at Winchester a grammar school on a scale of unexampled magnificence, which became the model for later foundations of equal splendour, like Eton. A certain proportion of the scholars were to be 'sons of noble and powerful (*valentium*) persons', a provision which the historian of our medieval schools has called the 'germ of the public school system' [84].[1]

The two ancient universities of England already existed; but scarcely yet as rivals, for Cambridge only rose to national importance in the fifteenth and sixteenth centuries.

In Chaucer's day, Oxford was the intellectual centre of England and Wyclif's influence was the chief fact in Oxford, until he and his followers were driven out or silenced by the interference of bishops and King with the independent life of the University (1382). If Oxford had been united, the invasion of her liberties would have been more difficult. But there had long been two academic parties, the secular and the regular clergy; the former took Wyclif's side, while the latter turned against him.

The 'regulars' were the monks and friars who had several great convents of their orders attached to the University. In the previous century the friars had been the leaders of academic thought, with their Grossetete, Roger Bacon, and Duns Scotus, and they were still a great power in Oxford.

The 'seculars', who regarded themselves as the University proper, consisted of secular clergy, priests like Wyclif, or deacons and clerks in lower orders. These men were academicians first and churchmen second. They were as jealous for the 'liberties' of their University as a burgher for those of his town. They were always on guard against papal and episcopal

1. A. F. Leach, *Winchester College*, p. 96.

83. William of Wykeham's tomb in his chantry chapel, Winchester Cathedral

84. Winchester College

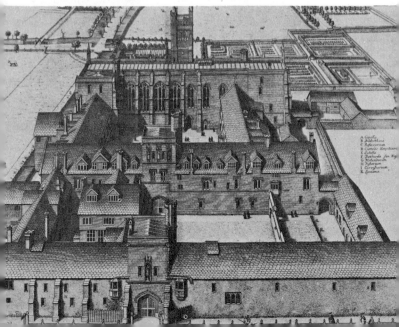

interference, royal mandates, and the claims and privileges of the town. Their rights were defended against all aggression by the hosts of turbulent undergraduates herding in the squalid lodging-houses of Oxford, who, when occasion called, poured forth to threaten the life of the Bishop's messenger, to hoot the King's officials, or to bludgeon and stab the mob that maintained the Mayor against the Chancellor.

Town and gown used daggers, swords, and even bows and arrows in their pitched battles in High Street. In 1355 the townsmen made a regular massacre of clerks and students: the survivors fled in terror from Oxford, and the University closed down until the King intervened to protect and avenge the scholars. At Cambridge, in the riots of 1381, the town destroyed the University charters and records.

The medieval student, before the development of the college system had done its work, was riotous, lawless, and licentious. He was miserably poor; he often learnt very little for want of books and tutoring, and left without taking a degree. Yet many were enthusiastically eager for learning or at least for controversy. Some were only fourteen years old, but most were of an age rather more nearly resembling that of modern undergraduates. Many were still laymen, but nearly all intended to become clerks if not also priests. There can be little doubt that the habits contracted at Oxford and Cambridge account for the violent and scandalous character of so many of the clergy in later life. The authorities of the universities, imitating the folly of authorities in Church and State elsewhere, forbade athletic exercises among the youth in their jurisdiction, but made no great effort to keep them out of the tavern and the brothel; some of them roamed the countryside in robber bands.

But England found a remedy for these evils. The college system, though it had originated in Paris, became in the end the unique characteristic of the two English universities. In the late thirteenth century several colleges had been founded at Oxford, and Peterhouse at Cambridge. But college life was still the exception, and in the early part of Wyclif's career it may be doubted whether more than a hundred of the three thousand Oxonians were under any such discipline – except the monks and friars in their convents. But before Wyclif died,

William of Wykeham had already founded his magnificent New College, with its quadrangular buildings and its 'hundred clerks'. With such a pattern to copy, the English college system grew apace with ever new foundations during the next two centuries [85].

The demand for colleges and the readiness of founders to supply the need were stimulated by religious controversy. The orthodox desired to place the boys, who were to be the clergy of the next generation, in the safe keeping of such institutions and masters as would preserve them from the Wyclif heresy, which raged in the lodging-houses and inns where the students lived crowded together, discussing all things in heaven and earth with the freedom of irresponsible and ardent youth. And, apart from all questions of divinity, parents and practical men saw the advantage of academic homes to shelter the young from material and moral dangers possibly as bad as the intellectual errors of Wyclif. The college system struck root in England and flourished as nowhere else. The business management of the college revenues at this period seems to have been more often efficient than the management of monastic finance.

And so, in the fifteenth century, while the forcible suppression of debate on religious and ecclesiastical questions crippled for a hundred years the intellectual vigour of the English

85. New College, Oxford

universities, the rapid growth of the college system brought about an improvement in morals and discipline, and a civilizing of academic life, for which later generations of Englishmen stand deeply in debt to the Oxford and Cambridge of the late medieval period.

One very important branch of learning had found for itself a home that was neither Oxford nor Cambridge. The lay lawyers, who were building up the common law administered in the King's Courts, had formed for themselves the Inns of Court between London and Westminster, where legal education, other than that of the ecclesiastical courts, was carried on. Maitland has thus described them:

> They were associations of lawyers which had about them a good deal of the club, something of the College, something of the trade union. They acquired the *inns* or *hospices* – that is, the town houses – which had belonged to great noblemen: for example, the Earl of Lincoln's inn. The house and church of the Knights of the Temple came into their hands. . . . The serjeants and apprentices who composed the inns of court enjoyed an exclusive right of pleading in court.[1]

These common lawyers were, as a class, the first learned laymen, and as such were of great importance to the growth of the nation.

1. *Collected Papers*, II, p. 482.

BOOKS FOR FURTHER READING FOR CHAPTERS ONE AND TWO

H. S. Bennett, *Life on the English Manor, 1150–1400*; Eileen Power, *Medieval English Wool Trade*; Trevelyan, *England in the Age of Wycliffe*; E. Lipson, *Economic History of England*, vol. I; *Social England* (edited by Traill), vol. II; Prof. Postan, *The Chronology of Labour Services*, in *R.H.S.* 1937; G. R. Owst, *Preaching in Medieval England*; B. L. Manning, *The People's Faith in the Time of Wyclif*; Coulton, *Chaucer and his England*; Chaucer's *Canterbury Tales* and Langland's *Piers Plowman*, ed. Skeat; *Medieval England*, edited by H. W. C. Davis, 1924; Rashdall, *The Universities of Europe in the Middle Ages*; A. F. Leach, *The Schools of Medieval England*, and review of it by A. G. Little in the *Economic History Review*, 1915, pp. 525–9. For the Church a hundred years before, see *Church Life in England in the Thirteenth Century*, J. R. Moorman, 1945.

CHAPTER THREE

ENGLAND IN THE AGE OF CAXTON

HENRY VI, 1422 – EDWARD IV, 1461 –
EDWARD V, 1483 – RICHARD III, 1483 –
HENRY VII, 1485

It is difficult for us today to imagine how slow was the pace of change before the era of inventions. After the social and intellectual unrest of the English fourteenth century, it might have been expected that something big and dramatic would soon occur. Yet the fifteenth century proved markedly conservative in most aspects of life and thought.

If Chaucer in the ghost had haunted England during the lifetime of Caxton (1422–91), he would have found little to astonish him, except perhaps that nothing had come of all the talk against the Church. As he rode along the familiarly bad highways, still dangerously beset by robbers, and crossed the deep fords and ill-mended bridges, he would see the peasants with their oxen cultivating the same strips in the big open fields, and only if he attended the manor-court would he learn that very few of them were any longer serfs. The wayfarers who accosted him would still be the types he knew so well – pilgrims as many and as jolly as those with whom he had ridden to Canterbury [86]; friars, summoners, and pardoners still at their old games with simple folk; merchants guarding their pack-horse trains; gentry and churchmen with hawk and hound; lords' retainers with bow and spear bound on the same dubious errands as when John of Gaunt's men held the countryside in awe. From their talk of Red and White Roses and battles fought on English soil, he might surmise that disorder was even worse than it had been in his own day, but the nature and cause of misrule was the same: the terrorizing of

86. 'Pilgrims as many and as jolly as those with whom he had ridden to Canterbury'

honest folk by the retainers of great men, and the corruption and intimidation of the law courts and of the Privy Council itself. It would not take Chaucer long to discover from wayside chat that a battle at Agincourt had revived in the minds of his countrymen ideas first implanted there by Crécy when he himself was a boy, to the effect that one Englishman could beat three foreigners and that it was England's proper business and pastime to rule and rob France. And therefore England's own social ills remained incurable as ever. For her success in France had proved no more durable after Agincourt than after Crécy; again driven back over the Channel, the privately enlisted armies had again disturbed peace at home as the retainers of great men.

Most of the towns, our ghostly visitor might notice, had not grown since his day and some had even shrunk. But London

87. Tattershall Castle, Lincolnshire

and Bristol flourished and thrust out new suburbs. In town
and country there were some splendid new churches, guild-
halls, and chantries, and equally splendid enlargements of old
churches. They were all built in an intricate and ornate style of
masonry which would seem to Chaucer a 'newe guise', as also
would the brick buildings now to be seen in the eastern
counties – manor-houses, gatehouses, Cambridge colleges like
Queens' [89], and noblemen's palaces like Tattershall [87],
towering up in red brick – and the King's College at Eton.[1]

In the port towns, bearded mariners, much the same as a
certain 'Shipman' whom Chaucer had described long ago, told

1. There had been no bricks made or used in England after the
thin tile bricks of the Roman period, until in the fourteenth century
bricks began to come in from Flanders (the very name *bricks* is of
French or Walloon origin). In the fifteenth century brick was widely
used in parts of the eastern counties where there was little or no stone
except clunch and where timber was now running short. Already the
bricks were manufactured in England of local clay.

88. Brickmaking in Flanders

89. Queens' College, Cambridge

rough tales of trade and tempest in the Channel and the Biscay Bay; of the luck of English pirates who preyed on the merchandise of Spanish galleys, Genoese carracks, and Breton and Flemish ballingers, and of adventures with foreign pirates who tried to retaliate! And amid all this old, familiar chat about the home seas, might be noted a strange rumour of something new: that certain foreign shipmen were hoping to reach the Indies by sea, round Africa or across the Ocean westward, and that some folk in Bristol were inclined to give ear [90].

In the gentleman's manor-house, the nobleman's castle, and the King's Court, the poet's ghost would find the culture he loved still alive in a faded kind of way. It was good that they should still be reading his poems, but his successors did not seem to do much except imitate with indifferent success. The imagination of youth still seemed prisoner to the formal allegories of medieval love-longing and its conventional discipline, and still delighted in the war of the Greek knights against Troy – as interminable as the English war against

90. English ships at Lisbon

France. But the stories of King Arthur's Table were being newly rendered from the 'Frenssche book' into Malory's immortal English prose.

And if Chaucer's spirit could have peeped over the shoulders of Edward IV at the machine which Master Caxton had brought from Flanders, as it stamped off in quick succession copies of the *Canterbury Tales* to look almost like real manuscripts, the flattered poet would have smiled at so pleasant a toy. He would hardly have foreseen in it a battering-ram to bring abbeys and castles crashing to the ground, a tool that would ere long refashion the religion and commonwealth of England.

After the second expulsion of the English armies from France came the Wars of the Roses at home (1455–85). How far did they affect the social life of England? The answer depends on what we mean by 'the Wars of the Roses'. Very little, if we mean only those brief occasional campaigns conducted by 2,000 to 10,000 men a side, which ended in battles like St Albans, Towton, Barnet, and Bosworth Field.[1] The verdict of such a battle, even if fought far away in Yorkshire or in the Midlands, was usually accepted without more ado by London and by the whole realm, as deciding which group of noblemen was for the time being to govern England. It was not possible for the Houses of York and Lancaster to wage civil war after the manner afterwards employed by Charles I and the Long Parliament, when numerous and enthusiastic armies were maintained by systematic plunder and by national taxation, to make regular campaigns, to besiege walled cities by the score and castles and manor-houses by the hundred. The Lords of the Roses had no such hold over their countrymen: since they could make no appeal to any principle or to any popular senti-ment on behalf of rival pretensions to the Crown, neither side could venture to antagonize opinion by heavy war taxation, by the interruption of trade or the devastation of the countryside, according to the recent and evil example of our armies in France. In this sense it is true that 'the Wars of the Roses' were, mili-tarily speaking, only a skin eruption on the surface of English life.

But if by 'the Wars of the Roses' we mean a period of social disorder which gave rise at intervals to spurts of real warfare, it is clear that the whole social fabric was affected by the general state of misrule. So deep and so widespread was the damage done by 'overgreat subjects' and 'lack of governance', that in the succeeding century the Tudor monarchy was popular because it was strong and could 'bridle stout noblemen and gentlemen'.

In what did this social disorder consist? It was a rural pheno-menon, not much affecting the towns. But the population of England was nine tenths rural, and the social disorder was mainly a struggle of landowners among one another for land.

Most men's conduct is determined by the prevailing fashion of the society in which each lives. Just as in the eighteenth cen-tury the squire was little thought of who did not drain and enclose land, rebuild farm houses, plant trees, enlarge his hall and adorn his grounds – so in the fifteenth century, a country

1. These battles were still fought with the same infantry tactics as Crécy and Agincourt, by archers shooting arrows, and knights and men-at-arms dismounted to fight by the archers' side. But cannon were now occasionally used in the field with effect.

gentleman was likely to imitate his most highly esteemed neighbours, when he observed them devote their time and energy, partly indeed to holding their manor-courts and exacting their rents, but still more to increasing their family estates and fortunes by marriage treaties, and frequently by the armed occupation of a neighbour's estate on some trumped-up claim of law. And those who were themselves the victims of such injustice, could only defend their rightful heritage by a similar combination of legal proceedings and brute force. An English county such as the Pastons' Norfolk was not unlike Europe, with its great and small powers, its alliances sealed by child-marriage, its balance of power, its territorial claims and counterclaims always simmering and occasionally leading to some act of violence or legal chicane. The connexion between this state of society and the official Wars of the Roses is illustrated by the siege of Caister Castle in 1469 by an army of 3,000 men in the pay of the Duke of Norfolk, acting in a purely private quarrel over the right of possession.

The technique of estate-jumping included assault and battery, or downright murder, often committed in a public place and in the eye of day to produce the greater effect. For not only the rival claimant but the jurors in court must be made to go in fear of their lives. Justice was not to be had from juries on the mere merits of a case. The livery of a powerful lord or knight gave immunity for the cutting of purses and even of throats [91].

Under these conditions, any aspirant to importance in the county, any ambitious man covetous of his neighbour's lands, or any quiet man who wished to remain safe in possession of his own, had need to secure the patronage of some magnate of the realm to be 'good lord' to him, to overawe the judge and jury when his case came on, and to speak the word for him at the Privy Council that should invoke or prevent interference by the Crown in the course of local justice. Redress was not to be had, unaided by fear or favour, whether in the law courts or at the Council Board.[1]

1. For example, in 1451 the Sheriff of Norfolk told John Paston that it was useless to think of suing Robert Hungerford, Lord Moleyns, because the Sheriff had received 'writing from the King that he make such a panel [as] to acquit the Lord Molynes'.

In the following century the Tudors freed the Privy Council and the courts of law from the dictation of the nobility, put down retainers, and enforced order in the land. But even they could not change human nature, either in themselves or their subjects, and in the palmy days of Elizabeth, Shakespeare put into the mouths of Justice Shallow and his serving-man Davy the principle on which justice was conducted in the fifteenth century, and to a less degree in the later and better times in which Shakespeare himself lived:

DAVY: I beseech you, sir, to countenance William Visor of Woncot against Clement Perks of the Hill.
SHALLOW: There is many complaints, Davy, against that Visor; that Visor is an arrant knave on my knowledge.
DAVY: I grant your worship that he is a knave, sir: but yet, god forbid, sir, but a knave should have some countenance at his friend's request. An honest man, sir, is able to speak for himself when a knave is not. I have served your worship truly, sir, this eight years; and if I cannot once or twice in a quarter bear out a knave against an honest man I have but very little credit with your worship. . . .
SHALLOW: Go to: I say he shall have no wrong.

In the fifteenth century perpetual law-suits about title to land, often dragging on for years without settlement, were a serious matter for the farmer of the land in question, especially when both claimants for a manor sent in armed men and extorted the rents by force. The expense of retainers and actions at law, and the agricultural depression of the period, made landlords niggardly about repairs and exorbitant about rents. For the country gentleman looked to his rent-roll to keep him in ready money. In those days, unless he were a breeder of sheep, he had seldom any other source of income in cash other than his money rents, though food and clothing for his household might come off his home farm, or from rents paid in kind.[1]

1. The regular 'investments' by which the upper and middle classes live today did not then exist for ordinary people. But great lords and prelates often had other forms of acquiring wealth besides agriculture. Politics, though very dangerous, was a very lucrative profession. Moreover, statesmen in close touch with the great merchants were let in to good things in trade. Cardinal Beaufort was supposed to deal in wool and certainly worked silver mines in Cornwall

The relation of the landlord to the tenant – whether of open-field strips or of an enclosed farm – was assimilating itself year by year to modern practice. Feudalism proper and serfdom were dying out. But the quasi-feudal position of the landlord still survived in his powerful chairmanship of the manor-court or court-leet, exercised by himself in person or by his steward. There the affairs of lord of the manor and his copyhold tenants were decided and registered, as well as the internal relations of the community of farmers of the open field and sharers of the common pasture and waste. It might not always be possible in practice for the tenants to override the will of the lord or his steward, but the tenants were judges in the court, and the procedure of an open court guided by the traditional custom of the manor was a real check on landlord tyranny, as well as an exercise in self-government for all, in which 'the poorest he' might take his part.

Disputes between landlord and tenant as to the obligation to do repairs, and as to the amount and regularity of rent payments, characterized this period of transition from the old feudal ways to a new leasehold money-system, of which the rules had not yet been regularized by tradition. Landed proprietors, as their correspondence shows, were kept busy over these controversies, and their agents, lay and clerical, had no easy task with a recalcitrant peasantry. James Gloys, the Pastons' chaplain and factotum, who acted as tutor to their sons, and as confidential secretary and land-agent, distrained and threatened to distrain cattle and ploughs. But he too was human: one tenant he declared he could never touch – 'I could never do it, unless I would have distrained him in his mother's house, and this I durst not for her cursing.'

The functions of land-agent were often performed by a gentleman's private chaplain, or even by the parish priest who

---

and Devon. Henry VI paid Adam Moleyns, Privy Seal and Bishop of Chichester, £1,000 to cancel a patent that had authorized him to ship wool where he pleased (Ramsay, *York and Lancaster*, ii, p. 79). This Moleyns was a characteristic figure of that epoch; Clerk of the Council and a politician useful to the great men, he was rewarded for his services to the State with the Bishopric of Chichester and licence to impark 12,000 acres and to fortify twelve manor-houses.

'visited' his flock in this secular capacity. Such mundane employment by the patron of the living must often have involved the parson in questionable proceedings.[1] The use of the beneficed clergy by the laity for their own secular purposes, deriving from a past age when only the clergy could read and write, still prevailed from top to bottom of society. For did not the saintly King Henry VI pay his civil servants with bishoprics and other Church preferment? How else indeed could he pay them, in a land whose people would not endure taxation?

Sometimes the parish priest spent most of his time as a farmer, cultivating his own glebe farm (normally forty to sixty acres of the open field) like the peasant born that he was, and even hiring other lands. Parson Trulliber, the agricultural enthusiast in Fielding's *Joseph Andrews*, was a survival from medieval custom.

Very occasionally the open field was enclosed and divided up into consolidated farms by agreement among the peasant cultivators themselves. And always there was a free land-market among the customary tenants. The thrifty peasant of fifteenth-century England, like the peasant of nineteenth-century France, often saved up money to enlarge his little holding by purchase of his neighbours' strips.

Taken as a whole, the fifteenth century was a good time for the peasant and labourer and a bad time for the landlord. Owing to the continual recurrence of plague, the shortage of the population had not yet been made up since the Black Death, and the decay of serfdom enabled the labourer to take full advantage of this fact by putting a high price on his free service. Not only did the landlord find it very expensive to work his demesne land by hiring labour, but he found it equally difficult to let farms, whether on the demesne or in the open field of the village. The land-hunger of the thirteenth century,

1. The relation of the parson, Sir Oliver Oates, to his master, Sir Daniel Brackley, in Stevenson's *Black Arrow* is, like most other social facts in the book, taken from a close study of the Paston Letters, in spite of the fact that R. L. S. does not seem to have known the difference between a friar and a monk. Another illuminating and more learned study of fifteenth-century thought and social practice is to be found in Mr Evan John's *Crippled Splendour* (1938).

so favourable to the landlord, had been replaced by a glut in land and a hunger for men to cultivate it, and this state of things lasted throughout most of the fourteenth and fifteenth centuries, until the beginning of the Tudor period.

England during the Wars of the Roses was poorer than she had been owing to the unsuccessful French war, followed by civil strife at home, and owing also to the fall in population. The recurrence of plague was most frequent in the towns and ports, where the flea-bearing rats multiplied most; that is to say, the part of the community where wealth was chiefly made was the part most often disorganized and reduced by epidemics. For these reasons the total national income was less than in Chaucer's day; but it was more evenly distributed. The general economic situation was favourable to the peasant and the poor.[1]

This period of rural society is best known to us from the letters of the Paston family and other smaller collections, like the Stonor and Cely Papers. The fifteenth century was the first in which the upper classes of both sexes, and their agents, lay as well as clerical, customarily wrote letters – in 'English tongue' it is to be observed. The times might be out of joint, but education had clearly made great strides since the time when kings and barons had set their seals and inked their crosses to documents they had not the skill to read.

In the age of Caxton, letters were not written for pastime or gossip, but had some practical purpose in view, usually of law,

1. Similarly, today the national income is less than it recently was, but is more evenly distributed. See Professor Postan's important article, 'The Fifteenth Century', in the *Economic History Review*, May 1939:

'Of the 450 odd manors for which the fifteenth-century accounts have been studied, over four hundred show a contraction of land in the hands of tenants and a corresponding fall in the rents. The effect of a falling population and depressed prices on the condition of the peasants is easily imagined. It meant a greater supply of land and lower rents. The improvement in the position of the landholder was accompanied by an improvement in the position of the hired labourer. The real sufferers from the agricultural depression were therefore the landlords.'

See also the article by Mr John Saltmarsh entitled 'Plague and economic decline in England in the later Middle Ages' in the *Cambridge Historical Journal* for 1941.

business, or local politics. But they tell us by the way something of domestic customs. The picture of family life, love, and marriage that emerges from these fifteenth-century letters is well worth consideration; and some of the aspects so revealed which modern readers will find strange, were, we have reason to think, equally or yet more characteristic of earlier ages which have left no such intimate records.

The extreme and formal deference that children were made to show to their parents, the hardness of home and school discipline, the constant 'belashing' of boys and girls and of servants will perhaps cause no surprise. But to some readers, vaguely accustomed to think of the Middle Ages as a period of chivalry and love, with knights ever on their knees to ladies, it may come as a shock to realize that, in the knightly and gentle class, the choice of partners for marriage had normally nothing whatever to do with love; often the bride and bridegroom were small children when they were pledged for life, and, even if adults, they were sold by their parents to the highest bidder. The Pastons and other county families regarded the marriages of their children as counters in the game of family aggrandizement, useful to buy money and estates, or to secure the support of powerful patrons. If the victim destined for the altar resisted, rebellion was crushed – at least in the case of a daughter or a female ward – with physical brutality almost incredible. Elizabeth Paston, when she hesitated to marry a battered and ugly widower of fifty, was for nearly three months on end 'beaten once in the week or twice, sometimes twice in one day, and her head broken in two or three places'. Such were the methods of her mother Agnes, a highly religious, respectable, and successful controller of the large Paston household. Many parents seem to have cared very little who married their children, provided they themselves got the money; John Wyndham, one of the Pastons' neighbours, proposed to sell to a London merchant the right to dispose of his young son in marriage.

These old-established medieval customs, still vigorous in the fifteenth century, may at first seem inconsistent with the tone of medieval literature; for three centuries past, poetry had been the analysis of love-longing, the service and devotion of the knight to his lady, sung in strains of rapture and in forms of mystic allegory [92, 93]. Such indeed was literature as known to the Pastons and their neighbours. But this poetry of love, from its most heavenly flight in Dante's chaste worship of another man's wife, to the more usual idealization of courtly adultery, had seldom anything to do with marriage.

To the educated medieval man and woman, marriage was one relation of life, love another. Love might indeed chance to grow out of marriage, as doubtless it often did. If it did not, the wife tried to assert her rights by her tongue, sometimes with success. But the 'lordship' was held to be vested in the husband, and when he asserted it by fist and stick he was seldom blamed by public opinion. In this unequal struggle, the woman also laboured under the handicap of constantly bearing children – most of whom soon died and had to be replaced. Such marriage was not an ideal state of things, but

92. The garden

93. Courtly love

for centuries it served to people England, a difficult task in those days of plague and medical ignorance.

A nobler view of what marriage might and should mean had not yet been envisaged by general opinion. Even the Church had scarcely been helpful, for her ascetic ideal was unsuited to average human nature. The Fathers had regarded women with suspicion as potential snares of Satan. The Church had indeed endeavoured to protect them by her authority from lawless lust and violence, and her support of the marriage tie had at least made it more difficult for a man to discard his wife – though divorce was sometimes obtained for money. But ecclesiastical authority, which insisted that priests must be celibate, regarded marriage as a lower state. In this imperfect world the laity must be permitted to marry, but the relation of man and wife was not held to touch a high spiritual plane. It was not therefore wonderful that the clergy sanctioned by their ceremonials the customs of child betrothal and child marriage, thereby accepting the materialistic view of the laity, that the rational choice of the parties most concerned was not necessary, and that the marriage of a boy and girl might be a proper subject for barter between other persons.[1]

Since, therefore, love was not the normal basis of marriage, the Troubadours of Languedoc at the end of the eleventh century, and the French and English poets who succeeded them in chanting the service of a pagan 'God of Love' regarded the passion of love as being under no obligation to respect so irrelevant a thing as the marriage bond. It has been shrewdly said that 'any idealization of sexual love in a society where marriage is purely utilitarian, must begin by being an idealization of adultery'. But it need not so end.[2]

The great gift of the medieval poets of the Western world was this new conception of the love of man and woman as a

1. The degree to which the Church tried to limit and in fact allowed child marriage is discussed in Coulton's *Chaucer and his England*, pp. 204–8, ed. 1921.

2. It was said that a Court of Love had pronounced that married persons could not be in love with one another. I would refer the reader to a very remarkable and scholarly book on the whole subject – *The Allegory of Love*, a study in medieval tradition, by C. S. Lewis of Magdalen College, Oxford, 1936.

spiritual thing – the best of all spiritual things, raising men and women above their normal selves in all gentleness and virtue.

> The God of love, a benedicite!
> How mighty and how great a lord is he!
> For he can make of low hertes high,
> And of high low, and like for to die,
> And hard hertes he can maken free. . . .
>
> And thereof cometh all goodnesse,
> All honour and all gentilnesse,
> Worship, ease and all hertes lust,
> Parfit joy and ful assured trust,
> Jolitee, pleasaunce and freshnesse,
> Lowlihead, largesse and curtesye,
> Semlihead and true companie,
> Drede of shame for to doon amis;
> For he that trewly love's servaunt is
> Were lother be shamed than to die.[1]

Here was a new and constant source of inspiration to the life of mankind, based on the facts of nature. It was an idea unknown to the Ancients,[2] and unknown to the early Church. Could this thrice precious concept of the medieval poets be allied, by a further revolution, to the state of marriage? Could the lovers themselves become husband and wife? Could the bond of young love be prolonged till age and death? This change has actually taken place in England in the gradual evolution of the idea and practice of marriage. It was not an inevitable change. In France, for instance, the arranged marriage is still normal, though of course the civilized French parent pays far greater consideration to the wishes and mutual compatibility of the young people than did Mistress Agnes Paston. And such marriages are often very happy. But in England the arranged marriage has given place to the love match; the parents have yielded to the children the choice of their own destiny. The battle of Gretna Green has been won.

This victory of freedom and love has behind it a long roll of

1. Sir Thomas Clanvowe, *The Cuckoo and the Nightingale*, time of Henry IV, formerly attributed to Chaucer.
2. There is a very shrewd analysis of marriage and love in the Graeco-Roman world in John Buchan's *Augustus*, p. 244.

unknown warriors and martyrs. No doubt there were many cases of lovers marrying, all through the Middle Ages. Men did not always obey their fathers, and fathers were sometimes human, and often died young. Chaucer's *Franklin's Tale* is a beautiful story of a marriage made and maintained by love. And in the fifteenth century things were slowly moving. The poet-King, James I of Scotland, made his love his Queen, and wrote *The Kingis quair* in her honour.

Even in the society of the prosaic Pastons we have epistolary record of at least two love marriages. In the first case, that of Margery Brews and John Paston in 1477, the girl won over her soft-hearted mother to the romantic view. Here, in the original spelling, is Margery's love letter to John while the matter was still being negotiated, not very hopefully, on the usual purely financial ground:

Right reverent and wurschypfull, and my ryght welebeloved Voluntyne [Valentine]
. . . My lady my moder hath labored the mat[t]er to my ffadur full delygently, but she can no mor gete [namely she can get no more dowry provided with me] than ye knowe of, for the wheche God knowythe I am full sory. But yf that ye loffe [love] me, as I tryste verely that ye do, ye will not leffe [leave] me therefor.

Her next letter on the same situation, though not very grammatical, is as moving as anything in English prose (I give it in modernized spelling):

Wherefore, if ye could be content with that good [namely, that amount of dowry] and my poor person, I would be the merriest maiden on ground. And if ye think not yourself so satisfied, or that ye might have much more good as I have understood by you before; good, true, and loving Valentine, that ye take no such labour upon you as to come [any] more for that matter but let it pass and never more be spoken of, as I may be your true lover and bede-woman during my life [namely, pray for you the rest of my life].

This was too much for John. He was more his own master than many young men, for his father was dead, and he put the matter through in spite of the doubts of his mother and relations.

The other Paston love story had a longer and rougher course but reached an equally happy haven. Margery Paston had the

137

courage secretly to plight herself to Richard Calle, the bailiff of the Paston estates. Such betrothals were regarded as binding and the Church could not refuse to maintain them, but they were sometimes broken by the consent of the parties. For years the girl stood out against the fury and bullying of her family, till at last, wearied out by her obstinacy and still desiring to retain the indispensable services of their too aspiring bailiff, the Pastons allowed the lovers to complete their marriage.

Already in the popular ballad literature of the later fifteenth century the motif of the love marriage was more and more making itself heard, as in the 'Nut-Brown Maid' [94], ancestress of the 'Bailiff's Daughter of Islington' and a hundred other romantically married heroines of ballad. When we reach the age of Shakespeare, literature and the drama treat mutual love as the proper, though by no means the invariable, basis of marriage. The struggle of children against parents for matrimonial freedom has got hold of the sympathetic popular imagination, and the commonest interest on the Elizabethan stage is the devotion of lovers aiming at marriage, and the adventures of runaway couples like Master Fenton and Anne Page. Clearly the love marriage was more frequent by the end of the Tudor period, but child marriages were still all too common: in this matter the reformed Church was at first as much in fault as the medieval. In 1582, Bishop Chaderton married off his only daughter Joan, aged nine, to a boy of eleven: the result was bad. On another occasion John Rigmarden, aged three, was carried in the arms of a clergyman who coaxed him to repeat the words of matrimony to a bride of five. Before the end he struggled to get down, saying he would learn no more that day; but the parson said, 'You must speak a little more and then go play you.'[1]

And so the slow and long contested evolution towards the English love match goes on throughout our social history, until in the age of Jane Austen and the Victorians free choice in love is accepted as the basis of marriage, even in the best society, and any more mercenary arrangement is regarded as exceptional and suspect. The lawless and pagan 'God of Love', whose altar the medieval poets had erected, has been baptized,

1. Early English Text Society, 1897, *Child Marriages*, etc., p. xxii.

¶To pay at the ferp for a man and his bagage.iiij.miȝ
¶Item a hors the man and his bagage.i.gȝ.
¶Item an emty hors onlp i ð.   Brokers to pay for a cloth vnder pl.
ȝ.the broker shal haueij.gȝ.
¶Item for a cloth aboue xl. ꝭ.the broker hath iiij gȝ.
¶Item C.ellis Cotton cloth payth lpke a clothe iiij.gȝ.ꝛc.

Be it right or wrõg.these mē a mong.on womē do cõplaine
Affermyng this.how that it is.alabour spent in vaine
To loue thē wele.for neuer a dele.they loue a man agayne
For lete a man do.what he can.ther fouour to attayne
Yet yf a newe.to them pursue.ther furst trew louer than
Laboureth for nought.and from her though.he is a bannisshed mã

Say not nay.bat that all day.it is bothe writ and sayde
That womans fapth.is as who sapthe.all vtterly decaped
But neutheles.right good witues.i this case might be lap
That they lone trewe.& cõtynew.recorde ꝑ Nutbrowne maide de
Which fre in her loue.whã her to proue.he cam to make his mone
Wolde not departe.for in her herte.she loupd but hym allone

Than bettwene vs.lete vs discusse.what was all the maner.
Betwene them too.we wyl also.telle all they peyne in fere
That she was in.now I begynne.soo that ye me answere.
Wherfore ye.that present be.I pray you geue an eare
I em the knyght.I cum be nyght.as secret as I can
Sayng alas.thus stondyth the cause.I am a bannisshed man

And I your wylle.for to fulfylle.in this wyl not refuse
Trusting to shewe.in wordis fewe.ꝑ men haue an ille vse
To other owne shame wymē.to blame.& causeles thē accuse.
Therfore to you.I answere now.alle wymen to excuse.
Myn owne hert dere.wꝑou what chiere.I pray you telle anoon
For in my mynde.of all mankynde.I loue but yon allon

i   It stõdith so.a dede is do.wherfore moche harme shal growe
        My destenp.is for to dye.a shamful dethe I trowe
Or ellis to flee.the ton must dye.none other wey I knowe.
But to wdrawe.as an outlaw.and take me to my bowe
                                    xru

LIFE AT THE MANOR

95. Spinning and weaving

96. The farm

and has settled down as a married man in the England of Alfred Tennyson and Mr and Mrs Robert Browning.

Among the poor, it is probable that marriage choice had always been less clogged by mercenary motives. We have but slight evidence on the subject, but we may presume that among the peasantry in the Middle Ages, as in all ages, Dick and Nan walked together in the wood and afterwards to church for reason of loveliking, added to the belief that Nan would make a good mother and housewife, and that Dick was a good workman, or 'had a pig put up in a stye' besides some strips in the open field. Marriage to legalize the consequences of incontinence was exceedingly common, especially in the lower ranks of society where maidens could not be so carefully guarded at all hours. But girls of the class of the Pastons were under their mother's strict watch and ward, so that the licentious amours of the gentry had usually to be conducted with either the daughters of the poor or the wives of the rich.

When once a lady was married, she entered on a sphere of activity, influence, and even authority. The Paston letters tell the tale of several generations of matrons by no means slaves to their husbands, but rather their counsellors and trusted lieutenants. They seem utterly devoted to their lords' interests, to which their numerous children must be sacrificed. They are better wives and housekeepers than mothers. Their letters show them taking part in the legal and business interests of the family, as well as in the purely domestic sphere where they ruled supreme.

To organize the feeding and clothing of the inhabitants of one or more manor-houses was in itself a task for a life, requiring the same sort of administrative ability as ladies in our day so often devote to public work or professional employment. The household requirements could not in those days be met by hasty 'shopping'. Everything that could not be supplied by the estate must be ordered in the requisite quantities months beforehand – wines of France, sugar grown in the Mediterranean, spices, pepper, oranges, dates, and the better kinds of cloth. It was the lady's business to make these provident calculations of coming needs and to see that orders were placed with solid merchants of the county capital or more often in

London, for even Norwich failed to supply such overseas goods as would now be found in the shops of any small market town. As to home produce, the preparation, curing, and storing of the meal, meat, and game off the estate and the fish from the ponds, besides the command of the dairy, the brew-house, and of the kitchen with its fire of logs roaring up the great chimney, were all under the supervision of the lady châtelaine. Much of the clothing, too, of the inmates of the manor-house was spun and woven, cut out and made up in the house or the neighbourhood under the lady's orders. Her daughters did not go to town to buy their dresses, though one might hope to have the stuff for one's best dress fetched from London. The young men, as brightly and fancifully clothed as their sisters, having more liberty to travel, could more often deal with a city tailor [95, 96].

Thus we can imagine the innumerable and constant activities of a wealthy matron, and *mutatis mutandis* the housewife's round of work in all ranks of life.

The walls of manor-house rooms in this period were hung with cloth: the hall and better chambers with the rich 'cloth of Arras', tapestries today of museum value, representing hunting scenes or religious or allegorical subjects [41, 97]; the commoner rooms with woven hangings either of one bright colour or of variegated stripes. Framed pictures had as yet no place in the English mansion, but the walls themselves were often painted. To judge by what is left of the mural painting in Eton College Chapel, done by an English artist, William Baker, between 1479 and 1488, there must have been much fine painting on walls in the England of the Wars of the Roses – almost all perished long ago [98].

Chimneys in the wall were more and more replacing the open hearth in the middle of the room, whence the smoke had escaped as best it could through open windows. The Pastons were making this great improvement in their manor-houses as early as the reign of Henry VI, but the change was gradual, for as late as the reign of Elizabeth, William Harrison remembered and regretted the old system:

Now have we manie chimnies, and yet our tenderlings complaine of rheumes, catarhs, and poses. Then had we none

97. Flemish tapestry at St Mary's Hall, Coventry

but reredoses [braziers in the centre of the hall], and our heads did never ache. For as the smoke of those daies was supposed to be a sufficient hardning of the timber of the houses, so it was reputed to be a far better medicine to keep the good man and his family. (Book II, chap. XXII)

Harrison would have sympathized with the most conservative remark ever made by Doctor Johnson, who in 1754 said to Thomas Warton about the old 'Gothic' halls: 'In these halls the fire-place was anciently always in the middle of the room, till the Whigs removed it on one side.' But this terrible innovation had been going gradually forward for three or four hundred years before there was a Whig in the world! [99, 100].

In the somewhat hard conception of family life that prevailed in manor-house and castle, there was little welcome extended to a superfluity of maiden aunts or elderly spinsters. If a girl were not married off, she must if possible be placed in a nunnery. To be well rid of her, money was piously paid and there was the girl respectably settled for life. It was rarely possible to become a nun without a dowry. In this way the English nunneries were recruited and in part financed, at least

98. Medieval domestic wall-paintings at Longthorpe Tower, near Peterborough

in the fourteenth and fifteenth centuries [101, 102]. Whatever they may have been in theory, or in the distant past, they were not in this era refuges for the poor, or houses for women with a special call to the religious life. The records of the frequent episcopal visitations show that there was a good deal of female human nature in the nunneries, and that discipline was relaxed, though scandal was only occasional. The nun, and particularly the lady abbess or prioress, seldom forgot that she was a lady born and bred. Like Chaucer's Madam Eglentyne, she was a model of fashion and deportment rather than of devotion.

The rules for dress and conduct drawn up long ago by founders with ascetic ideas were very generally neglected: 'for more than six weary centuries the bishops waged a holy war against fashion in the cloister and in vain'. The episcopal visitor was often deafened by a flood of shrill female eloquence, the prioress complaining of the nuns, and all the dozen nuns together accusing the prioress, till the good man fled before the storm, having effected little by his visitation. In vain the bishops attempted to dislodge the regiments of 'hunting dogs and other hounds' – and sometimes the monkeys[1] – with which, contrary to rule, the poor ladies solaced their long leisure. 'At one nunnery in the Lincoln diocese, when the bishop came and deposited a copy of the Bull in the house and ordered the nuns to obey it, they ran after him to the gate and threw the Bull at his head, screaming that they never would observe it.'

The nunneries, though numerous, were very small. Of the one hundred and eleven Houses in England only four had over thirty inmates. The total number of nuns in the country was

---

1. We know how the nuns' monkeys reached this island. The author of the *Libel of English Policy* (1436) complained that

> ' The grete galees of Venees and Florence
> Be well ladene wythe thynges of complacence,
> All spicerye and other grocers ware,
> With swete wynes, all manere of chaffare,
> Apes and jades and marmusettes taylede,
> Nifles, trifles that litell have availed,'

in return for which they take away our good cloth.

99. The Great Hall, Penshurst Place, Kent, showing the open hearth or brazier in the centre

100. Fireplace at Tattershall Castle, Lincolnshire

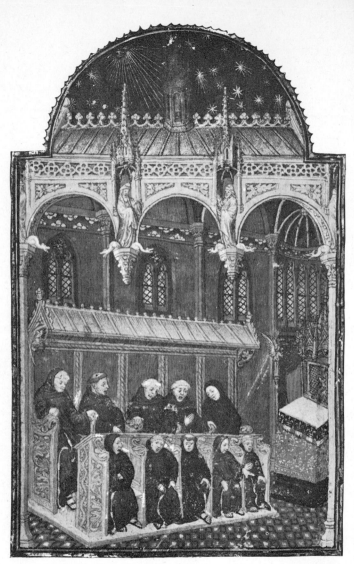

101 and 102. Monks and nuns in choir

between 1,500 and 2,000. But of course each nunnery had also servants attached and one or more priests.

In the fifteenth century these establishments were going downhill financially and otherwise. Before Henry VIII took the matter so drastically in hand, eight nunneries had been suppressed in the course of forty years at the instigation of orthodox bishops. For example, Bishop Alcock of Ely in 1496 founded Jesus College, Cambridge, in place of St Radegund's nunnery, of which he procured the dissolution on the ground of 'the negligence and improvidence and dissolute disposition and incontinence of the religious women of the same house, by reason of the vicinity of Cambridge University'. The successors of those two Cambridge scholars who visited the Trumpington Mill in Chaucer's day had apparently been paying too much attention to the nuns of St Radegund. At the very end there were only two nuns left, one an absentee and the other an 'infant'. So at least said the Bishop, anxious to clear the ground for a more useful institution.

St Radegund's was an exceptionally bad case, but it remains true that the nunneries of England were less useful and admirable houses of religion in the later Middle Ages than they are today.[1]

Between the time of Wyclif's criticism on the great endowments of the Church, and the onslaught of Henry VIII, gifts of land and money were still commonly made, but they now went less often to houses of monks, nuns, and friars than to chantries and schools. In these latter days, wealthy gentry and burghers in their gifts and bequests seemed to be thinking more of themselves and of their fellow laymen, and less of Holy Church. The endowment of a school was in the fifteenth century as useful for the education of laymen as of priests. And the foundation of a chantry was largely a self-regarding act: in a chantry, one or more priests were paid to say mass for the soul of the founder. And whatever one's expectations about the next world, it was clearly a way of endowing a living monument to one's own memory here below. A chantry often took

1. The authoritative works which I have quoted on the subject are Eileen Power's *Medieval English Nunneries* and her chapter on 'Madame Eglentyne' in *Medieval People*.

the architectural form of a delicately wrought side-chapel in a church, with the founder's tomb large therein; sometimes it was a separate building, a small church or chapel, carrying down to posterity the founder's name. 'There's hope a great man's memory may outlive his life half a year: but by'r lady he must build churches, then, or else shall he suffer not thinking on. . . .' [103–5].

The fifteenth century, for all its troubles, was a great time for increased educational facilities and endowments. There had been many schools in Chaucer's England, but there were many more on the eve of the Reformation. The fifteenth-century bishops, often worldly-wise men of a good type, loved to endow schools. Municipal guilds and individual burghers and merchants, increasing in wealth and in family connexions with

103. John Rous, chantry priest of Guy's Cliff, near Warwick, compiling the Warwick Roll

104. Chantry Chapel, Wakefield Bridge, Yorkshire

the landed gentry, took pride in founding schools which would give to other boys of their town or shire the chance to rise, either to be future priests and bishops, or equally well to be future mayors, merchants, royal ministers and clerks, judges, and lawyers, gentry capable of managing their estates and ruling their county for the King.[1]

England, in fact, acquired a fine-system of secondary education. Many of these schools were endowed to teach 'the poor' gratis; but the poor who benefited by them were not the labouring class but the relatively poor, the lower middle class, the sons or protégés of small gentry, yeomen, and burghers who rose through these schools to take part in the government of the land. Thus were prepared the social and intellectual changes of the next century, by the training up of a new middle

1. Between 1390 and 1415 papal and episcopal registers frequently mention 'Literate laymen' – a phenomenon then coming into notice. As the fifteenth century goes on the expression drops out of use, because the class it describes has become too common for remark, and the grammar schools educated an ever increasing proportion of laymen (M. Deanesly, *The Lollard Bible*, 1920, p. 209).

105. The Waynflete Chantry, Winchester Cathedral

class of scholarly laymen and scholarly priests, for both had their part in the great movements that shortly took place. Grammar schools were not, as used to be thought, the result of the English Reformation: they were its cause.

Before the Greek and Ciceronian Renaissance reached our island at the end of the fifteenth century, secondary education, from aristocratic Winchester and Eton downwards, was based on the teaching of Latin – Virgil, Ovid, and some Christian authors. The medieval Church had long ago acquired a liberal reverence for the ancient writers in spite of their pagan errors, and out of the liberality grew much that was finest in European civilization. Boys in the grammar schools wrote Latin verse and prose compositions, and stood up in class to translate the Latin authors into English, already the universal medium of instruction; only in some schools French was used alternatively, not because it was any longer spoken by the boys at home, but on the contrary 'lest the French tongue be wholly lost'. But out of school hours no language must be talked except Latin! For some centuries to come this amazing rule was sanctioned by the usual brutalities of flogging. Sometimes a 'lupus' or spy was paid to sneak among the boys and report if any of them used an English word in their play. How fully, one wonders, did this harsh prohibition actually take effect? Was Latin less 'a dead language' and more a real medium of speech to the grammar-school boy of the fifteenth century than to the public-school boy of the nineteenth? There are many reasons to suppose that it was. Familiarity with Latin such as the grammar schools set out to supply was indeed essential in those days to any professional career. It was not merely the priest who needed it; it was required also by the diplomat, the lawyer, the civil servant, the physician, the merchant's accountant, the town clerk, in many of the documents connected with their daily work.

The sons of the nobility and gentry were educated in various ways, differing according to the rank or the personal views of their parents. Some stayed in the manor-house and were taught letters by the chaplain, field sports by the forester, and the use of arms by an old retainer or a neighbour knight [106–9]. More usually they were sent away from home, an English practice that seemed heartless to foreigners, but was perhaps more good

106. At school

than bad in its results. Some sat in the grammar schools,
conning Latin, cheek by jowl with the ablest sons of burghers
and yeomen. Others went to smaller private schools, even then
sometimes kept by a married master.[1] Others again were

1. *Stonor Letters*, I, p. 21.

107. Field sports

boarded in monasteries under the special care of the abbot.[1]
At some time between the ages of fourteen and eighteen they
might go on to Oxford or Cambridge, while others completed
their education as 'henchmen' or squires at the King's Court,
or in the Court-like households of great noblemen. There the
acquirements most valued were not Latin, but skill in riding,
jousting at tournaments, field sports, dancing, harping, piping,
and singing – and doubtless all the forms of love-making.
Moralists denounced these establishments as the ruin of the
youth trained in them. No doubt some were better than others,
but the noblemen as a class and their retinues were going
downhill at the latter end of the fifteenth century, and the men

1. Shortly before the Dissolution, the Abbot of Reading writes to
Lord Lisle, 'I have set your young gentleman with William Edwards,
my under-steward, that he may be well seen to by a woman for his
dressing, for he is too young to shift for himself. He is the most
forwardly child in learning that I have known' (G. Baskerville, *English
Monks and the Suppression of the Monasteries*, p. 37).

108. Students

from the manor-house, the counting-house, the grammar
school, and the university, were coming up. To them the new
age was destined to belong. Many of the gentlemen's sons who
did best in after life were those who had been apprenticed to
craftsmen and merchants, a custom which increasingly

109. A scholar

differentiated English from French society, merging the gentles
with the burghers.

William of Wykeham's Winchester, and Eton College founded by Henry VI in 1440, were gradually approximating to the
character of 'public schools' in the English sense of the word –

schools where the sons of the gentry were educated. Winchester from the first had a contingent of this class, and from the first was a national, not merely local, grammar school; it drew boys from all over the south, the Midlands, and even from Cheshire and Lancashire. Many of the scholars stayed till the age of eighteen. Eton was in great financial difficulties during the Wars of the Roses. But this, says Mr Leach,

perhaps hastened rather than retarded the development of the school into a great public school for the upper classes and the aristocracy, who while paying nothing for their education, paid large sums for boarding in the houses of the fellows, and in the town of Eton, whence they came to be called Oppidans.[1]

And so in 1477 young William Paston was sent from the Norfolk manor-house to Eton, to learn Latin translation and composition in verse and prose, and to consort with other young gentlemen, though his parents were lamentably slow at paying his boarding expenses, which fell nine months in arrear. His tutor on one occasion lent him twenty shillings, which we should multiply many times to get the modern equivalent.

In a previous generation, the first John Paston had gone to the neighbouring University of Cambridge, to learn law at Trinity Hall, prior to going on to the Inner Temple. In that litigious era, a squire had need to know law to preserve his property, as his worldly-wise mother, Agnes, wrote to him:

I advise you to think once of the day [every day] of your father's counsel to learn the law, for he said many times that whosoever should dwell at Paston should need to conne [know how to] defend himself.

John's son, Walter Paston, was sent to the more distant Oxford under charge of the family chaplain and man-of-all-works, James Gloys. His mother Margaret was anxious lest the clerks of the University should persuade him to take Holy Orders: 'I would love him better to be a good secular man than a lewit [unworthy] priest.'

While Walter Paston was at Oxford in 1474, he must have seen the walls of Magdalen, the college founded by Bishop

1. Leach, *Schools of Medieval England*, p. 259.

110. Grammar Hall, Magdalen College, Oxford

Waynflete two decades back, at length beginning to rise after a long delay caused by the Wars of the Roses. Wykeham's New College, already a hundred years old, had a fair rival in the architecture of Magdalen, where the quadrangle received the novel form of a roofed cloister adorned with stone figures. At Cambridge also the building of Henry VI's King's College was retarded by the troubles of his reign: even the chapel had to wait till the Tudor age for completion, with the happy result that it obtained the modern splendour of its fan-vaulted roof.[1] But Queens' College on the riverside, founded by Margaret of Anjou, rose in the lifetime of her meek husband, giving, with his own Eton, proof of what fine things could now be done with brick [89, 110–13].

Throughout the fifteenth century, Cambridge was gaining ground as a serious rival to Oxford. Though Church and State had in 1382 successfully purged the older university of Wycli-

1. Willis and Clark, I, p. 494.

fism, it was still suspect of heresy in the minds of pious parents choosing a university. Partly for this reason, the number of Oxford students fell, and the number of Cambridge students rose during the next hundred years, and royal patronage was turned to the foundation of colleges on the banks of the hitherto neglected Cam. By the end of the century a high proportion of bishops were Cambridge men. But though the younger university was rising fast in numbers, wealth, and importance as a place of education, neither Cambridge nor Oxford added much to scholarship or thought until the coming of the New Learning in the first years of the Tudor Kings. Speculation and scholarship had to be orthodox, and orthodoxy was no longer mentally creative, as in the days of the great medieval schoolmen.

But during this conservative age the college system took firm root, and thereby an end was put in England to the uncared-for and undisciplined life of the medieval student. It is the tendency of all movements to go too far in the first blush of

111. Magdalen College, Oxford; the roofed cloister with stone figures

112. Duke Humphrey's Library in the Bodleian, Oxford

success, and undergraduate discipline became in some respects too strict in the fifteenth and sixteenth centuries. At least this must have been so if all the college and university rules of Yorkist and Tudor times were actually carried out, for in that case the undergraduates were treated like schoolboys. One of the sanctions was flogging, previously unknown in universities. This is the more remarkable as the age of undergraduates was tending to rise: when Erasmus was at Oxford and Cambridge there were more students of seventeen and fewer of fourteen than in the days of Wyclif. But it is always difficult to know how far and how often rules were enforced, and presumably matters adjusted themselves to circumstances and cases. At any rate the time had gone by for ever when there was no such thing as academic discipline. Already by the end of the fifteenth century the framework of collegiate Oxford and Cambridge had been created once for all.

With the increase in the numbers of readers taught in the schools and universities of England, what were the books they

113. Fan-vaulting at King's College Chapel, Cambridge

read ? Works of piety and religion were much in demand, but the Bible was little known. Its possession in English without licence was regarded by the Church authorities as presumptive evidence of heresy. Lollardry, now without learning or leadership, was confined to the poor. It was proscribed and driven underground; it was not dead, but ready to sprout up again as soon as times changed. A score of heretics were burned alive in the fifteenth century; many more recanted to evade the stake; many escaped notice or at least arrest.

Apart from books of piety, Latin classics taught at school, and heavy tomes of learning for real scholars, the commonest types of reading among gentry and burghers were chronicles of England and of France in verse and in prose, endless romances in prose and in 'rhyme doggrel' about Troy, King Arthur, and a hundred other traditional tales.[1] The constant reproduction of copies of Chaucer, Langland, and Mandeville's *Travels* (how the crocodile weeps as it eats men), proved the abiding popularity of those old authors. Political satires in English verse were much circulated in manuscript; so was the *Libel of English Policy*, written in 1436 to urge that the first duty of government was to keep the home seas with an adequate royal fleet, alike for reasons of military defence and commercial policy.

> Kepe thou the see abought in speciall
> Which of England is the rounde wall,
> As though England were lykened to a cité
> And the wall environ were the see.

Besides private libraries, public libraries were being formed, such as Duke Humphrey's at Oxford, the University Library at Cambridge, Whittington's at Grey Friars in London, and

---

1. Roger Ascham, Queen Elizabeth's schoolmaster, wrote retrospectively: 'In our forefathers' time, when papistry, like a standing pool, covered and overflowed England, few books were read in our tongue saving certain books of chivalry, as they said for pastime and pleasure. . . . As one, for example, *La Morte d'Arthure*, the whole pleasure of which book standeth in two special points, in open manslaughter and bold bawdry. . . . Yet I know when God's Bible was banished the Court, and *La Morte d'Arthure* received into the Princes Chamber.'

another at Guildhall. Of lighter literature there was little except ballads, and they were more often recited or chanted than written and read. The eternal human appetite for stories was for the most part satisfied by word of mouth. To kill the long hours, men and women still practised the social art of story-telling, besides music on all sorts of instruments, and singing of songs.

Such was the state of society and letters when Caxton set up his printing-press in England.

William Caxton (1422–91) was a product of the new middle class and its improved education. He was an early and a noble example of a well-known modern type that has done so much for the world, the individualistic Englishman following out his own 'hobbies' with business capacity and trained zeal. As a successful merchant of the London Mercers' Company, he made enough money during his thirty years residence in the Low Countries to be able to devote his later years to the literary pursuits he loved. He began by translating French books into English. While so engaged, he fell in with the new mystery of printing with movable types, and studied it at Bruges and Cologne. In 1474–5 he produced abroad two of his own translations (one of them a medieval romance and the other *The Game and Playe of Chesse*), the first books to be printed in our language [114–16].

114. The Merchant Adventurers' House, where Caxton lived in Bruges

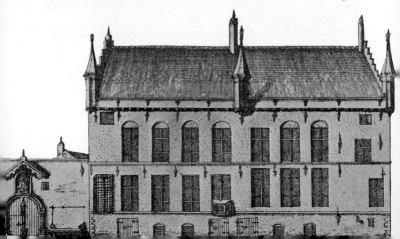

Prelũ Ascẽsianũ

115. The oldest known representation of a printing-press (Paris, 1507)

Then in 1477 he brought over his press to England, set it up at Westminster, under the shadow of the abbey, and there, during the remaining fourteen years of his life, under royal and noble patronage, he poured out nearly a hundred books, many of them in folio, and most in the English tongue. Among them were Chaucer, Gower, Lydgate, Malory's *Morte Darthur* and translations of Cicero and of Aesop's *Fables*. His industry was

116. A German printing-press (1568)

prodigious. Besides his constant and arduous labours at the press he translated as many as twenty books. He had indeed a missionary zeal for the dissemination of good and useful books among his countrymen 'in our English language'. His diligence and success as translator, printer, and publisher did much to lay the foundations of literary English, and to prepare the way for the great triumphs of our language in the following century.

His own use of the machine which he established as part of our island life was at once ideal and practical, but it was not controversial. Yet the press would henceforth be the weapon of every political or religious controversy; the tempo of the spread of ideas and of knowledge would be immensely accelerated. But in the year Caxton died that consequence had scarcely yet been realized.

On the other hand, Caxton was well aware of the importance of his work in fixing the form of the English language for educated people, and he therefore gave much thought and asked much advice as to the dialect into which he had best translate the books he printed. He described these difficulties in his Prologue to the *Eneydos*,[1] his translation from a French paraphrase of Virgil's *Aeneid*:

> After dyuerse werkes made translated and achieued, hauing noo werke in hande, I, sittyng in my studye where as laye many dyuerse paunflettis and bookys, happened that to my hande came a lytyl booke in frenshe, whiche late was translated oute of latyn by some noble clerke of fraunce, whiche booke is named *Eneydos* made in latyn by that noble poete and grete clerke Vyrgyle.
>
> And whan I had aduysed me in this sayd boke, I delybered and concluded to translate it in-to englysshe, And forthwyth toke a penne and ynke, and wrote a leefe or tweyne whyche I ouersawe agayn to corecte it. And whan I sawe the fayr and straunge termes therin, I doubted that it sholde not please some gentylmen whiche late blamed me, sayeng that in my translacyons I had ouer curyous termes whiche coude not be vnderstande of comyn peple and desired me to vse olde and homely termes in my translacyons. And fayn wolde I satisfye euery man; and so to doo, toke an olde boke and redde therein and certaynly the englysshe was so rude and brood that I coude not wele understand it. . . . And certaynly our langage now vsed varyeth ferre from that whiche was vsed and spoken when I was borne. . . . And that comyn englysshe that is spoken in one shyre varyeth from another. In so moche that in my dayes happened that certayn marchauntes were in a shippe in Tamyse, for to haue sayled ouer the see into Selande, and for lacke of wynde thei taryed atte Forlond [North Foreland in Kent], and wente to

1. Early English Text Society, 1890, pp. 1–4.

lande for to refreshe them; And one of theym named Sheffelde, a mercer, cam in-to an hows and axed for mete; and specyally he axyed after eggys; and the goode wyf answerde, that she coude speke no frenshe. And the marchaunt was angry, for he also coude speke no frenshe, but wolde haue hadde 'egges' and she vunderstode hym not. And theene at laste another sayd that he wolde haue 'eyren' then the good wyf sayd that she vnderstod hym wel. Loo, what sholde a man in thyse dayes now wryte, 'egges' or 'eyren'?

Certainly it is harde to playse euery man by cause of dyuersite and chaunge of langage. And som honest and grete clerkes haue ben wyth me, and desired me to wryte the moste curyous termes that I coulde fynde. And thus between playn, rude and curyous, I stand abasshed, but in my judgemente the comyn termes that be dayli vsed, ben lyghter to be vnderstonde than the olde and auncyent englysshe. And for as moche as this present Booke is not for a rude vplondyssh man to laboure therein ne rede it, but onely for a clerke and a noble gentylman that feleth and vnderstondeth in faytes of armes, in loue, and in noble chyualrye, therefor in a meane bytwene bothe I haue reduced and trans-lated this sayd booke in to our englysshe, not ouer rude ne curyous, but in suche termes as shall be vnderstanden, by goddys grace, accordynge to my copye.

We thus see that Caxton had a choice to make. He had no dictionaries to cramp or to guide him. As he sat in his book-littered study considering the matter, he had not, as we have and as even Shakespeare had, an English language 'given' whose limits he might extend but whose framework he must accept. The number of dialects were almost as numerous as the counties of England, and moreover they were perpetually changing. The northerner, the west country man, even the housewife of Kent with her 'eyren', could not easily under-stand either the London merchant or one another. The victory of the speech of London and the Court may perhaps have been ultimately inevitable, but it was rendered certain and rapid first by Chaucer and his fifteenth-century imitators, who drove the west-midland dialect of *Piers Plowman* out of the field among the educated classes; then by the products of Caxton's press; and last and most of all by the English Bible and Prayer Book, which in Tudor times, thanks to the printing-press, reached everyone who could read and many who could only listen. Thus, in the course of the fifteenth and sixteenth centuries, the educated English obtained a common dialect, corresponding to 'literary English'; and, as education spread, this dialect became the language of all the land.

Throughout the troubled reigns of the Lancastrian and Yorkist kings, London remained peaceful and her wealth constantly increased: the pomp and parade of her magistrates on solemn occasions grew ever more imposing in the streets and on the river; her civic, ecclesiastical, and domestic architecture grew more rich and beautiful, till no wonder at the end of the century the Scottish poet Dunbar exclaimed: 'London, thou art the flower of cities all!'[1]

The government of London during this period was conducted, not by the democracy of manufacturing crafts but by members of the great merchant companies. The Mercers, Grocers, Drapers, and to a lesser extent the Fishmongers and the Goldsmiths, supplied nearly all the mayors and aldermen of fifteenth-century London. The members of these great companies, whatever their names might portend, were not in fact confined to the business of mercers, drapers, and so forth: their chief profits came from the export overseas of all kinds of goods, principally of corn, wool, and cloth. They had their houses and their agents, like William Caxton, established in Bruges and other great trading cities of Europe. They owned good plenty of English ships, not only in London but in other ports, and traded also in hired foreign bottoms. But the merchants of Italy and of the north German Hanse still brought their own goods in their own ships to London. The wharves, crowded with vessels of many nations, stretched down the river from the Bridge, battlemented with tall houses and

1. In the reign of Henry VII an Italian traveller wrote: 'in one single street, named *Strada*, leading to St Paul's, there are fifty-two goldsmiths' shops, so rich and full of silver vessels, great and small, that in all the shops in Milan, Rome, Venice, and Florence put together, I do not think there would be found so many of the magnificence that are to be seen in London' (*Italian relation of England*, Camden Society, 1847, p. 42). *Strada* is probably not the Strand, but Cheapside: see Miss J. Davis's article in *History*, April 1932.

117. 'The wharves, crowded with vessels of many nations,
stretched down the river from the Bridge . . . to the Tower.'

decorated with ever fresh supplies of traitors' heads, to the
royal palace and armoury at the Tower [117].

The merchant aristocracy that ruled the capital wisely
resisted the temptation to take an active part in the struggle of
the rival families for the Crown (it was only in Stuart times that
London was in a position to make and unmake kings). But
they compelled the armies of the Red and White Roses to
respect London's liberties and commerce, and each successive

government, whether of Henry VI, Edward IV, Richard III, or Henry VII, regarded the friendship of her merchants as indispensable to the solvency of the national exchequer. Edward IV courted their friendship in personal and domestic visits to the City, almost beneath the dignity of a king. The Staplers continued to lend money to government. The wool off the royal estates, and off the land of political magnates like Lord Hastings and the Earl of Essex, was sold abroad through the good offices of London merchants. Gentry like the Stonors, owning West Country sheep runs, were proud to be styled Merchants of the Staple. The 'landed and monied interests' were often indistinguishable, even at this early date. Wealth acquired in trade already flowed into and fertilized the land. The younger sons of the gentry, apprenticed to London masters, rose to be City magnates.

Not only London but the other towns enjoyed peace during the Wars of the Roses by the practice of virtual neutrality, and by paying small sums for presents to the King and other political personages, national and local, as also to the judges for their favour in court. Thus in the accounts of the Borough of Cambridge in 1484-5 we read such items as:

For a present given to the Lord the King, namely, in fishes £6 5s. 0d.

In a present given to the Chief Justice of the Lord King, namely in wine, spice, fish, and bread 5s.

In a present given to the Bishop [sic] of York 8s. 8d.

For a present given to the Duke of Norfolk 6s. 8d.

To William Copley for having his friendship 6s. 8d.

In wine to the Duke of Norfolk 2s. 8d.[1]

Cambridge town also paid its burgesses of Parliament 12d. a day each during the session, total 33s., though one of the two members 'released his part'. The new mayor had 20s. each year to buy his magnificent robes, and much money was paid for 'minstrels', and for their 'vestments'. These sums of course represented something very much larger in terms of modern money: a country parson who had £10 a year from all sources was considered to have a tolerable income.

1. Cooper's *Annals of Cambridge*, I, pp. 230-31.

From the middle of the fourteenth century onwards, the manufacture and export of cloth were growing at the expense of the export of raw wool. In other words the Merchant Adventurers were gaining ground at the expense of the Staplers. The cloth trade enriched inland towns like Colchester, where it was collected, and the ports whence it was shipped, especially London. But the actual manufacture of the cloth was carried out chiefly in rural areas, and many country villages acquired a richer and more varied life that was partly industrial. The skilled manufacture of cloth for the open market had, ever since the thirteenth century, been leaving the towns and migrating to the country. The day was still far distant when the mechanical inventions of the eighteenth and subsequent centuries would reverse the movement and herd English workmen back into the cities. Except London, most English towns in the fifteenth century were stationary or declining in wealth and population.[1]

The migration of the cloth trade to the country was bound to be unpopular with the clothing guilds in the towns, who attempted to prevent the competition of rival manufacture by prohibiting the merchants of their towns from dealing with country cloth-makers. But these restricting efforts were spasmodic and vain. For in this question the town merchants had the opposite interest to the town craftsmen, and were more influential in the control of municipal policy. The great merchants therefore continued on an ever increasing scale to operate the cloth trade in both town and country on a capitalist system. They supplied the raw material to the village craftsman who owned his own loom. They then took back the woven

1. See Professor Postan (*Economic History Review*, May 1939, pp. 164–5): according to him the great increase in the cloth trade had been made in the second half of the fourteenth century, and was resumed in Tudor times in the last twenty years of the fifteenth. During most of the fifteenth century the total production of cloth remained nearly stationary – it was expanding in the villages and towns of East Anglia, Yorkshire, and the West, but decreasing in the older clothing towns. But the Staplers' export of raw wool was declining still more rapidly, and 'even at the topmost fifteenth-century level, the cloth exports were not large enough to account for the whole decline of the wool trade'.

cloth, passed it on to other workers for the finishing processes, and finally put it on the market.

All over Essex there lay villages famous for cloth-making, Coggeshall and Braintree, Bocking and Halstead, Shalford and Dedham, and above all Colchester, the great centre and mart of the trade. The villages throve on the industry and there was hardly a cottage which did not hum with the spinning-wheel, and hardly a street where you might not have counted weavers' workshops, kitchens where the rough loom stood by the wall to occupy the good man's working hours. Hardly a week but the clatter of the pack-horse would be heard in the straggling streets, bringing in new stores of wool to be worked, and taking away pieces of cloth to the clothiers of Colchester and the surrounding villages. Throughout the fifteenth century Coggeshall was an important centre second only to the great towns of Norwich, Colchester, and Sudbury, and to this day its two inns are called the Woolpack and the Fleece.[1]

In Coggeshall lived the famous cloth merchant, Thomas Paycocke, and there he built his fine house with carved timbers, now belonging to the National Trust. Such mansions in the village street and brasses in the parish church mark the rise of a new rural class, as wealthy as the neighbouring gentry with whom they were not long in forming marriage alliances, and whose privileged circle they entered by the purchase of landed estates [118-21].

And it was the same in the West; after two more centuries had passed, Defoe observed that 'many of the great families who now pass for gentry in the western counties have been originally raised from and built up by this truly noble manufacture' of cloth. In the fifteenth century, Cotswold wool was considered the best in England and therefore in Europe. It was the basis of the prosperity of that lovely region, of which the record still stands in magnificent stone farm-houses, and old fulling-mills beside the streams of the valleys.

The character of an English merchant of this period is made very real to us by the life and letters of Thomas Betson.[2] He was a wool merchant of the Staple [53], often resident at

1. Eileen Power, *Medieval People*, p. 149.
2. op. cit., chap. v.

118. Brass of Thomas Pownder, his wife and family, at St Mary's Quay, Ipswich (note the arms of Ipswich and the Merchant Adventurers, and Pownder's merchant marks)

Calais on his business, but well acquainted with the West Country manor-houses of gentlemen like the Stonors; for he bought the wool of their sheep-runs to sell at Calais. These business connexions were cemented by matrimonial alliance. Betson married Katherine Ryche, a relation and ward of the Stonors. He did not in fact marry her till she was fifteen and the marriage proved a happy one, but they had been betrothed some years before, and we have a letter of Thomas to his Katherine, then aged twelve or thirteen; he writes in 1476 from his business house in Calais to Katherine at Stonor in Oxfordshire. If one must be engaged to a girl of twelve this is certainly a good way to write to her. He bids little Katherine:

Be a good eater of your meat alway, that ye may wax and grow fast to be a woman . . . and to greet well my horse and pray him to give you four of his years to help you withal. And I will at my coming home give him four of my years and four horse-loaves to make amends. Tell him that I prayed him so. . . . And Allmighty Jesus make you a good woman and send you alway

119. Thomas Paycocke's house, Coggeshall, Essex

120. A fifteenth-century stone manor-house, Little Sodbury, Gloucestershire

many good years and long to live in health and virtue to his pleasure. Written at Calais the first of June, when every man was gone to his dinner, and the clock smote noon and all our household cried after me and bad me come down. 'Come down to dinner at once!' And what answer I gave to them ye know of old.

More than four and a half centuries have slipped by since that old clock 'smote noon' at Calais, but Thomas Betson as he rises from his writing-desk and folds the letter with a smile on his face is an Englishman we can all understand and like.[1]

1. *Stonor Letters*, Camden Society, II, pp. 6–8 (spelling modernized). The English merchants of the Staple, like Betson, were the principal buyers of wool in the western shires, but they had to compete with Italian merchants who rode about the Cotswolds on a like errand. The Staplers shipped to Calais the English wool that supplied the Low Countries and northern Europe, but they did little business in the Mediterranean. The Italian merchants had royal licence to ship English wool direct by the Straits of Gibraltar to the Italian looms.

The hours of labour in field and workshop were very long by the standards of today. But men rested on Sundays and on an indefinite number of the greater saints' days. Custom enforced this good rule, and the Church courts did useful service in exacting penance or fine for work on Sundays and Holy Days. Much besides work went on in old England, which in all ages has been both 'merry England' and miserable England, though the forms of misery and merriment have changed from age to age. The joyful background of country life was hunting and hawking, snaring and fishing, conducted with all the pomp of 'venery' by the inhabitants of castle and manor-house, monastery and parsonage – and more quietly by the unprivileged poacher from farm and cottage. Much money was spent on 'stage-plays, enterludes, maye games, wakes, ravells', and much money changed hands in 'wagers at shootinge, wrestlinge, runninge, and throwing the stone or barre'.

It was during this period that playing-cards came in, very much in the form in which we have them today: the dress of

121. The Wool Hall, Lavenham, Suffolk

our court cards is still based on late fifteenth-century costume. Cards served, like chess, to while away the tedious winter evenings of the manor-house and supplied the gambler with an alternative to dice.

Shooting at the butts was encouraged by proclamation and statute at the expense of rival forms of amusement, such as 'handball, football, or hockey', in order to preserve England's military monopoly of archery with the long-bow. It remained a monopoly, because it was an art not easily acquired. Hugh Latimer described how his yeoman father in Henry VII's reign:

taught me how to draw, how to lay my body in my bow. . . . I had my bows bought me according to my age and strength; as I increased in them, so my bows were made bigger and bigger. For men shall never shoot well unless they be brought up to it [see note, p. 43].

At the archery competitions, leaders dressed in the parts of 'Robin Hood' and 'Little John' led the village procession to the butts.

In towns and wealthier villages, many guilds – not merely the craft guilds – helped to organize pageantry and merriment. On every possible occasion, national or local men rejoiced in solemn processions, of which the Lord Mayor's Show and the King's opening of Parliament are today among the few survivors. In those times, before it was easy to invest one's savings, much money was spent on splendour. Rich men wore the most magnificent and expensive clothes, and showed their wealth in plate upon their sideboards. The guilds, from which priests were generally excluded, represented the growing intelligence and initiative of the laity. But they were permeated, as was most of life and thought, by religious ideas. The line between religion and daily life was not so strictly drawn as in modern times. Men combining in a guild for a benevolent, a useful, or even a convivial purpose, liked to give a religious tinge to their proceedings and to invoke a saint's blessing on their association. Even if they were anti-clerical, they were not irreligious.

Besides the maintenance of a chantry, a school, an almshouse or a bridge, one of the chief activities of guilds was the staging

122. The stage for the Passion Play of Valenciennes (1547), showing

of miracle plays 'in a scaffold hye'. Such plays were very popular in the fifteenth century, and taught versions of the Bible stories, and many legends beside, in an age when the Bible as a book was known to few [122–4].

The actors announced themselves as *I am Abraham* or *I am Herod*. They dressed in contemporary clothes, and contemporary clothes were symbolical of status. God Almighty was bearded and wore a tiara, a white cope, and gloves. Wicked kings wore a turban and swore by Mahound. High priests were vested as bishops and sat 'in convocation'. Doctors of the law wore round caps and furred gowns. Peasants and soldiers wore the dress of the day, and Mary Magdalene before her conversion was tricked out in overmuch finery. Angels went up to heaven and came down by real ladders, and the gloomy portal called Hell's-mouth was contrived to open and shut. Black, blue, and red devils came out to claim the damned, while a clanging of unseen pots and pans signified the discord that prevailed within.[1]

1. Canon Maynard Smith's *Pre-Reformation England* (1938), p. 146; it is a book much to be recommended.

the various scenes across which the action moved

Such was the drama a hundred years and more before Shakespeare.

So too the Christmas Carols represented the homely religious feeling of the laity on the eve of the Reformation.

> The shepherd upon a hill he sat;
> He had on him his tabard and his hat,
> His tarbox, his pipe and his flagat [flageolet],
> His name was called jolly, jolly Wat,
> > For he was a good herd's boy
> > > With hoy
> > For in his pipe he made so much joy.
>
> Now must he go where Christ was born:
> Jesus I offer thee here my pipe
> My skirt, my tarbox, and my scrip;
> Home to my fellows now will I skip,
> And also look unto my sheep,
> > For he was a good herd's boy
> > > With hoy
> > For in his pipe he made so much joy.

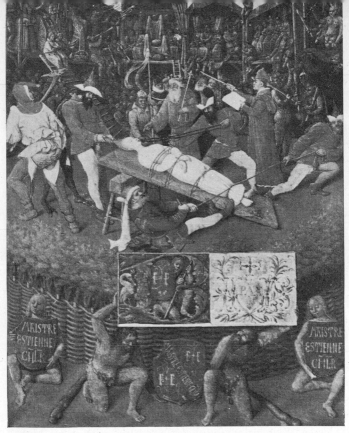

123. A mystery play in France in the fifteenth century (the martyrdom of St Apollonia is being enacted on a wattled stage)

More directly under the patronage of the clergy were the 'Church ales', forerunners of the religious tea and philanthropic bazaar. Men and women sold and drank ale in the church itself or the churchyard, to raise funds for the fabric or for some other good purpose. Church ales were very common in the fifteenth century though they had been frowned upon by the more ascetic churchmen of earlier times. The nave of the church was the 'village hall' for most communal purposes.

The ceremony of the Boy Bishop, very strange to modern

124. A play of Terence being mimed with masked actors

ideas, was patronized equally by the high-and-dry orthodox clergy and by the reforming Dean Colet. On the day of St Nicholas, patron saint of boys, or on Holy Innocents' Day, a boy dressed up as a bishop in schools and cathedrals, went in procession, and preached a sermon, to which not only his schoolmates but the Church dignitaries were expected to listen with reverence. Sometimes regular endowments were left to meet the expense and pageantry of this pretty scene, in which the Dean knelt for the child's blessing.

BOOKS FOR FURTHER READING

H. S. Bennett, *The Pastons and their England*; C. L. Kingsford, *Prejudice and Promise in Fifteenth Century England*; Eileen Power, *Medieval People*; Professor Postan, article on the fifteenth century in the *Economic History Review*, May 1939; *Cambridge Hist. Journal*, 1941; J. Saltmarsh's *Plague and Economic Decline*; Alice Stopford Green, *Town Life in the 15th Century*; E. Lipson, *An Economic History of England*, vol. 1; H. Maynard Smith, *Pre-Reformation England*; Rashdall's *Universities of Europe in the Middle Ages* (ed. Powicke and Emden), vol. III; *Libel of English Policy* (1436), ed. Sir George Warner, 1926; *Paston Letters, 1422–1589*, ed. James Gairdner.

CHAPTER FOUR

TUDOR ENGLAND: INTRODUCTION

THE END OF THE MIDDLE AGES?

HENRY VII, 1485 – HENRY VIII, 1509 –
DISSOLUTION OF MONASTERIES, 1536–9 –
EDWARD VI, 1547 – MARY, 1553 –
ELIZABETH, 1558–1603

Dates and periods are necessary to the study and discussion of history, for all historical phenomena are conditioned by time and are produced by the sequence of events. Dates, therefore, apply a necessary test to any historical statement, and are apt to be found inconveniently cumbering the path and tripping up the heels of glib generalization rushing forward with head in air. There is no appeal from the verdict of a date.

But, unlike dates, 'periods' are not facts. They are retrospective conceptions that we form about past events, useful to focus discussion, but very often leading historical thought astray. Thus, while it is certainly useful to speak of 'the Middle Ages' and of 'the Victorian Age', those two abstract ideas have deluded many scholars and millions of newspaper readers into supposing that during certain centuries called 'the Middle Ages', and again during certain decades called 'Age of Victoria', everyone thought and acted more or less in the same way – till at last Victoria died or 'the Middle Ages came to an end'. But in fact there was no such sameness. Individual character, variety, and an urge to change were marked features of the English over whom Victoria presided; and the end of her reign was very different from the beginning. So, too, medieval society can only be studied fruitfully if we conceive it not as a static order but as a continuous evolution, without any definable date for its beginning or end.

The habit of thinking about the past as divided into water-tight 'periods' is most dangerous of all in economic and social history. For 'periods' have usually been assorted, as their names imply, for purely political reasons – 'the age of the Tudors', 'the age of Louis XIV', and so forth. But economic and social life takes little heed of the deaths of kings or the accession of new dynasties: absorbed in its own daily task it flows on, like an underground river, only occasionally making eruption into the upper daylight of politics, though it may all the time be their unacknowledged and unconscious arbiter.

And it is all the more difficult to think about economic and social history in 'periods', because there is always an overlap of the old and the new continuing side by side in the same country for generations and even for centuries. Different systems of production – craft and domestic and capitalist – all went on in England both in late medieval and in modern times. So, too, in the agricultural world, open fields, and enclosures. Anglo-Saxon and modern methods were found together, from the Middle Ages to the nineteenth century [49, 50, 125]. And in the social sphere, the feudal and the democratic spirit have had a marvellous aptitude for coexistence in our tolerant island.

If, then, we are asked to name a date, or even a period, when 'the Middle Ages came to an end', what can we safely say? Certainly not '1485', the year when Tudor rule began, though it has been found by teachers and examiners a convenient point at which to wind up the Middle Ages in England. But in the real year 1485, when our simple ancestors 'gaped and rubbed the elbow at the news' that Henry Tudor and his Welshmen had overthrown Richard III at Bosworth, they had no thought that a new era was beginning. They supposed merely that the Lancastrians had again got the better, for the time, of the Yorkists, in the endless and tiresome Wars of the Roses. It is true that the events of the next twenty years showed that in fact the Wars of the Roses had, almost but not quite, ended on Bosworth field. But the end of the Wars of the Roses is by no means the same thing as the end of the Middle Ages – in whatever way the Middle Ages are defined.

The victory of Henry the Welshman made no change distantly comparable in importance to the victory of William the Norman at Hastings. For half a century after 1485, until Henry's son took the papal power and the monastic wealth into

125. Part of the manor of Feckenham, Worcestershire, showing the court-house, the lord's mill, open fields with 'strip' cultivation, and the encroachment thereon by enclosure (note that Ralph Bowes (DD) is shown encroaching on Chesterfield and Edward Robinson (NN) on Perry Hill Field)

KEY A† Lord's domain, etc.
     H Corporate parish lands
     * Common lands
     DD and NN Landholders

his own hands, English society continued very much as I have described it in the last chapter. The agricultural changes still continued at a slightly accelerated pace. The Church went on just as before, though exposed to renewed unpopularity and denunciation, very similar to the anti-clerical outcry in the days of Langland, Chaucer, and Wyclif; but there was no evident certainty that such strictures would have any more practical outcome this time than so often of old. Henry VII and young Henry VIII were both zealous in their orthodoxy; they were dutiful in the roasting of heretics; they frequently employed bishops as their counsellors of State, after the medieval custom, culminating in the grand finale of Cardinal Wolsey, who displayed on a colossal scale the pride and power of the medieval Church. Himself the instrument of papal power, he greatly increased its control over the *Ecclesia Anglicana*. He treated the lay nobles and gentlemen like dirt beneath his feet, thereby helping to prepare the anti-clerical revolution that accompanied his fall. He kept a household of nearly a thousand persons, and marched in state with silver pillars and pole-axes borne before him. Besides many other sources of wealth, he drew the revenues and neglected the duties of Archbishop of York, Bishop of Durham, and Abbot of St Albans; the biographer of Wolsey and of Henry VIII estimates that the Cardinal was almost as rich a man as the King.[1] He obtained for his natural son four archdeaconries, a deanery, five prebends, and two rectories, and only failed in his endeavour to have him succeed in the fabulously rich see of Durham. In proportion to Wolsey's pride, luxury, and greed was his munificence in founding schools and colleges of splendour then unparalleled. Here was a prince indeed, of the cosmopolitan hierarchy of Europe before which men had bowed for centuries, but should never again bow in England. Yet he served the King as Chancellor with far more devotion than he served the religious interests of the Church. In all this, Wolsey is one of the greatest and the most characteristic of 'medieval' figures in our history, and his power was at its fullness more than forty years after Bosworth field [126].

Another aspect of that half century of calm before the storm,

1. Pollard's *Wolsey*, pp. 320–21.

126. Cardinal Wolsey

was the Renaissance of classical scholarship and biblical exegesis under Grocyn and Linacre, Colet and More, the English friends of Erasmus. Their work, more than all Wolsey's

GVLIELMVS TINDALE MARTYR
OLIM EX AVLA MAGD

Hac et luce tuas dispers
Sponte extorris era
ma tenebros
Sacrificium.

127. William Tyndale

pride, was preparing the future, but it was not much altering the present. None of those friends thought that their new knowledge of the classics and of the Greek Testament would destroy the 'Medieval' Church, which they hoped to liberalize and to reform. More radical was the intention of William Tyndale, as in penury and danger he translated the Bible into words of power and beauty that unborn millions were to have daily on their lips, and to interpret in a hundred different ways disruptive of the past [127–9].

In the secular sphere, Henry VII restored order to the countryside, and put down retainers. That was an important social change, but it was not 'the end of the Middle Ages'; rather it was the belated fulfilment of a hope of medieval Englishmen. One medieval institution indeed, Parliament, was in grave danger under Henry VII and under Wolsey of perishing through disuse; but in England, unlike France and Spain, the medieval Parliament was destined to be revived and strengthened by Henry VIII for modern purposes. So, too, another great medieval institution, the English Common Law, survived the Tudor period to become the basis of modern English life and liberty.

In the early sixteenth century, English trade, though again on the increase after a period of relative stagnation, still ran in its old medieval channels along the coasts of northern Europe, with a new thrust into the Mediterranean, for vent of cloth. In spite of Cabot's voyage from Bristol to Newfoundland in the reign of Henry VII, the wider outlook across the Atlantic did not greatly affect Englishmen before Elizabeth was on the throne. Until the reign of her sister Mary, the English were still a French-hating, not a Spaniard-hating, people, for the quarrel about the Inquisition and about the possession of the New World had not yet arisen.

It is indeed useless to look for any date, or even for any period, when the Middle Ages 'ended' in England. All that one can say is that, in the thirteenth century, English thought and society were medieval, and in the nineteenth century they were not. Yet even now we retain the medieval institutions of the monarchy, the peerage, the Commons in Parliament assembled, the English Common Law, the Courts of Justice interpreting the rule of law, the hierarchy of the established Church, the parish system, the universities, the public schools and grammar schools. And unless we become a totalitarian state and forget all our Englishry, there will always be something medieval in our ways of thinking, especially in our idea that people and corporations have rights and liberties which the State ought in some degree to respect, in spite of the legal omnicompetence of Parliament. Conservatism and Liberalism, in the broadest sense, are both medieval in origin, and so are

128. Sir Thomas More

trade unions. The men who established our civic liberties in the seventeenth century, appealed to medieval precedents against the 'modernizing' monarchy of the Stuarts. The pattern of history is indeed a tangled web. No simple diagram will explain its infinite complication.

As to the economic side of things in town and country, Mr Tawney, the social historian of the sixteenth century, regards the Tudor epoch as a 'watershed' whence things moved downward with ever increasing momentum towards the big estates and farms of the eighteenth and nineteenth centuries, and the industrial capitalism of modern times. This may well be true. But it is a question whether 'the end of the Middle Ages' might not as well be sought in the consummation of economic and social change in the reign of George III, as in the Tudor beginnings. Nor in fact did these things begin first under the Tudors: as noted in former chapters of this book, 'capitalism' was established in some important trades long before. So too the emancipation of serfs and the consequent break-up of the medieval manor system had actually been accomplished before ever Bosworth Field was fought.

Where then shall we place the end of medieval society and economics – in the fourteenth, the sixteenth, or the eighteenth centuries? Perhaps it matters little: what does matter is that we should understand what really happened. It is probable that ere long a new perspective of periods in the past will replace the old. Owing to the mechanization of life, man has changed more in the last hundred years than in the previous thousand. It is not unlikely therefore that the real beginning of 'modern times' – if 'modern times' are to include our own – will be allocated to the growth of the Industrial Revolution rather than to the Renaissance and Reformation. And even in the realm of thought and religion, the impact of science and Darwin may come to seem as memorable as the impact of Erasmus and Luther.

It is of course the Renaissance and the Reformation of which people are chiefly thinking when they ascribe the end of the Middle Ages to the sixteenth century.[1] In the spheres of thought and religion, of clerical power and privilege, we may indeed say that the medieval scheme of things was abolished in Tudor England. Yet even this is not true without qualification about the land that Elizabeth ruled. The Protestantizing and secularizing of England was not complete till after the Puritan Rebellion and the Whig–Tory Revolution – or rather

1. Another alleged reason is the 'rise of National Monarchies'. But England, unlike France and Spain, had already been a 'national Monarchy' in the days of Crécy and Agincourt. No doubt Henry VIII's assumption of religious power carried nationalism one step further.

129. Title-page of the Fourth Great Bible

it has never yet been made complete. The Church of England, both in its organization, its privileges, its ceremonies, and in its thought has always remained in part 'medieval'.

The Elizabethan system, the grand finale of Tudor triumph,

was as much a triumph of the Renaissance as of the Reformation. The two became one, and partly for that reason Shakespeare's England had a charm and a lightness of heart, a free aspiring of mind and spirit not to be found elsewhere in the harsh Jesuit-Calvinist Europe of that day. And at the same auspicious moment England's old song of the sea became a new ocean song. The Elizabethan adventurers – Drake, Frobisher, Hawkins, Ralegh, and the rest – were sailing the wide world, discovering 'islands far away', opening to their countrymen at home new realms of hope and fancy – committing indeed crimes in Ireland and in the slave-trade but without knowing that they were crimes or what the dreadful consequences were to be in the deep of time. The music of the Elizabethan madrigal and the lyric poetry to which it was wedded expressed the reasonable joy in life of a people freed from medieval and not yet oppressed by Puritan complexes and fears; rejoicing in nature and the countryside in whose lap they had the felicity to live; moving forward to a healthy agricultural and mercantile prosperity, and not yet overwhelmed by the weight of industrial materialism.

All this found its perfect expression before it passed away – in Shakespeare's plays. In them we see the immense step forward that had been taken in the realm of thought and feeling, away from the ancient limits. The play of *Hamlet*, that at least is modern. Also in the English church service in every parish, and in the wide study of the English Bible in the homes of rich and poor, we can say the English mind and imagination had in those respects already ceased to be medieval. But society, politics, and economics still very much more closely resembled those of the fourteenth than of the twentieth century; the author of *Richard II* and *Henry IV* found it easy to understand and portray that not very distant world.

If all aspects of life are taken into consideration, we may perhaps agree with the historian of the reign of Henry VIII, that 'of all the schisms which rend the woven garment of historical understanding, the worst is that which fixes a deep gulf between medieval and modern history'.[1]

But before this brief golden age corresponding to the lifetime

1. A. F. Pollard, *Wolsey*, p. 8.

130. The coronation procession of Edward VI

of Shakespeare (1564–1616), Tudor England had known a long period of *malaise*. She did not, indeed, suffer from 'wars of religion' such as devastated France, because here monarchy was stronger and religious fanaticism less strong. But the Tudor Reformation was not carried through without attendant misery and violence. And the disturbances caused by the quick changes of ecclesiastical policy under Henry VIII, Edward VI, and Mary coincided with a grave economic crisis in trade and agriculture, due chiefly to a rise in prices. That rise we must ascribe partly to world causes and partly to Henry's wanton debasing of the coinage. Of these things, among much else, it will be my business to deal in the chapters that follow [130, 131].

CHAPTER FIVE

ENGLAND DURING THE
ANTI-CLERICAL REVOLUTION

The advent of the first English antiquary, John Leland, may, if we wish, be taken for a sign that the Middle Ages were indeed passing away and becoming matter for retrospect. For nearly ten years (1534–43) Leland travelled through the length and breadth of Henry VIII's kingdom, diligently seeking out and observing things new and old.[1] He noted much that was flourishing, but he had also a loving and learned eye for the past, to discern

> by Time's fell hand defaced
> The rich-proud cost of outworn buried age.

Many 'lofty towers' he saw 'downrazed', especially three kinds of ruin – dilapidated castles, crumbling walls of towns, and the housebreakers beginning their work upon the roofs of the abbeys.

Many castles indeed Leland saw that had been adapted to the domestic uses of a later age, and had long years of splendour still before them. But many others (like royal Berkhamsted where the Black Prince kept court) had after the Wars of the Roses been abandoned by the frugal policy of Henry VII; while private owners often condemned their ancestral fortresses as fit neither to withstand cannon planted on a neighbouring eminence, nor to house nobles and gentlemen with modern comfort. Leland, therefore, reports on many a feudal strong-hold that 'tendith to ruin', some stripped of their roofs, their

1. *The Itinerary of John Leland*, edited by Lucy Toulmin Smith, 1906–10.

132. 'The thin stone curtain' of the old city wall in the grounds of New College, Oxford

walls a quarry for the village or the new manor-house, the slighted remains sheltering poor husbandmen and their cattle.

In the Middle Ages, the glory and safety of every town had been its encircling walls, but military, political, and economic reasons had combined to bring about their decay. The thin stone curtain, such as can still be seen in the grounds of New College, Oxford, could no longer avail to protect a town against the cannon of Tudor times [132]. A hundred years later, in the wars of Charles and Cromwell, places like London, Oxford, and Bristol were defended by earthworks thrown up on newer principles of military engineering, well outside the too narrow circuit of the medieval walls. Indeed such prosperous cities had already in Leland's day outgrown their antique suits of stone armour, and had thrust out suburbs and 'ribbon development' along the roads of approach. Other less fortunate towns, shrunk and impoverished by economic change, had no money to waste on keeping up walls which the Tudor peace rendered no longer needful. More generally, the decadence of the walls was a symptom of the decline of that intense civic patriotism which had inspired medieval townsfolk. National control and individual initiative were taking the place of the corporate spirit of town and guild, not only in matters of government and of military defence, but in trade and industry, as witness the

THE PASSING OF THE MONASTERIES

cloth manufacture continuing to move ever more rapidly into the rural parts to escape municipal and guild regulation.

But the third kind of ruin that Leland saw was the most recent. The crash of monastic masonry resounding through the land was not the work of the 'unimaginable touch of time' – not at least in the physical sense – but the sudden impact of a king's command, a demolition order to resolve at one stroke a social problem that had been maturing for two centuries past [133–6].

During the decade in which Leland was travelling and making his notes, Henry VIII, through the instrumentality of Parliament, effected the anti-clerical revolution which more than any other single event may be held to mark the end of medieval society in England. The claim of national independence for a Church repudiating the Pope's authority rendered possible the subjection of the clergy to the laity, and the division of the vast estates and social influence of the monasteries among laymen. Taken together, these proceedings constitute a social revolution. It was accompanied by just that amount of religious change which Henry VIII, a child of the

133. 'The crash of monastic masonry resounded through the land';
Bury St Edmunds Abbey, the ruins by 1779

134. Bury St Edmunds Abbey, the ruins adapted for dwelling-
houses by 1787

THE PASSING OF THE MONASTERIES

135. Castle Acre Priory, Norfolk, the west end of the Priory Church and the Prior's Lodging

136. Fountains Abbey ruins (see also 166)

new learning, approved – the diffusion of the English Bible among all classes [129], the destruction of the cruder forms of idolatry and relic-mongering, the substitution at Oxford and Cambridge of Renaissance scholarship for scholastic philosophy and canon law – measures which constituted in Henry's eyes an orthodox and Catholic reform. Having done all this, he continued to abhor and persecute Protestants, and if he had not done so he might have lost his throne in the then state of opinion. None the less, he had created a new social and ecclesiastical order of things which, as the changing years went by, could only be maintained on a more definitely Protestant basis.

The Reformation in England was at once a political, a religious, and a social event. All three of its aspects were closely interwoven but, so far as division is possible, this volume is concerned only with its social causes and effects. Anti-clericalism is a social phenomenon, compatible with many different forms of belief about religion. And anti-clericalism was the keynote of the movement of opinion, equally felt among the learned and the vulgar, which rendered possible the breach with the Papacy and the Dissolution of the Monasteries, at a time when English Protestants were still a persecuted minority.

Henry VIII had himself been educated in the scholarly anti-clericalism of Erasmus and his Oxford friends – men sincerely religious and in the main orthodox, but inflamed with indignation at the tricks by which the baser sort of clergy conjured money from the ignorant and superstitious. They were specially hostile to the monks and friars, as protagonists of obscurantism, upholders of scholastic philosophy, and opponents of that direct study of the Greek Testament to which Erasmus and Colet appealed as a criterion of religious truth.

Some, indeed, of the writings of Erasmus conveyed the most uncompromising spirit of anti-clericalism. In the *Praise of Folly* he denounces the monks for

observing with punctilious scrupulosity a lot of silly ceremonies and paltry traditional rules,

for which Christ cares nothing, yet managing therewith to lead a life of luxury,

gorging the carcase to the point of bursting.

The 'contemptible friars' and their preaching come off no better:

> Their whole demeanour in preaching is such that you might swear they had taken lessons from a set of itinerant mountebanks, though indeed the mountebanks are out and out their superiors.

and so forth for pages together.

If the most learned and polished man in Europe, who deprecated Luther's robust and headlong proceedings, could write thus in Latin about the monks and friars, it can be imagined what was the tone of popular anti-clerical writers, appealing to the common English in their own tongue. The printing-press busily circulated such attacks, making direct appeal to the greed of the laity in view of the vast landed wealth of a Church that had for a while lost its only defences against spoliation – moral influence and religious awe.

For example, a few years before the Dissolution of the Monasteries, Henry VIII read without apparent disapproval, and Londoners read with loudly expressed delight, the pamphlet of Simon Fish entitled *Supplication of the Beggars*. Its form was an address to the King:

> In the times of your noble predecessors past, craftily crept into this your realm an other sort, (not of impotent but) of strong, puisant and counterfeit, holy and idle beggars and vagabonds . . . the Bishops, Abbots, Priors, Deacons, Archdeacons, Suffragans, Priests, Monks, Canons, Friars, Pardoners, and Sommoners. And who is able to number this idle, ruinous sort, which (setting all labour aside) have begged so importunately that they have gotten into their hands more than the third part of all your Realm? The goodliest lordships, manors, lands, and territories, are theirs. Besides this they have the tenth part of all corn, meadow, pasture, grass, wool, colts, calves, lambs, pigs, geese, and chickens. . . . Yea, and they look so narrowly upon their profits, that the poor wives must be countable to them of every tenth egg, or else she [sic] getteth not her rights at Easter, shall be taken as a heretic. . . . How much money get the Sommoners by extortion in a year, by citing the people to the Commissaries Court, and afterwards releasing their appearance for money? . . . Who is she that will set her hands to work

to get 3d. a day, and may have at least 20d. a day to sleep an hour with a friar, a monk or a priest?

The conclusion reached by the pamphleteer is that the clergy, especially the monks and friars, should be deprived of their wealth for the benefit of the King and Kingdom, and made to work like other men; let them also be allowed to marry and so be induced to leave other people's wives alone.

Such crude appeals to lay cupidity, and such veritable coarse anger at real abuses uncorrected down the centuries, had been generally prevalent in London under Wolsey's régime, and at his fall such talk became equally fashionable at Court. In those days, whenever the capital and the Court were agreed on a policy, the battle was already half won. And judging by the readiness with which the Reformation Parliament followed Henry's lead, similar feelings must have been widely spread in the country at large, though least in the northern counties, where feudal and religious loyalty to the Church and the monasteries still prevailed.

In the face of this storm of opinion, now directed to practical issues by the King, what would be the attitude of the clergy, thus threatened and arraigned? Their submission or their resistance would be an event of the utmost importance to the whole future development of English society. If the clerical body – bishops, priests, monks, and friars – had stood together for the high privileges and liberties of the Medieval Church, and had arrayed themselves under the papal banner, they would scarcely have been overcome; certainly not without a struggle that would have rent England to pieces. But in fact the clergy were not only scared by the union against them of the King and so many of his subjects; they were themselves genuinely divided in opinion. A large number of clergymen were in close and daily contact with laymen and understood their way of thinking. The English priesthood had not got the spiritual isolation or the discipline of a caste, like the Roman Catholic clergy of today.

The bishops, for example, were first and foremost royal nominees and civil servants. And in like manner parish priests and chaplains, as has been noted in an earlier chapter, often acted as business agents and trusted confidants of lords, squires, and other lay patrons. Even the monks were wont to have their estates managed for them largely by laymen and to submit in many things to the wishes of the patrons and founders' kin, who were not infrequently lodged in the abbey precincts.

It was not therefore natural to the clergy to draw together to defend themselves against lay attack. The hostility with which bishops and parish priests regarded monks and friars was centuries old and was in no degree abated. So too was the feeling against the papal authority which had so long mercilessly bled and exploited the Church in England. And of recent years Wolsey, as the Pope's *legatus a latere*, had infuriated the English clergy by overriding episcopal authority and clerical freedom. 'Better the King than the Pope' was a general feeling among them at the time of his fall. There was no third choice before Convocation. Wolsey, says his biographer, 'always rode furiously; he rode papal jurisdiction in England to its death'.[1]

Moreover, the reforming doctrines, whether of Erasmus or of Luther, had many secret sympathizers and open missionaries among the clergy; otherwise there would never have been a reformation in England, but only a brutal struggle of anti-clerical hatred with clerical privilege, such as seemed to be foreshadowed in propaganda like Fish's *Supplication of the Beggars*, such as in later times has actually taken place in countries that rejected the Reformation.

Many different currents of thought were moving in the English clerical mind. Just as the Oxford reformers responded

1. Professor Pollard adds:
'The essential difference between Wolsey and Henry VIII was that the Cardinal was the protagonist of the *Sacerdotium* and the King of the *regnum*; and that, rather than any question of theology, distinguished the Roman from the Anglican Church. The one was a priest-ridden, the other a king-ridden body. . . . Wolsey had reduced the Church to a despotism whose liberties consisted in its jurisdiction over the laity and not in its government of itself. By Henry's conquest and annexation the *Ecclesia Anglicana* was saved from sinking into a church of Wolsey's conception, purely papal and autocratic and incompatible with the spirit of self-determination which was informing and transforming the nation as a whole. And into the sphere of church government were thereby injected the discords and debates which are the representative signs of popular interest and intellectual life' (*Wolsey*, pp. 369–70).

to Erasmus in the reign of Henry VII, so in the reign of his son the Cambridge reformers, including Cranmer and Latimer, Tyndale and Coverdale, responded to the impulse of Luther from oversea. And without being definitely Lutherans, many of the clergy sincerely desired to reform their own profession and were by no means in love with all its privileges. Many even of the expropriated monks and dissolved friars became Protestant clergymen under Edward VI, and there is no reason to suppose that they were hypocrites.

English opinion, lay and clerical, was a shifting kaleidoscope. It was not yet divided between two fixed and clearly divided parties, one of reform, the other of reaction. And in the confusion the King's eclectic will prevailed. His anti-papal, anti-monastic policy, in the year that it was challenged by the northern rebellion known as the Pilgrimage of Grace (1536), was saved by the support of conservative noblemen like Norfolk and Shrewsbury, and bishops like Gardiner and Bonner, all of whom desired to burn Lutherans as much as Henry himself.[1] On the other hand, two chief lights of academic renaissance and reform, More and Fisher, the dear friends of Erasmus, suffered death rather than agree to the repudiation of papal authority and the subjection of the Church to the State.

The dissolution of the orders of monks and friars was a natural outcome of the attitude towards religion, life, and society that Erasmus and his English friends had done so much to propagate. The men of the new learning in classical and Biblical study, now dominant at Court as well as in the Universities, had been taught to regard the monks and friars as the obscurantist enemies of the new movement. And the ascetic ideal, which had founded the monasteries in ages long ago, was no longer either admired by the world or practised by the monks. Why, then, should the monasteries any longer be maintained at vast expense?

1. 'It is indeed worthy of comment that of the leading figures concerned in the Dissolution [of the monasteries] in Cornwall, not one was a Protestant; Sir Thomas Arundell, no more than Sir John Tregonwell, neither Prideaux nor Prior Mundy. The sympathies of each were unmistakably Catholic' (Rowse's *Tudor Cornwall*, p. 222).

That question was asked by the man in the street, particularly in London. And it was pressed by certain interested parties. The weakest of these were reforming clergymen, like Latimer, who hoped that the monastic wealth would go to endow education and religion; they were the more deceived. Then there were the lay neighbours and patrons of the monasteries, who looked to succeed to their estates on easy terms of purchase, and who were seldom disappointed. Next, the King himself, whose profligate finance and foolish wars in France had emptied his treasury, sought to refill it by confiscation. And lastly, the House of Commons was only too glad to evade the unpopularity of voting taxation of their constituents, by passing the Bills for the disendowment of the monasteries.

An obstinate refusal to pay taxes was a characteristic of the English at this period. A new tax of any weight, even though voted by Parliament, was liable to produce a rebellion in some part of the country, and the Tudors had no standing army. Henry, therefore, in the last part of his reign sought relief for his financial embarrassments from two sources, first the monastic wealth, and, after that, the debasement of the coinage. Both these expedients had, as we shall see, important social consequences.

For a short while the sale of the monastic lands replenished the King's treasury. If Henry had not been bankrupt, he might never have dissolved the monasteries at all; or he might have kept all their lands and tithes for the Crown, and so perhaps enabled his successors to establish absolute monarchy in England; or again, he might have given more of their wealth to education and charity, as at first he intended to do, had not his financial needs been so pressing. Even as it was, he founded Trinity as a college on a larger scale than any other at Cambridge. He was probably inspired to that good deed by the example of Cardinal College (Christ Church) which Wolsey had recently founded at Oxford, also out of the spoils of monasteries; for the diversion of monastic lands and tithes was not an invention either of Henry or of the Reformation [137, 138]. But considering the enormously greater opportunities of the King, he did very little for the endowment of institutions beneficial to the public. Some indeed of the monks' money he spent on fortifying the harbours of the Kingdom and the arsenals of the Royal Navy.

Henry did not, as it is sometimes stated, distribute any large proportion of the monastic lands and tithes gratis among his courtiers. He sold much the greater part of them.[1] He was driven by his financial necessities to sell, though he would have preferred to keep more for the Crown. The potential value of the estates, enjoyed in times to come by the lay purchasers or their heirs, was very great compared to the market prices they had actually paid to the necessitous King or to the merchant speculators who bought them up from Henry to re-sell to the local squirearchy. Therefore the ultimate beneficiary of the Dissolution was not religion, not education, not the poor, not even in the end the Crown, but a class of fortunate gentry, of whom more will be said when we come to consider the changes going on in social and agricultural life.

A good deal of monastic, chantry, and other ecclesiastical land and tithe remained in the hands of the Crown for several generations. But financial necessity induced Elizabeth, James, and Charles I gradually to part with it all to private purchasers.

The coalfields, particularly in Durham and Northumberland, had been, to a predominant extent, ecclesiastical property. But owing to the action of Henry VIII this source of future wealth, which from Stuart times onwards was to be developed on an immense scale, passed into the hands of private gentlemen, whose descendants founded many powerful and some noble families out of coal. Yet even from the remnant left to the Church, the Ecclesiastical Commission a few years ago was drawing nearly £400,000 a year – a seventh part of all coal royalties.[2]

Besides the gentry, another class that benefited by the Dissolution of the Monasteries were the citizens of towns like St Albans and Bury St Edmunds, now released from the stranglehold of monastic lordship, against which they had been in fierce rebellion for centuries past. On the other hand, the

1. See Appendix II, pp. 497–9, of H. A. L. Fisher's vol. v of the *Political History of England* – table of Disposition of Monastic Lands.
2. Nef, *Rise of the British Coal Industry*, i, pp. 134–5.

destruction of great monastic establishments and the suppression of popular centres of pilgrimage reduced the wealth and importance of some towns and some rural districts, which were not in a position to make good the loss as independent centres of industry and trade. The destruction of many monastic libraries with their irreplaceable manuscripts was a cruel injury to learning and literature.

The monks suffered personally much less than used to be supposed until recent research has revealed the facts.[1] They

1. See G. Baskerville, *The English Monks and the Suppression of the Monasteries*, 1938. See also Rowse's *Tudor Cornwall*, 1941, chaps. VIII–IX.

137. Trinity College, Cambridge, in the late seventeenth century

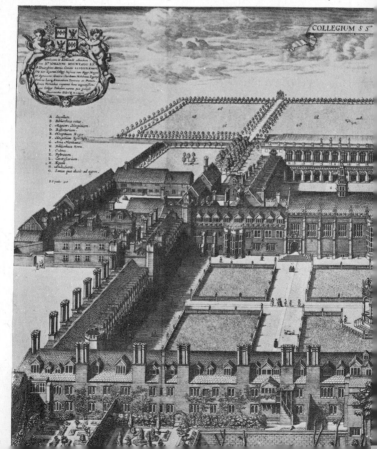

wcre given adequate pensions, which were really paid. Many of them found employment, particularly as beneficed clergymen and some even as bishops. Under the successive Catholic and Protestant régimes of Henry, Edward, Mary, and Elizabeth, the Church was served by former monks and friars, who appear to have been as well able as the rest of the clerical body to adapt their views to the frequent changes of the times. A few of the heads and inmates of the dissolved houses resisted the new order of things and were ruthlessly executed by the tyrant King. But the great bulk of the monks and friars accepted changes which to many of them were not unwelcome as opening to them personally a freer life and greater opportunity

in the world. They did little to build up a party against Henry's innovations, except in the north where social conditions still resembled those of feudal ages gone by.

With the monks disappeared also the preaching friars, so long the auxiliaries and rivals of the parish clergy. The familiar grey and black-gowned figures of Franciscan and Dominican were no longer seen upon the roads of England, tapping at the cottage door, or perorating to an audience of rustics. Their functions were in part taken over by 'hot gospellers' and itinerant Protestant preachers, working sometimes for, sometimes against the authorities of the Church. The life of Bernard Gilpin, 'the Apostle of the North', in his religious peregrinations of the Border Counties under Mary and Elizabeth, recalls the earlier days of the friars, and looks forward to Wesley.

In all, about 5,000 monks, 1,600 friars, and 2,000 nuns were pensioned off and sent out into the world. The disappearance of the nunneries made the least social difference. Their wealth and estates were not comparable to those of the monks, nor their popular activities to those of the friars. The nuns of this period

138. Christ Church, Oxford, in the late seventeenth century

were ladies of good family whom their relations had provided for in the life of religion, as they could not be suitably married. The convents were not an important factor in English social life.[1]

But the social consequences of the Dissolution of the Monasteries require more consideration. How far did their tenants, their servants, and the poor suffer by the change?

As regards estate management, there is less than no reason to suppose that either the secular or regular clergy were easier landlords than laymen before the Dissolution. The Domesday of Enclosures of 1517 shows that evictions were as common on ecclesiastical as on lay estates and that 'while the average rental value of lands in the hand of owners are considerably lower in the case of ecclesiastics than of lay owners, the rents of lands let by ecclesiastics are higher'.[2] The abbeys were accused by Sir Thomas More of turning tillage into pasture and by popular rhymers of extortionate renting as well as of enclosing:

1. For the nuns in the fifteenth century see Eileen Power's *Medieval English Nunneries*. Something has been said of them on pp. 144–50.

2. R.H.S. *Domesday of Enclosures*, Leadam, pp. 48, 65.

> How have the abbeys their payment?
> A new way they do invent
> Letting a dozen farms under one,
> Which one or two rich franklins
> Occupying a dozen men's livings
> Take all in their own hands alone. . . .
>
> Where a farm for twenty pounds was set,
> Under thirty they would not it let.[1]

In fact the monks had to a large extent handed over the control of their estates to laymen. The abbey lands were often managed, and the farms taken on lease and sublet, by noblemen, gentlemen, and 'franklins', who ran them very much as other estates were run, enclosing land where it was profitable to enclose, turning copyholders into tenants at will, and raising rents if prices rose or the value of the farms increased. When, at the Dissolution, the monastic property passed into lay ownership, the existing lay management continued as before in much the same spirit towards the tenants. But as, owing to Henry VIII's debasement of the coinage, the reign of his son was a period of soaring prices, all landlords new and old, if they would not be ruined, had to raise their rents whenever leases and copies fell in. The 'new men' were therefore denounced, sometimes rightly but very often unfairly, for doing what the monks would have had to do in like price-conditions, and for continuing an estate policy for which abbots had, in former times, been abused with equally good or bad reason. As years went by, the past was seen through a golden haze, and a tradition grew up that the monks had been particularly easy landlords – a tradition that modern research has not confirmed.[2]

Apart from the tenants of the monastic lands, who cannot be positively said to have either gained or lost by the Dissolution, there was also a great army of servants, more numerous than

1. Date 1527–8; Tawney and Power, *Tudor Ecclesiastical Documents*, III, pp. 20–21.
2. For what I say about the monasteries in this chapter, see Baskerville, *English Monks and the Suppression of the Monasteries*; Savine, *English Monasteries on the Eve of the Dissolution* (*Oxford Studies*, edited by Vinogradoff, 1909); Snape, *English Monastic Finances*, 1926.

the monks themselves, who were employed in the domestic service of the abbeys. It had been the custom to denounce them as 'idle abbeylubbers, apt to do nothing but only to eat and drink'.[1] They were probably no better and no worse than the great households of serving-men that noblemen and gentlemen loved to keep up, after Henry VII had disarmed their military retainers. 'Serving-men' were not admired, even in Shakespeare's day. These monastic dependants were many of them taken over by the new proprietors, especially by such as converted the abbey buildings into a manor-house. But no doubt a certain proportion lost their places and swelled the ranks of the 'sturdy beggars', which the monks themselves had no need to do owing to their pensions.

Many of the abbey 'servants' had been young gentlemen of the squire class attached to the monastery, 'wearing its livery, administering its estates, presiding over its manorial courts, acting as stewards, bailiffs, gentlemen farmers'. Besides these gentlemen servants, paid officers of the monks, there were wealthy guests and corrodians living in the abbey at its charges. And there were noblemen and gentlemen who, as patrons or founders' kin, exerted great influence over the administration of the House. The lay upper class had got its fingers deep in the monastic pie long before the Dissolution. In some aspects, the secularization of the monastic lands was a gradual process, and the Dissolution only a last step.[2]

But there were always the poor at the gate. They duly received broken meats and a dole of money. The custom represented an ancient tradition and doctrine of Christian duty which was of priceless value. But in practice, according to the historian of our Poor Law, the monastic charity being 'unorganized and indiscriminate' did 'nearly as much to increase beggars as to relieve them'.[3] Presumably the cessation of the dole at the abbey gate did something in the first instance to increase the number of beggars elsewhere, but there is no evidence that the problem which mendicancy presented was

1. Starkey's *England, temp. H. VIII*, Early English Text Society, p. 131.
2. Baskerville, chap. 11 and *passim*; Savine, op. cit., pp. 244–67.
3. Leonard, *Poor Law*, p. 18.

THE PASSING OF THE MONASTERIES
139. Much Wenlock Abbey, Shropshire, the Prior's house,
continuously inhabited by lay owners since the Dissolution

seriously worse after the Dissolution than it had been before.
It was certainly less bad at the end of the reign of Elizabeth.

How far, when the new order of things was well established,
did the heirs of those who had purchased the abbey lands carry
on the work of charity? Did the lord and lady of the manor in
Elizabethan times give more or less of their incomes to the poor
than the monks before them? It is impossible to say; probably
some gave more and others less.[1] Early in the Stuart era the

1. In 1539, while the Dissolution of the Monasteries was still
proceeding, Robert Pye wrote to Thomas Cromwell on the state of
opinion in the country about the King's ecclesiastical changes:
'I asked what relief they had since the suppression of religious houses
and was told they were never in so good case, were it not for the
unreasonable number of hounds and greyhounds which the gentlemen
keep and compel their tenants to keep, and many tenants keep them
for their own pleasures. These dogs eat up the broken meats and
bread which should relieve the poor. [Exactly the same complaint
had been made against the monks!] They say they must keep dogs,
or the foxes would kill their lambs. There are men enough if they
might be suffered with traynes [traps] who would not leave a fox
in the country. Howbeit they have always been resisted by gentlemen
for killing their game' (Cal. L. and P., H. VIII, vol. XIV (2), p. 354).

140. Titchfield Abbey, Hampshire

care of the village was a duty recognized by many a squire's wife, sometimes even by a peeress, like Letice, Lady Falkland, who used to visit the sick, dose them, and read to them. The 'Lady Bountiful' of the manor-house and her lord often did as much for the poor as had been done by the later monasteries.

How far the poor positively lost by the dissolution of the monasteries remains obscure, but it is plain as noonday that a great chance was missed of endowing the poor, as well as education and learning. This was realized by many at the time, especially by the reforming clergy, like Latimer and Crowley. About 1550 Crowley wrote:

> As I walked alone, and mused on things
> That have in my time been done by great Kings,
> I bethought me of the Abbeys that sometimes I saw,
> Which are now suppressed all by a Law.
> O Lord (thought I then) what occasion was here
> To provide for learning and make poverty cheer!
> The lands and the jewels that hereby were had
> Would have found godly preachers which might well had led
> The people aright that now go astray,
> And have fed the poor that famish every day.

Instead of that, a further impetus had been given to a tendency already strong enough, the rise to dominance of the class of landowning gentry, whose power replaced that of the great nobles and ecclesiastics of the feudal ages and whose word was to be law in the English countryside for centuries to come [134, 135, 139–47].

The bands of 'sturdy beggars' who alarmed society in the early Tudor reigns were recruited from many sources – the ordinary unemployed, the unemployable, soldiers discharged after French wars and the Wars of the Roses, retainers disbanded at Henry VII's command, serving-men set adrift by impecunious lords and gentry, Robin Hood bands driven from their woodland lairs by deforestation and by the better enforcement of the King's peace, ploughmen put out of work by enclosures for pastures, and tramps who prudently pretended to belong to that much commiserated class. All through the

Tudor reigns, the 'beggars coming to town' preyed on the fears of dwellers in lonely farms and hamlets, and exercised the minds of magistrates, Privy Councillors, and Parliaments. Gradually a proper system of poor relief, based upon compulsory rates, and discriminating between the various classes of the indigent, was evolved in England, first of all the countries of Europe. It was soon found that the whipping of 'sturdy beggars' was by itself no solution. The double duty of providing work for the unemployed and charity for the impotent was gradually recognized by Tudor England as incumbent not merely on the Church and the charitable, but on society as a whole. In the reign of Henry VIII some great towns, like London and Ipswich, organized the administrative relief of their poor. At the end of Elizabeth's reign and under the early Stuart kings, it had become a duty prescribed by national legislation, enforced upon the local magistrates by a vigilant Privy Council, and paid for by compulsory Poor Rates.[1]

After the monasteries, the chantries! Henry VIII was already preparing an attack upon them when death took him where Kings can steal no more. On the accession of Edward VI (1547) Protestant doctrine triumphed, and prayers for the dead were pronounced 'superstitious'. As that was the specific purpose of chantries, their spoliation had now the cover of religious zeal. The 'ramp', as our generation would call it, of greedy statesmen and their parasites at Court, and of rural gentry living near to chantry lands, became more shameless under the boy King than under his formidable old father; Henry had at least

1. About the year 1550 Robert Crowley thus writes in his *Epigrams*:
   I heard two beggars that under an hedge sate,
   Who did with long talk their matters debate.
   They had both sore legs most loathsome to see,
   All raw from the foot well most to the knee.
   'My leg,' quoth the one, 'I thank God is fair.'
   'So is mine,' quoth the other, 'in a cold air,
   For then it looketh raw and as red as any blood,
   I would not have it healed for any world's good.
   No man would pity me but for my sore leg,
   Wherefore if I were whole I might in vain beg.
   I should be constrained to labour and sweat,
   And perhaps sometime with scourges be beat.'

THE MONASTIC LIFE
141. A medieval library, Hereford Cathedral Chained Library

142. The Abbot's Kitchen, Glastonbury

143. The great gate of St Augustine's Abbey, Canterbury, where the dole was given to the poor

144. The south cloister of Gloucester Cathedral, showing the 'carrels' where the monks studied or illuminated MSS.

145. The refectory, Chester Cathedral (note the stone lector's pulpit on the right)

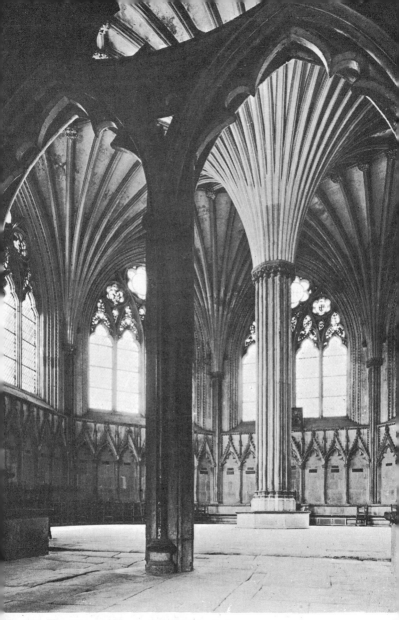

146. The Chapter House, Wells Cathedral

protected the interests of the Crown, so far as his financial incompetence permitted.

The chantries were not purely ecclesiastical establishments. Many of them were the property of lay guilds, and their endowments went to pay not only for prayers on behalf of the dead, but for the maintenance of bridges, harbours, and schools. When therefore their 'superstitious' uses were to be suppressed, the secular purposes for which the endowments were also used ought clearly to have been separated off and protected. In some cases this was done; the burgesses of Lynn secured the funds of their Holy Trinity Guild to maintain their piers and seawalls [148]. But many public services suffered in the scramble, especially in the case of the poorer and less influential guilds. School endowments lost heavily.

For three hundred years after his death, Edward VI enjoyed an undeserved reputation as a very good boy who had founded schools. But in fact the 'Edward VI Grammar Schools' were simply those old establishments which his counsellors refrained from destroying and to which his name was sycophantically appended. Most of the chantry and guild schools affected by the legislation of this period suffered, some more, some less. Lands of great potential value were taken from them, and they were compensated with fixed stipends in a rapidly depreciating currency.[1]

Another great chance had been missed. If all, or even half, the endowments of masses for the dead had been devoted to schools, and if at the same time those schools had been left with their old landed property, England would soon have had the best secondary education in the world, and the whole history of England and of the world might have been changed for the better. Latimer denounced the waste of opportunity – and appealed for a new form of endowment more suited to the religious needs of the time:

1. Christ's Hospital, indeed, was really founded by Edward VI on the site of Grey Friars Monastery, originally as a foundling hospital, though it soon became the famous 'blue-coat school'. Some monastic hospitals had been destroyed by Henry VIII, but 'Bart's', St Thomas's, and Bedlam were saved and refounded under lay control. The disendowment of hospitals was more injurious to the poor than the disendowment of monasteries. The hospitals had been founded to help the poor and had been placed where they were most needed [149].

147. The Abbot's Tribunal (or court house), Glastonbury

Here I will make a supplication that ye would bestow so much to the finding of scholars of good wits, of poor men's sons, to exercise the office of salvation, in relieving scholars, as ye were wont to bestow in pilgrimage matters, in trentals, in masses, in parsons, in purgatory matters.

Such appeals had little effect on the policy of the councillors and courtiers who were greedily exploiting the minority of Edward VI. But they were not without influence on individuals. The Tudor English were not all of a piece. Members of the rising class of gentry and individual lawyers, merchants, and yeomen did much by private beneficence to retrieve the educational position. In Elizabeth's reign, Camden notices newly founded schools at Uppingham, Oakham, and other towns; the yeoman, John Lyon, founded a free grammar school for boys at Harrow, where Greek was to be taught in the upper forms. In the first year of King James, a grammar school was founded in the remote but flourishing dale of Dent in

148. The Guild Hall at King's Lynn, where the Holy Trinity Guild funds maintained the piers and sea walls

149. Edward VI granting the Royal Palace of Bridewell for a hospital

Yorkshire, by subscription among its 'statesman' freeholders, and thence for centuries to come the University of Cambridge and the parsonages of the north drew many valuable recruits, down to the days of Professor Adam Sedgwick. The grammar school at Hawkshead, where the poet Wordsworth was educated, had been founded in the reign of Elizabeth by Archbishop Sandys.

A typical 'new man' of the Tudor age was Nicholas Bacon, father of Francis and son of the sheepreeve to the Abbey of Bury St Edmunds [150, 151]. Nicholas Bacon rose by law and politics to be owner of many of the farms on which his father had served the monks as one of their bailiffs. He founded a free grammar school on those lands, with scholarships thence' to Cambridge, and gave other endowments to his old College of Corpus Christi. At Cambridge he had first met his lifelong friends Matthew Parker and William Cecil, the future leaders of Church and State under Elizabeth. The younger and hitherto lesser university was coming rapidly to the front, and her sons played the leading part in the great changes of the period.

At the same time the educational methods and ideals of the men of the new learning, eager to study the classics and the Bible in the original tongues, gave an increased value to school and university teaching. The influence of John Cheke and Roger Ascham, the 'Grecians' of St John's, Cambridge, had a profound and lasting effect. Shakespeare got a classical education of the new type at Stratford Grammar School, and he got it free of charge, which was fortunate, as his father was at the time gravely embarrassed. Our humble and hearty thanks are therefore due to the medieval founders of Stratford School and to the educational reformers of the English Renaissance [152].

If under Henry VIII and Edward VI the Catholic families had refused to purchase confiscated Church property, it is probable that their children and grandchildren would less often have become Protestants. In the days of Elizabeth, when a vigorous Catholic reaction threatened England from overseas, the new owners of abbey and chantry lands found their own interest had become involved in that of the Reformation.[1]

Throughout Tudor times, as for centuries before, 'enclosure' of land with permanent hedges was going on in various forms: the enclosure of waste and forest for agricultural purposes; the enclosure of open-field strips into a smaller number of hedged fields to promote better individual tillage; the enclosure of village commons; and the enclosure of arable land for pasture. All of these forms of enclosure increased wealth, and only some of them defrauded the poor or reduced the population. Some were carried out with the active collaboration of the peasants themselves. Others, especially the enclosure of commons, were deeply resented, and provoked riot and rebellion [125].

In the reign of Henry VII a cry arose against the throwing together of small peasant holdings into pasture farms, as being injurious to population and leading to the 'pulling down of towns' (namely, villages). In 1489 and 1515 Acts were passed

1. On the treatment of chantries and schools under Edward VI, see Pollard, Longmans' *Political History of England*, vol. VI, 1547–1603, pp. 15–20; and Leach, *English Schools at the Reformation*.

150. A typical 'new man' of the Tudor age: Sir Nicholas Bacon

151. Gorhambury, built by Sir Nicholas Bacon partly with stone from the dissolved abbey of St Albans

to restrain this practice, apparently without result. After that, the proclamations, commissions, and statutes of Henry VIII's middle and later years indicate a growing alarm at the increase of pasture at the expense of arable, and the consequent reduction of the village population. But enclosure does not appear to have been conducted on any large scale except in certain Midland shires where Royal Commissioners were sent to report. And even in the Midlands, enclosure, whether for arable or pasture, must in fact have been very limited, for in these same counties, in the eighteenth century, we find that the open fields and commons of the medieval manors are, with few exceptions, still unhedged and waiting to be enclosed by Hanoverian Acts of Parliament.[1]

The amount of noise made over economic and social change

1. Gonner, *Common Land and Enclosure.*

is determined, not by the extent and importance of the changes that actually occur, but by the reaction of contemporary opinion to the problem. For example, we hear much of rural depopulation in Tudor times, because it was then regarded as a grave evil. Enclosures for pasture were therefore denounced by More and Latimer and a hundred other writers and preachers, Catholic and Protestant alike. 'Where forty person had their livings, now one man and his shepherd hath all' – such was the outcry. There were some such cases, and there would have been more but for the agitation and the consequent action by government to restrain such enclosure. But the 'rural depopulation' in Tudor times was only sporadic and local, and was more than made up elsewhere. When, however, 'rural depopulation' really set in on a national scale about 1880, as a result of the import of American foodstuffs, the later Victorians looked on with indifference at this tremendous social disaster, as a natural and therefore acceptable outcome of Free Trade, and did nothing to check it at all. Only in our own day, the fear of

152. The Grammar School, formerly Guild House, Stratford on Avon

island starvation in time of war has attracted some general interest to a problem of rural depopulation twenty times more serious than that which four centuries ago occupied the thoughts of our ancestors as much perhaps as the Reformation itself.

Social and economic grievances caused Kett's rising in Norfolk (1549), when the rebellious peasantry, encamped on Mousehold Heath, slaughtered 20,000 sheep as a protest against the landlords who kept an unconscionable number of their own sheep upon the common lands. But enclosure of arable for pasture was not the grievance in Norfolk, where, a generation later, Camden recorded that the county was 'almost all champion', to wit unenclosed, though he also notes its 'great flocks of sheep'.

Agrarian trouble had not been to any large extent aggravated by the Dissolution of the Monasteries. But it was aggravated, as we shall presently see, by Henry's next financial expedient, the debasement of the coinage. The bottom of the trouble lay deeper, in the growing pains of historic change. Society was passing from a system of wide distribution of land among the peasants at easy rents which had prevailed during the shortage of labour of the fourteenth and fifteenth centuries, to a gradual abolition of peasant holdings and their consolidation into larger, highly rented farms. This implied a further reduction of mere 'subsistence agriculture', and a greater production for the market. It may or may not have been a change from a better form of life to a worse, but it was certainly a change from a poorer to a richer countryside. And some such change was necessary in order to feed the increasing number of inhabitants of the island; to multiply the nation's wealth; and to allow the rise of the general standard of living, which modern conditions ultimately brought about at the expense of the old order of life.

Sixteenth-century England was ahead of Germany and France in having got rid of the servile status of the peasant, of which little was left in the reign of Henry VII and practically nothing in the reign of Elizabeth. But the agrarian changes of the epoch were beginning another evolution less to the peasants' advantage, which in the course of the seventeenth and eighteenth centuries gradually got rid of the peasant himself, converting him either into farmer or yeoman, or into the landless labourer on the large leasehold farm, or into the town workman divorced from the land. Agrarian discontent in Tudor times was the protest against an early stage of this long process. The circumstances under which it began require further examination here.

Long ago, in the thirteenth century, there had been 'land-hunger' – too many men and not enough land in cultivation – greatly to the advantage of the landlords. But, as has already been noticed, during the next two centuries, largely owing to the Black Death, there had been a glut of land and a hunger for men to till it – to the advantage of the peasant, who had effected his emancipation from serfdom under these favouring conditions. And now in the sixteenth century there was land-hunger again. The slow advance of the birth-rate against the death-rate had at last made good the ravages of the Black Death – though its local recurrence still periodically took toll of London and other towns. Only the rich had medical attendance of any value, and even their children died off at a rate that would appal modern parents, but was then taken as a matter of course. But in spite of the 'dance of death', a favourite subject for the artists at that time, the population was slowly on the rise, probably reaching four millions for all England [153, 154]. So there was again under the Tudors a

153. Medical attendance

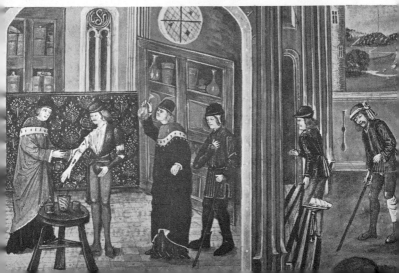

154. The Dance of Death – the blind leading the blind

surfeit of labour in proportion to the land available. And as yet there was no colonial and little industrial development to absorb the superfluous men. Hence the 'sturdy beggars'; hence increased deforestation and taking in of waste land for agriculture, which had been held up in the fifteenth century; hence also the economic opportunity of the landlord to do what he liked with land so much in demand, and to exact higher rents so far as the character of his tenants' leases allowed him.

While the land-hunger enabled the landlord to effect changes in rent and in agricultural method, the rise in prices compelled him to do so or be ruined. Between 1500 and 1560 the prices that the landlord had to pay for the things he bought for himself and his household had much more than doubled; food had nearly trebled. Unless then the landlords were to accept ruin they must raise rents when leases fell in, and they must turn land to its most profitable use – even in some cases to pasture instead of arable.[1]

But this excuse was scarcely considered at all by popular anger and religious sentiment. Catholic and Protestant alike applied medieval ethical judgements to economic actions. For example, in spite of the long established practice of business-men, law and opinion still attempted to forbid as usury all interests on money lent. So far did legislation lag behind reality that as late as 1552 an Act of Parliament prohibited all taking of interest as 'a vice most odious and detestable'. At length, in 1571, this Act was repealed and interest not exceeding ten per cent ceased to be criminal.

It is not surprising then that preachers, pamphleteers, and poets denounced enclosure as immoral and higher rents as extortionate. Some of them were so, no doubt; but on the whole the landlords were acting under financial compulsion. 'Economic necessity' became indeed the tyrant's plea for much oppression, and was too glibly used in later centuries when the 'dismal science' of Political Economy bore iron rule over the minds of men. But much of the Tudor writing on these questions suffered from the opposite fault and was not economic enough. It blamed the wickedness of individuals alone, instead of looking for root causes and remedies.

1. There were three stages of the price-rise under the Tudors: (1) 1510–40. Owing to production of silver in Germany, and the dispersal of Henry VII's hoarded treasure by Henry VIII, prices of foodstuffs go up 30 per cent. Other prices rise less. (2) 1541–61. Owing to Henry VIII's debasement of the coin (and a little later to American silver-mines beginning to take effect) prices of all kinds rush up about 100 per cent more. (3) 1561–82. Owing to Mary's better finance and Elizabeth's re-coinage, prices are stabilized, and rise more slowly. Then in early Stuart times American silver-mines again raise prices to peak 1643–52; after that prices fall.

But there were exceptions. A remarkable dialogue, written at the height of the social trouble under Edward VI, entitled *A Discourse of the Common Weal*, managed to elucidate the real truth with fairness to all parties, perceiving the unavoidable effect that the price-rise must have on rent, as well as its main cause in Henry's debasement of the coinage. And early in Elizabeth's reign Thomas Tusser grew lyrical as well as economic in praise of the much abused enclosures:

> More plenty of mutton and beef,
> Corn, butter, and cheese of the best,
> More wealth anywhere (to be brief)
> More people, more handsome and prest,
> Where find ye (go search any coast)
> Than there, where enclosures are most?

But, more usually, indiscriminate abuse was poured on all enclosure, which might better have been reserved for the cases of real injustice, when lords of the manor 'enclosed from the poor their due commons'. Equally indiscriminate was the attack on the gentry as 'cormorants and greedy gulls' because they 'raise our rents'. Yet owing to the price-rise, peasants and farmers were selling their produce at two or three times the old money, while their landlords were paying proportionately more for all they bought.[1] How then could rents fail to rise? But the mind of the community, still essentially medieval in outlook, thought the right basis of social economics was not competition but immemorial custom, even when the fall in the value of money and the soaring of prices was rendering old custom every day more impossible and unfair.

A chief cause of social *malaise* was the casual and irregular incidence of the price-rise on various classes of men. One part of the peasantry, who were lucky enough to have long-term

---

1. This point, though noted in the *Discourse of the Common Weal*, is shirked in most of the literature of the time. But the poet Gascoigne early in Elizabeth's reign says of the peasants in his *Piers Plowman*:

> Nor that they can cry out on landlords loud
> And say they rack their rents an ace too high,
> When they themselves do sell their landlords' lamb
> For greater price than ewe was wont be worth.

leases or copyhold tenures of the kind that was by law not breakable, reaped the full advantage from the soaring prices of their products because their rents could not be raised. Since therefore the landlords could not raise rents all round in moderation, they recouped themselves by extorting high rents and heavy fines for renewal of leases from the other less fortunate part of the peasantry and farmers, whose leases were renewable annually or fell in upon death or after a period of years. The result was that one group of peasants was coining money without paying an extra penny of rent, while another group, not socially distinguishable except by the date of their leases or the legal forms of their tenure, were being oppressed all the more to make up for the immunity enjoyed by the others. Meanwhile the yeoman freeholder, who paid no rent or a purely nominal one to the lord of the manor, was selling his corn and cattle for three times the price that his grandfather had been able to ask.

Thus, while some men flourished exceedingly, others, including many lords and squires, were in real distress during the reigns of Edward VI and Mary, largely as a result of their royal father's unscrupulous juggle with the coinage. For the same reason the landless labourer suffered from the time-lag of wages behind prices.[1] But the landless labourer was then a much smaller proportion of the working-class than he is today, and as he was to some extent paid in kind, his loss from the fall of the value of money was often not very great. On the other hand, the craftsman, manufacturer, and merchant gained by the rise of prices as much as the peasant whose rent could not be raised. More generally, the rise of prices, which brought poverty to some and wealth to others, had the effect of stimulating trade, production, and enterprise both in the towns and on the land. It was a factor in the development of the new England of adventure and competition, replacing the old England of custom and settled rights.

Before the end of the century equilibrium had been reached for a time. In the last years of Edward VI a real financial reform had been begun which Mary continued and Elizabeth

1. Between 1501 and 1560 food prices had gone up as from 100 to 290, while wages in the building trade had gone up only from 100 to 169. Agricultural wages cannot be given.

carried to fruition. As early as the second year of her reign (1560–61) the great Queen was able to restore the purity of the currency. Prices were for a while stabilized. Gradually, as more and more leases fell in, rents were adjusted all round, and in the age of Shakespeare there was agrarian peace and a high general level of prosperity and content, except in times of bad harvest.

By the time that this new balance had been adjusted, important changes had been brought about under the pressure of the bad times. The number of farmers in the modern sense of the word, men with a considerable acreage held on terminable leases, was greater than before, and the typical peasant holder of the Middle Ages was rather less common. But there were still many small peasants, and the bulk of the best arable land in the Midlands was still cultivated in open-field strips, either in large or small holdings.

The continuous effort of successive Tudor governments, by legislation, commissions, and the judicial action of the Star Chamber and Court of Requests, had done something to check the abuses of enclosure and to protect the old-fashioned peasant against his landlord. But it had not stopped the gradual process of inevitable change.

As a result of these conditions, the class denominated 'yeomen' was more numerous, more wealthy, and more important than in any former age. The term 'yeoman' covered at least three different classes, all now prosperous: the freeholder cultivating his own land; the capitalist farmer, who might be a tenant-at-will; and the peasant who was lucky enough to enjoy a secure tenure at an unalterable rent. All these three types of yeoman might be cultivating either land enclosed by hedges, or scattered strips in the open field. The wealth of many of them was derived wholly or in part from the fleeces of their sheep. The praise of the yeoman as the best type of Englishman, holding society together, neither cringing to the high nor despising his poorer neighbour, hearty, hospitable, fearless, supplies a constant motif of literature under Tudors and Stuarts. And it corresponded to a social fact.

The yeomen were held to be the real strength and defence of the nation. Of old they had won Agincourt and but yesterday

Flodden, and were still the nation's shield and buckler. 'If the yeomanry of England were not, in time of war we should be in shrewd case. For in them standeth the chief defence of England.'[1] Other nations, Englishmen boasted, had no such middle class, but only an oppressed peasantry and the nobles and men-at-arms who robbed them.

A strong feeling already existed among the English against professional soldiers, largely derived from memories of what had been endured by quiet folk at the hands of the lords' retainers. The Tudor kings had put all that down, and had no standing army of their own: hence their popularity. The English were conscious and proud of their liberty, not yet defined as the liberty of governing their king through Parliament, or of printing what they liked against the authorities of Church and State, but simply freedom to live their own lives undisturbed either by feudal or royal oppression. In the *Discourse of the Common Weal* in Edward VI's reign, the Husbandman and Merchant discuss whether there should be a standing force in England to repress tumults:

HUSBANDMAN: God forbid that we have any such tyrants amongst us; for, as they say, such will in the country of France take poor men's hens, chickens, pigs, and other provision and pay nothing for it; except it be an evil turn, as to ravish his wife and daughter for it.

MERCHANT: Marie, I think that would be rather occasion of commotions to be stirred, than to be quenched, for the stomachs of Englishmen would never bear it.

The English yeomen would not stand that kind of thing!

The new age was bringing into increasing prominence not only the yeoman, but the squire. He survived the difficulties of his family budget during the price-crisis, and emerged under Elizabeth as the principal figure in the life of the countryside. The wealth and power of the country gentleman had been increased, partly by their easy purchases of monastic land, partly by the recent changes in the agricultural economy of their estates, which the land-hunger had enabled them, and

1. Starkey's *England, temp. H. VIII*, Early English Text Society, p. 79.

the price-rise had forced them, to accomplish. And many of them had other interests besides land, in the cloth trade and commerce overseas.

Apart from the absolute increase in their wealth, they had acquired a new relative importance by the disappearance of their former superiors, the feudal nobles and the abbots and priors. The gentry who now governed the counties for the Crown as justices of the peace had no longer cause to dread interference in their duties by 'overgreat subjects' and their retainers. The old nobility who had disturbed and terrorized Plantagenet England had lost their lands and their power in the confisca-tions of the Wars of the Roses; and the policy of the early Tudor Kings continued to depress their order, as in the Attainder of the lordly Buckingham. The last nobles of the old type maintained their feudal power along the Scottish border, where men said 'there was no King but Percy'. They too were broken by Elizabeth after the rebellion of the northern earls in 1570. In other parts of England, such semi-sovereign nobles had disappeared long before.

The families whom the Tudors raised up in their stead, the Russells, Cavendishes, Seymours, Bacons, Dudleys, Cecils, and Herberts, rose to influence not because they were feudal magnates but because they were useful servants of the Crown. Their social affinities were with the rising class of gentry, whence they derived their origin, and to whom they still essentially belonged even when they were raised to be peers of the realm [155-8].

Not only political but economic causes were depressing the old nobility. They suffered from the fall in the value of money even more than the gentry, because they paid too little personal attention to the management of their far-flung properties, and were less quick than the smaller landlords to evict tenants, terminate leases, impose fines, and raise rents. In the Tudor period taken as a whole, the gentry rose while the nobles declined.

A distinguishing feature of the English gentry, which astonished foreign visitors as early as the reign of Henry VII, was their habit of turning their younger sons out of the manor-house to seek their fortunes elsewhere, usually as apprentices

155. William Cecil, Baron Burghley

to thriving merchants and craftsmen in the towns. Foreigners
ascribed the custom to English want of family affection. But it
was also, perhaps, a wise instinct of 'what was best for the
boy', as well as a shrewd calculation of what was best for the
family fortunes. The habit of leaving all the land and most of
the money to the eldest son built up the great estates, which by
steady accumulation down the years became by Hanoverian
times so marked a feature of English rural economy.

The younger son of the Tudor gentleman was not permitted
to hang idle about the manor-house, a drain on the family
income like the impoverished nobles of the Continent who

were too proud to work. He was away making money in trade or in law. He often ended life a richer and more powerful man than his elder brother left in the old home. Such men bought land and founded county families of their own, for they had been bred in the countryside and to the countryside they loved to return.

Foreigners were astonished at the love of the English gentry for rural life. 'Every gentleman', they remarked, 'flieth into the country. Few inhabit cities and towns; few have any regard of them.'[1] Though London might already be the greatest city in Europe, England was still in its essential life and feeling a rural community, whereas in France and Italy the Roman had deeply implanted the civilization of the city, that drew to itself all that was most vital in the life of the surrounding province. The English squire did not share the feelings of the 'Italian gentlemen of quality' described by Robert Browning, pining unwillingly in his country home –

> Had I but plenty of money, money enough and to spare
> The house for me, no doubt, were a house in the city square.

The place for the squire, whether he were rich or poor, was at home in his manor-house, and he knew and rejoiced in the fact.

Owing to the habit among the gentry of apprenticing their younger sons to trade, our country avoided the sharp division between a rigid caste of nobles and an unprivileged *bourgeoisie* which brought the French *ancien régime* to its catastrophe in 1789. Unlike the French, the English gentry did not call them-selves 'nobles' – except the select few who sat in the House of Lords. The manor-house, its hospitality open to neighbours and friends of many different classes, was not ashamed to acknowledge a son in trade, besides another at the Inns of Court and a third perhaps in the family living. The 'landed' and 'moneyed' men might talk as if they were rivals, but in fact they were allied by blood and by interest. Recruits from the landed class were constantly entering town life, while money and men from the towns were constantly flowing back to fertilize the countryside.

1. Starkey's *England, temp. H. VIII*, Early English Text Society, p. 93.

156. The Lord Protector Somerset

Throughout Tudor, Stuart, and early Hanoverian times, successful lawyers formed a large proportion of the 'new' men who introduced themselves into the county circle by purchase of land and by building of manor-houses. The number of English county families who were founded by lawyers is even greater than those derived from the cloth trade. The process had begun in the Middle Ages: the fortunes of the Norfolk Pastons had been founded by one of Henry VI's judges. And the road opened yet wider before the men of law in the exciting, litigious, and rapacious times of Henry VIII and his children, when lawyers of an adventurous turn had unusual opportunities to serve the Government, and receive a very full reward, especially when, as in the case of the Bacons and Cecils, law was blended with courtiership and politics. Many of the lovely Tudor homes, small and great, that still adorn the English landscape, were paid for by money made in the courts of law.

There was much in common between the squire, the lawyer, the merchant, and the yeoman. They were all men of the new age, not hankering after feudal ideals now passing away. And they tended to become Protestant, alike from interest and conviction. They evolved a kind of religion of the home, essentially 'middle-class' and quite unmedieval.

The tendency of Protestant doctrine was to exalt the married state, and to dedicate the business life, in reaction against the medieval doctrine that the true life of 'religion' was celibacy and monastic separation from the world. The permission to marry, conceded to the clergy under Edward VI and Elizabeth, was one symptom of this change of thought. The religious home was the Protestant ideal, with family prayer and private

157. 'Looking stiffly out at posterity from the painted boards'

Bible reading in addition to the services and sacraments of the Church. These ideas and practices were by no means confined to the dissident Puritans: in the late Tudor and Stuart times they were the practice of Anglican families who loved and fought for the Prayer Book. The religion of the home and of the Bible became a social custom common to all English Protestants. It was found most often, perhaps, in the households of squires, yeomen, and tradesmen, but it was widely extended among the cottages of the poor.

The new type of English religion idealized work, dedicating business and farming to God. As George Herbert quaintly and nobly wrote:

> Who sweeps a room as for Thy laws
> Makes that and the action fine.

It was a good religion for a nation of shopkeepers and farmers.

The seed-time of these practices and ideas, which in the following century became so general, was the reign of Edward VI and his elder sister, while Cranmer was producing the Prayer Book to stand beside the Bible, and Queen Mary was providing English Protestantism with a martyrology. The anti-clerical revolution of Henry VIII, with its unedifying scramble for Church property, had lacked a moral basis, but the martyrs recorded in Foxe's book provided one for the new national religion beginning to emerge out of chaos. When Elizabeth came to the throne, the Bible and Prayer Book formed the intellectual and spiritual foundation of a new social order.

The institutions of a country are always reflected in its military system. During the Hundred Years War there had been two military systems. Home defence, against domestic rebellion and Scottish invasion, was conducted chiefly by local militia levied on a conscript basis. The more difficult war in France, which required a more professional soldiery, was conducted by war-bands following fighting nobles and gentlemen who enlisted and paid them; the King indented with their employers to furnish him with so many of these professionals for so much money. This dual system continued under Henry VII and Henry VIII, with this difference, that the destruction of the

158. Burghley House, Northamptonshire, begun by Burghley in 1575

military power and landed wealth of the old nobility by the confiscations of the Wars of the Roses had taken the value out of the indenture system. Indeed, the system of indenting with private individuals to supply an army for foreign war was incompatible with the Tudor domestic policy of suppressing the retainers and military establishments of great subjects. But as the Kings could not afford to keep up a standing army of their own, the troops hastily levied for occasional foreign service were undisciplined, mutinous, and often useless, as the history of the Tudor war on the Continent was to show again and again. The steady, devoted bands who had followed the great lords to Crécy and Agincourt no longer existed. And as yet there was no royal army.

English archery was still so good that firearms had not yet displaced it. Flodden was won by the archers. Bow and bill for the infantry, the lance for the cavalry was still the rule. The artillery, of which the King had a monopoly in his realm, was becoming an important arm, not only for sieges but for battles against rebels or Scots, as at Loose-Coat Field and Pinkie Cleugh. Under these conditions, the democratic conscript

militia sufficed to make the King safe at home, so long as his policy was not too unpopular. But he was powerless to make conquests in Europe.

While the royal army did not exist, the royal navy was growing strong. Sole reliance could no longer be placed on conscripted merchant ships to hold the narrow seas in time of war. Henry VIII has been called 'the father of the English navy', though Henry VII might perhaps dispute the title. The navy was placed under a separate government department and organized as a standing force in the King's pay. Henry VIII spent much of the royal and monastic wealth on this project. He not only built royal ships, but established dockyards at Woolwich and Deptford, where the Thames estuary made a surprise raid difficult, developed Portsmouth as a naval base, and fortified many harbours such as Falmouth Roads.

The formation of a professional navy for war purposes only was the more important because naval tactics were, after 2,000 years, entering on a new era. The placing of cannon in the broadside of a vessel transformed naval war from a mere grappling of ship with ship (the method used from the days of the ancient Egyptians and Greeks till late medieval times) into the manoeuvring of floating batteries, which first showed their strength against the Armada. By proficiency in that new game England was to attain her sea-power and Empire, and Henry VIII's naval policy first put her in a way to win it [159–61].

In spite of much economic trouble, the standard of life was slowly going up in the early and middle Tudor period. When the more marked advance under Elizabeth had diffused a general sense of prosperity, William Harrison, the parson, recorded in 1577 the improvement in household conditions that had taken place since his father's day, 'not among the nobility and gentry only but likewise of the lowest sort in most places of our south country'.

Our fathers [he writes] yea and we ourselves have lien full oft upon straw pallets, covered only with a sheet, under coverlets made of dagswain or hop harlots (I use their own terms) and a good round log under their heads instead of a bolster. If it were so that our fathers or the good man of the house had a mattress or flockbed and thereto a sack of chaff to rest his head upon, he

159. Dover Harbour, at the time of Henry VIII, showing fortifications

thought himself to be as well lodged as the lord of the town [village], that peradventure lay seldom in a bed of down or whole feathers. Pillows were thought meet only for women in childbed. As for servants, if they had any sheet above them, it was well, for seldom had they any under their bodies, to keep them from the pricking straws that ran oft through the canvas of the pallet and razed their hardened hides.

Straw on the floor and straw in the bedding bred fleas, and some fleas carried plague.

Harrison also notes that chimneys have become general even in cottages, whereas 'in the village where I remain', old men recalled that in 'their young days' under the two Kings Harry, 'there were not above two or three chimneys if so many, in uplandish towns [villages], the religious houses and manor places of their lords always excepted, but each one made his fire against a reredoss in the hall where he dined and dressed his meat'. The increasing use of coal instead of wood for the domestic hearth made it more disagreeable not to have chimneys, and the increasing use of bricks made it easier to build them, even if the walls of the house were of some other material.

160. The *Anne Gallant* carrying forty-five guns (1546)

Common houses and cottages were still of timber, or of 'half-timber' with clay and rubble between the wooden up-rights and cross-beams. Better houses, especially in stone districts, were of stone. But brick was gradually coming in, first of all in regions where stone was not to be had on the spot, and where timber was running short owing to the process of deforestation – chiefly, that is to say, in the eastern counties [162, 163].

Harrison also records a change during his own lifetime 'of treen [wooden] platters into pewter, and of wooden spoons into silver or tin'. The age of forks was not yet come; where knife and spoon would not avail, even Queen Elizabeth picked up the chicken bone deftly in her long fingers. Until her reign 'a man should hardly find four pieces of pewter in a farmer's house' [164]. Of china there was as yet no question at all.

So primitive, in the early Tudor period, had been household conditions. Such or worse they had been in all previous ages. But things were now on the way to the marked improvement noted by the Elizabethan parson. We must never forget, in picturing the past and specially the remoter past, the want of comforts and luxuries which we take for granted. Yet they have only been made general by slow process of change, some of which, like the new farming, we call in question as having been in some respects unjust to the poor.

In the reign of Henry VIII, the long predominance of Gothic architecture may be said to have come to an end, after bursting out into the final magnificent flourishes of Wolsey's hall at Christ Church, Oxford, and the fan-vaulted roof of the chapel of King's College, Cambridge, completed by his royal master [113]. Then the new age came in. Italian workmen ornamented the new quadrangle of Hampton Court with terracotta busts of Roman emperors, entirely Renaissance in feeling and in design.

The Tudor period was not one of church building. Rather the lead and stones of abbey churches were requisitioned for the 'gentleman's seats' that took their place, or for the yeomen's

161. St Mawes Castle, Cornwall, part of Henry VIII's fortification of Falmouth Roads

162. Tudor Cottages, Chiddingstone, Kent (note the use of brick between the timber uprights)

farms of the new age [136, 166]. In the manor-houses, now everywhere being built or enlarged, spacious rooms, well-lighted galleries, wide lattice windows and oriels, instead of narrow loopholes, proclaimed the Tudor peace and comfort. The commonest form of large manor-house was now an enclosed court, entered through a turreted gateway of gigantic proportions, frequently of brick. A generation later, under Elizabeth, when the need for fortifying a house had even more completely disappeared from men's minds, it became usual to build an open courtyard with three sides only, or to adopt the E-shaped form [158, 165–70].

Every manor-house of any pretensions had a deer-park dotted with clumps of fine trees at various stages of growth,

163. Tudor house, Lavenham, Suffolk

the whole enclosed by a high wooden pale. Sometimes two parks, one for fallow deer and one for red, diminished the arable land of the demesne, and sometimes, it is to be feared, the common lands of the village. On hunting mornings, the chime of hounds 'matched in mouth like bells' chased the deer round and round the enclosure, while the gentlemen and ladies of the manor and their guests followed easily on horseback – and Lady Jane Grey stayed indoors and read Plato! But there were also plenty of deer at large beyond the park pales, to be hunted more nobly 'at force' across the countryside. Great herds of red deer roamed over the Pennines, the Cheviots, and the northern moors. In the south, fallow deer ran wild in the forests, woods, and fens, often issuing forth to attack the crops. One use of the enclosure was to provide fences against these visits made while the village slept.

Hunting did not usually mean fox-hunting: farmers for the

164. 'A man should hardly find four pieces of pewter in a farmer's house'

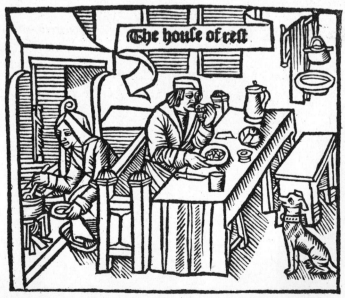

165. 'Tudor peace and comfort'; Compton Wynyates, Warwickshire

166. Fountains Hall, built in 1611 from the abbey stones

167. Tudor wall-painting in the gatehouse at West Stow Hall, Suffolk

168. The Abbot's Parlour, Thame Park, Oxfordshire

169. East Barsham, Norfolk

170. West Stow Hall, Suffolk

most part were free to kill the red thief as best they could.[1]
Gentlemen hunted the deer; and everyone, on foot and horseback, hunted the hare – 'poor Wat, far off upon a hill!' Horse-
men and greyhounds pursued the swift-footed young bustards
over the downs. The poaching of deer was a great feature of
life; the scholars of Oxford openly hunted Radley Park, till the
owner was fain to throw down the pales in despair. As to fowl-
ing, though the hawk, the bow, and the crossbow were still the
most usual methods, the 'birding-piece' was sometimes employed.[2] But snaring, liming, and trapping all sorts of birds
and beasts were still conducted not only for use but for sport.

The English were already notorious in Europe for their
devotion to horses and dogs, of which they bred and kept many
varieties in great numbers. But the horse was still a cumbrous
animal. The slim racer and hunter of eastern blood had not yet
come in, and a gentleman's mount was still bred to carry a
knight in his armour at full trot, rather than a huntsman at full
gallop. The farm-horse was gradually beginning to share with
the ox the labours of the plough.

It was still the age of the tournament [171], ridden before
the eyes of sympathetic ladies and critical populace,

> The gravelled ground, with sleeves tied on the helm,
> On foaming horse, with swords and friendly hearts,

as Surrey, Henry VIII's courtier poet describes it. He sings
also of other play at that Court:

> The dances short, long tales of great delight;
> With words and looks that tigers could but rue,
> When each of us did plead the other's right.
> The palme-play [courtyard tennis] where,
>   despoiled for the game
> With dazed eyes oft we by gleams of love
> Have missed the ball, and got sight of our dame,
> To bait her eyes that kept the leads above.

1. Yet in some districts in Elizabeth's reign foxes and badgers were
'preserved by gentlemen to hunt and have pastime withal' when they
would otherwise have been 'rooted out', Harrison says (book III,
ch. IV).
2. *Merry Wives of Windsor*, IV, ii, 58.

That gay Court owed its character to the young, athletic Henry, one of the best archers in his own kingdom, not yet grown an obese and angry tyrant, but himself the glass of fashion and the mould of form. Leaving policy to his still trusted Wolsey, he spent in delights and pageants and masques the treasure which his careful father had laid up for the nation's need. Not to have been at Court was indeed, in Touchstone's words, to be damned. There the gentlemen of England learnt not only the intrigues of love and politics, but music and poetry, and a taste for scholarship and the arts, seeds which they took back to their rural homes to plant there [172, 173, 174]. The culture, art, and scholarship of the Italian courts of the Renaissance had great influence on the courtiers and nobles of England, from the time of the Wars of the Roses until the reign of Elizabeth. The medieval distinction between the learned clerk and the barbarous fighting baron was coming to an end, blending in the ideal of the all-accomplished 'gentleman'. The 'courtier's, soldier's, scholar's eye, tongue, sword', the Elizabethan ideal afterwards realized in Sir Philip Sidney, had been rehearsed two generations before by Sir Thomas Wyatt (1503–42), a kind and faithful public servant in a hard-hearted and faithless Court. He was just as happy in the privacy of his country estate:

> This maketh me at home to hunt and hawk
> And in foul weather at my book to sit.
> In frost and snow then with my bow to stalk
> No man doth mark where I so ride or go;
> In lusty lees my liberty I take. . . .
> But here I am in Kent and Christendome
> Among the muses where I read and rhyme.

The 'cultivated country gentleman' already existed, often like Wyatt, half a courtier.[1]

At Court, Holbein and his studio were turning out apace portraits of Henry and of his chief nobles. Thence the fashion spread to the country houses, and family portraits took their place beside the tapestry that adorned the walls. Some of them

1. See E. K. Chambers's and E. M. Tillyard's books on Sir Thomas Wyatt.

were fine pictures by the Court painters, but most were creations of local talent – white-faced knights and ladies looking stiffly out at posterity from the painted boards [157]. It was the beginning of a fashion that led up to Gainsborough and Reynolds [174–7].

The music in the Chapel Royal was perhaps the best in Europe. And it was the fashion at that Court, from the King downwards, to compose musical tunes, and verses to go with them. The Tudor age was the great age of English music and lyrical poetry, two sisters at a birth, and the impulse may in part be traced to the Court of the young Henry VIII. But the whole country was filled with men and women singing songs, composing music, and writing the verses. It was a form taken in England by the free, joyful spirit of the Renaissance; but here it was a rustic spirit, mingled with the song of birds in the greenwood, and leading up to the full chorus of Shakespeare's England.

HENRY VIII
171. Jousting before Katherine of Aragon

172. With his harp and jester

173. Reading in his bedroom

174. The Darnley Brothers, by Hans Eworth

175. Henry VIII, after Hans Holbein

176. Princess Elizabeth, by a painter working in England about 1546

177. Thomas Howard, Duke of Norfolk, by Hans Holbein the Younger

When the Tudor age began, Venice still held the East in fee [178]. The precious goods of the Indies, still borne on camels' backs, continued as for ages past to reach the Levant overland. Thence Venetian ships carried the spices to England, returning with cargoes of wool to feed the looms on the Adriatic. The Venetian trader was therefore a well-known figure in our island. In 1497 one of them reported home the discovery of Newfoundland made by his countryman John Cabot, five years after Columbus's greater exploit.

The Venetian, our countryman, who went with a ship from Bristol in quest of new islands, is returned, and says that 700 leagues from hence he discovered land, the territory of the Grand Cham. He coasted for 300 leagues and landed; saw no human beings, but found some felled trees, wherefore he supposed there were inhabitants. He is now at Bristol with his wife. Vast honour is paid him; he dresses in silk, and these English run after him like mad people . . . This discoverer of these places planted on his new found land a large cross, with a flag of England and another of St Mark's by reason of his being a Venetian, so that our banner has floated very far afield.

But it was significant of the future that the flag of St Mark had not gone thus 'far afield' in a Venetian ship.

After this discovery, prophetic of an end of things for Venice and a beginning of things for England, nothing much came of it for two generations, except indeed cod-fishing by English, French, and Portuguese fishermen off the Newfoundland coast.[1] Throughout the early and middle Tudor period our commerce was conducted as before with the coast of Europe from the Baltic round to Spain and Portugal, most of all with the Netherlands, and above all with Antwerp, the centre of European business and finance. Even more rapidly than in the fifteenth century, the export of manufactured cloth

1. The increase of deep-sea fishing was a feature of early Tudor times, and helped to build up the maritime population and strength of the country, soon to be turned to such great account. The herring had recently moved from the Baltic into the North Sea, and our herring fishery had sprung to importance as a result. 'These herrings,' wrote Camden, 'which in the times of our grandfathers swarmed only about Norway, now in our times by the bounty of Providence swim in great shoals round our coasts every year.'

by the Merchant Adventurers gained on the export of raw wool by the Staplers, and the volume of London's foreign trade continued to increase. In the reigns of Henry VII and VIII English ships began to trade in the Mediterranean as far as Crete. In 1486 an English consul was established at Pisa, where there were English merchants exploiting Florentine rivalry against the Venetian monopoly. But our goods still reached Italy chiefly in Italian ships.

Meanwhile the Portuguese were rounding the Cape of Good Hope and opening the oceanic route to the Eastern trade, a fatal blow to Venice. More slowly the English followed them along the west coast of Africa, in defiance of their claim to monopolize the Dark Continent. As early as 1528 William Hawkins, father of a great line of seamen, traded in friendly fashion with the Negroes of the Guinea coast for ivory [179]. It was his more famous son John who in Elizabeth's reign

178. Venetian trading ships: Marco Polo sets out from Venice

made the Negroes themselves an article of export, and thereby almost destroyed the legitimate trade with the natives, who learnt to regard the white man as their deadly enemy. In the reigns of Edward VI and Mary the West African trade in its proper form was still being developed, besides voyages to the Canaries, to Archangel and ventures as far as Moscow; but except the cod-fishing off Newfoundland, nothing was done beyond the Atlantic by Englishmen before the reign of Elizabeth.

Although the 'vent of cloth' was still conducted mainly on the old lines and in the old European markets, it was constantly on the increase, supplied by the ever growing cloth manufacture in the towns and still more in the villages of England. After a stationary period in the fifteenth century, the cloth trade was again increasing by leaps and bounds. 'Enclosure for pasture' was a result. Even before such enclosures were much complained of, foreigners had marvelled at the incredible number of sheep in England.

The manufacture of wool into finished cloth involved a number of processes, not all carried on by the same folk or in

179. 'As early as 1528 William Hawkins . . . traded in friendly fashion with . . . the Guinea Coast for ivory'; map of the Guinea Coast (1556)

the same place [58, 59, 180]. The capitalist entrepreneur passed on the raw material, the half-manufactured and the finished cloth from place to place, employing various classes of workmen or buying from various classes of masters in the process. William Forrest, in Edward VI's reign, grows prosaically lyrical over the ubiquitous cloth trade that employed so many kinds of skill.

> No town in England, village or borough
> But thus with clothing to be occupied.
> Though not in each place clothing clean thorough,
> But as the town is, their part so applied.
> Here spinners, here weavers, there clothes to be dyed,
> With fullers and shearers as be thought best,
> As the Clothier may have his cloth drest.

In another stanza he urges the now popular policy of encouraging the cloth trade at the expense of the declining export of raw wool:

> The wool the Staplers do gather and pack
> Out of the Royalme to countries foreign,
> Be it revoked and stayed aback,
> That our clothiers the same may retain,
> All kind of work folks here to ordain,
> Upon the same to exercise their feat
> By tucking, carding, spinning, and to beat.

Most of the weaving was done on the domestic system; the loom, owned and plied by the goodman of the house, was set up in garret or kitchen. But the fulling-mills on the western streams must needs be more like factories, and some weaving was already done on what may be called the factory system. The clothier John Winchcombe was so rich and so princely that after his death in 1520 he became a legendary hero of ballad as 'Jack of Newbury', a rival in fame to Dick Whittington himself. Tradition said that he led a hundred of his prentices to Flodden Field and feasted King Harry at his house. The Elizabethan ballad proceeds to describe his factory of cloth:

> Within one room, being large and long
> There stood two hundred looms full strong.

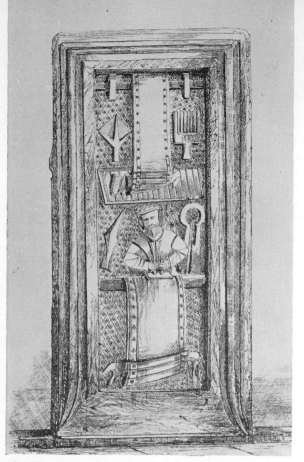

180. The cloth trade: the Fuller's Panel, bench-end at Spaxton
Church, Somerset

Two hundred men, the truth is so,
Wrought in these rooms all in a row.
By every one a pretty boy
Sate making quilts with mickle joy.
And in another place hard by
A hundred women merrily
Were carding hard with joyful cheer
Who singing sat with voices clear.

Possibly the cheerfulness, certainly the numbers, of the hands in the factory, are exaggerated by the retrospective ardour of the poet.[1] Jack of Newbury of course founded a county family. His son supported the King against the Pilgrimage of Grace, acquired abbey land, and sat in Parliament.

The volume of internal trade was far greater than the external. England still imported only luxuries for the rich. Her people were fed, clothed, housed, and warmed by home products.

The rivers were a great means of transport especially for the heaviest goods, like the railways today. Even inland towns like York, Gloucester, Norwich, Oxford, Cambridge, were to a large extent ports on rivers.

But the roads were used, then as now, for all local distribution and for much traffic in bulk. The badness of the roads, though execrable by our standards, was not absolute. In dry weather they were used by wagons, and in all weathers by pack-horse trains. As far as possible the roads followed by commerce kept to chalk and other hard soils, of which much of England is composed. Where they had to cross marshy or clay belts, the traffic was helped by causeways; some of these were built by the merchants who needed them, in the absence of any effectual road authority. Leland notes the causeway between Wendover and Aylesbury, ' else the way, in wet time, as in low stiff clay, were tedious to pass '.

Even for long-distance traffic of heavy goods the supremacy of water over road was not complete. Southampton, for example, flourished as a port serving London. Certain classes of goods were regularly unshipped at Southampton and sent by road to the capital, to save the vessels from the necessity of rounding Kent.

1. Elizabeth Power, *Medieval People*, p. 158.

Darby's *Historical Geography of England* (1936), chap. IX; Miss Toulmin Smith's edition of Leland's *England*; Lord Ernle, *English Farming*, chap. III; Tawney, *The Agrarian Problem in the Sixteenth Century*, and *Religion and the Rise of Capitalism*; *Social England*, ed. Traill, vols. II and III; Baskerville, *English Monks and the Suppression of the Monasteries*; Lipson, *Economic History of England*, II. In working on this chapter, I have been much indebted to the advice and notes of Mr John Saltmarsh of King's College, Cambridge.

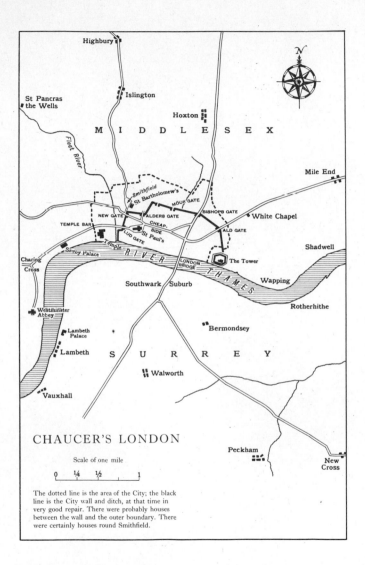

CHAUCER'S LONDON

Scale of one mile

0   ¼   ½   1

The dotted line is the area of the City; the black line is the City wall and ditch, at that time in very good repair. There were probably houses between the wall and the outer boundary. There were certainly houses round Smithfield.

DESCRIPTIVE NOTES TO
THE ILLUSTRATIONS

1

Gold noble of Edward III, struck between 1360 and 1369
(Dept of Coins and Medals, British Museum)

2

The Pageants of Richard Beauchamp, Earl of Warwick (B.M.
MS. Cott. Julius E. iv, art. 6, f. 20ᵛ; Flemish, late fifteenth
century)

This MS. consists of fifty-three pencil drawings depicting
various episodes in the life of the second Earl (1382–1439). It
was probably executed about 1493 by a Flemish artist working
for Anne, Countess of Warwick, youngest daughter of the Earl
and widow of the kingmaker. The drawings are of great delicacy
and the page reproduced is a spirited illustration of men and
horses in action.

3

'Open Field System', Laxton Village, Nottinghamshire (from
an air photograph by Aerofilms Ltd)

Note the 'strips' in the foreground running in different directions across the wide unfenced area (cf. 125, showing a map with
open fields).

4

'Lands' and green furrows at Crimscote, near Whitchurch,
Warwickshire (from an air photograph by Aerofilms Ltd)

5

Queen Mary's Psalter (B.M. MS. Royal 2 B. vii, f. 78ᵛ; English,
early fourteenth century)

This psalter owes its name to the fact that in 1553 it was
prevented by Baldwin Smith, a London Customs officer, from

being sent abroad and was presented by him to Queen Mary in October of the same year.

Besides its numerous full-colour miniatures this MS. is adorned with delicately tinted drawings which portray many scenes of contemporary life – all kinds of games, hunting and hawking, feasting and dancing. The decorations of the Calendar are in full colour and illustrate the occupations of each month and scenes dramatizing the zodiacal signs. The present illustration is that for August and shows peasants reaping corn under the direction of the reeve.

The tinted drawings are remarkable for their delicate yet lively style, their free and graceful treatment of drapery, their graphic delineation of animals in action and their close observation of the details of contemporary life.

6

The Luttrell Psalter (B.M. MS. add. 42, 130, f. 158; English, East Anglian, *c.* 1340)

This MS. was commissioned by Sir Geoffrey Luttrell of Irnham, Lincolnshire (1276–1345); it is richly illuminated throughout with miniatures and marginal drawings, as well as with decorative initials and borders. The marginal subjects are of great variety covering many activities of contemporary life; they are drawn with vigour and are full of broad humour and realistic detail, forming a valuable commentary on the social life of the period. The MS. is also remarkable for the fantastic monsters and grotesques, which posture in harsh colours alongside the moros peasants at their everyday work. In this illustration the man is riding to mill (as Clement Paston did) 'on the bare horseback with his corn under him' (cf. text, p. 40).

7

Queen Mary's Psalter (B.M. MS. Royal 2 B. vii, f. 74; for general description of MS. see note under [5] above)

This illustration is from the Calendar under March and shows two shepherds watching their flock.

8

The Luttrell Psalter (B.M. MS. add. 42, 130, f. 163^v; for general description of MS. see note under [7] above)

In this illustration the sheep are enclosed in a wattled pen; the woman in the foreground is milking a ewe, while two women carry away pitchers of milk on their heads. In the background a man appears to be doctoring one of the sheep.

9 and 10

The Luttrell Psalter (B.M. MS., add. 42, 130, ff. 170^v and 147^v; for general description of MS. see note under [7] above)

These contrasted scenes illustrate the English yeoman as farmer and archer:

[9] shows a man sowing grain; his dog chases one crow away, while yet another crow is busy feeding at the sack of grain;

[10] shows archery practice at a range. The man standing in front appears to be instructing five others and a bull's-eye has already been scored. Note the bracers on the instructor's and the first archer's left arms.

11

Chroniques de France et d'Angleterre, by Jehan Froissart, vol. ii (B.M. MS. Royal 18 E. i, f. 165^v; this MS. was probably one of those at Richmond Palace; Flemish, *c.* 1460)

The miniatures depict events which took place between 1377 and 1385. They are not of very good quality and suggest mass production. This scene portrays the Peasants' Revolt; John Ball (labelled with his name) rides in front of a most orderly array of helmeted peasants bearing the banners of England and St George.

12 and 13

Chroniques de France et d'Angleterre, by Jehan Froissart, vol. ii (B.M. MS. Royal 18 E. i, ff. 172 and 175; for general description of MS. see note under [11] above)

[12] shows the rebels murdering the Archbishop of Canterbury at the Tower;

[13] combines two incidents: on the left Wat Tyler meets his death as he threatens the young King, Richard II; and on the right Richard presents himself to the mob as their King and leader.

14 and 15

The Luttrell Psalter (B.M. MS. add. 42, 130, ff. 170 and 181; for general description of MS. see note under [7] above)

[14] shows a man ploughing with yoked oxen, while his fellow walks alongside with a long whip;

[15] shows a water-mill, built of brick and timber, with a thatched roof. In the foreground are the water-wheel and a wooden dam, while on the right can be seen two eel-traps set in the stream.

16

The Luttrell Psalter (B.M. MS. add. 42, 130, f. 173^v; for general description of MS. see note under [7] above)

A cart piled high with sheaves is being driven uphill, while various helpers push hard at the wheel or prevent the load slipping off.

17 and 18

Queen Mary's Psalter (B.M. MS. Royal 2 B. vii, ff. 161 and 160ᵛ; for general description of MS. see note under [5] above)

These two illustrations show archery practice and a wrestling match. In the latter scene one of the spectators holds up a pole with a cock, presumably the prize for the victor.

19

Alnwick Castle, Northumberland (from an air photograph by Aerofilms Ltd)

Alnwick Castle was originally a Norman work of the early twelfth century. Extensive additions, including a barbican and flanking towers, were made by the Percys at the beginning of the fourteenth century. The castle was much restored in the eighteenth and nineteenth centuries. Note how closely the layout in its essentials corresponds with that of the humble peel tower in [20].

20

Smailholm Tower, Roxburghshire (from the engraving by J. Grieg after the painting by H. Weber, from *Border Antiquities of England and Scotland*, by Sir Walter Scott, 1814)

Note the situation on a rocky outcrop. The tower itself formed the home of the laird and was surrounded by a strong outer wall within which the peasants and their cattle could be housed when danger threatened (cf. [19]).

21

The fortified tower of Great Salkeld Church, Cumberland (from a photograph in the Library of the National Buildings Record)

The village of Great Salkeld was frequently exposed to attack since the Kings of Scotland laid claim to its manor. This fortified tower was built about the time of Richard II, apparently as a place of refuge; it is four storeys high with an embattled parapet and a staircase turret. Underneath it is a dungeon. The walls are some six feet thick and perforated with smoke vents.

22

Li romans du boin roi Alexandre, by Lambert di Tours and Alexandre de Bernay (ff. 1–208 of Bodleian MS. 264; this illustration is on f. 128; French, the first half of the fourteenth century)

The illuminations are stated in a colophon to be the work of Jehan de Grise and to have been finished on 18 April 1344. In addition to the full-colour miniatures of the deeds of Alexander there occur in the lower margins many varied scenes of contemporary life, depicting indoor games and outdoor pastimes, windmills and forges, friars preaching and boys playing at school. They are vividly drawn, often with close attention to detail, but they lack the artistry of the secular scenes in the *Queen Mary's Psalter* (cf. under [5] above). This illustration shows people warming themselves at a fireplace. Note the fire-irons and the decoration on the chimney-piece.

23
Le Livre de Rusticon des prouffiz ruraulx, compile par Maistre Pierre Croissens, Bourgoiz de Boulogne (B.M. MS. add. 19, 720, f. 214; French, late fifteenth century)

The illuminations to this French translation of Piero di Crescenzi's treatise on gardening, agriculture, and rural pursuits are hard in outline and show fondness for rather harsh blues, reds, and greens. In this illustration the master of the house is discussing matters with a gardener, one of the ladies is examining a bush, while the others admire a flower with their attendant squire. Note the small formal beds and the high brick wall shutting in the garden. In both this illustration and those reproduced in [48] below, the rather skimpy little plants assort oddly with the assured conventional representation of the buildings and the blue distant landscape.

24
Haddon Hall, Derbyshire (from an air photograph by Aerofilms Ltd)

In spite of its apparent unity of design, Haddon Hall embodies some five centuries of building. Parts of the chapel and the outer walls are twelfth and thirteenth century, while the Great Hall (which separates the two courtyards) and the offices are fourteenth century. Most of the rest of the present fabric belongs to the fifteenth and sixteenth centuries. The actual building of Haddon therefore corresponds roughly to its tenure by the Vernons, though it was altered and embellished in the seventeenth century by the Manners.

25 and 26
The Luttrell Psalter (B.M. MS. add. 42, 130, ff. 193 and 166^v; for general description of MS. see note under [7] above)

[25] The woman on the left is turning her spinning wheel by means of a handle, while the one on the right is carding wool with two hand-cards.

[26] A woman, with her distaff tucked under her arm, is feeding her chickens. Note that the hen is tethered to a peg.

27 and 28
Queen Mary's Psalter (B.M. MS. Royal 2 B. vii, ff. 81^v and 75; for general description of MS. see note under [5] above)

[27] From the Calendar under November. Two men are knocking down acorns to feed their swine.

[28] From the Calendar under April (sign of Taurus, the bull), showing women driving cattle.

29
The Luttrell Psalter (B.M. MS. add. 42, 130, f. 172^v; for general description of MS. see note under [7] above)

Two women are reaping with sickles, while in the background a third appears to be suffering from backache. The man on the left is binding the sheaves.

30–32
Queen Mary's Psalter (B.M. MS. Royal 2 B. vii, ff. 73, 112, and 155^v; for general description of MS. see note under [5] above)

[30] From the Calendar for February (sign of Pisces, fishes). The men are hauling in a net, but seem to have caught very few fish in it.

[31] A man is catching partridges with a drop net.

[32] One woman is setting a ferret into a burrow, while another is netting a rabbit coming out of a hole on the other side.

33
The Luttrell Psalter (B.M. MS. add. 42, 130, f. 63; for general description see note under [7] above)

A clerk is netting a small bird; note the string being pulled to close the mouth of the net.

34–6
The Luttrell Psalter (B.M. MS. add. 42, 130, ff. 206^v, 207, and 208; for general description of MS. see note under [7] above)

The first two illustrations show kitchen preparations for the meal depicted in the third illustration. The top scene shows one man turning a spit on which are fowl and a sucking-pig, while his companion tends the fire itself. The second one shows other kitchen servants engaged in pounding and chopping and apparently examining the contents of the steaming cauldrons. The bottom scene shows Sir Geoffrey Luttrell at dinner, his cup-bearer kneeling in front of the table. It has been suggested that the two Dominicans on the left of the picture are probably his chaplain and his confessor. Note the shape of the knives and the lack of forks.

37–9
Queen Mary's Psalter (B.M. MS. Royal 2 B. vii, ff. 151^v, 150^v, and 151; for general description of MS. see note under [5] above)

Note that in the hawking scene the two women are riding astride; the hawk has already fastened on one of the duck while the man on foot is ready to recall it with the lure.

40
The Pageants of Richard Beauchamp, Earl of Warwick (B.M. MS. Cott. Julius E. iv, art. 6, f. 16; for general description of MS. see note under [2] above)

This scene shows a tournament in progress in the French lists, the king and his nobles watching from the gallery.

41
Hardwick Hunting Tapestry (from a painted photograph by W. G. Thomson in the Victoria and Albert Museum, Dept of Textiles; Flemish, mid fifteenth century)

This tapestry is one of a series of four wool tapestries woven at Arras or Tournai, belonging to the Duke of Devonshire, which at one time hung in the Long Gallery at Hardwick Hall, Derbyshire. They had been cut into pieces at some time unknown and were not restored and put together again until the beginning of this century.

The subjects cover bear- and otter-hunting, hawking, deer-hunting, and boar-hunting. The complete tapestry from which our section is reproduced shows (in the centre foreground) the end of the hunt with a dead stag and the huntsmen apparently proceeding to the gralloch; to the left are hounds in leash. In the right foreground water fowl are being caught with hawks. There is a general background of wood and hills, topped by a castle, and nearer lies a water-mill with the river pouring through the sluices. Plenty of by-play may be observed among the company. Note the elaborate horn-shaped head-dresses of the women, their netted hair and long hanging sleeves. The scenes were probably inspired by Gaston de Foix's *Livre de Chasse* of *c.* 1440–50.

42
Une povre et simple epistre dun vieil solitaire des Celestins de Paris adressant a tres excellent . . . prince Richart par la grace de dieu roy dangleterre, etc. (B.M. MS. Royal 20 B. vi, f. 2; French, 1395–6, probably the original copy presented to Richard II; one of the MSS. formerly at Richmond Palace)

The author of this allegorical work was possibly Philippé de Maizières, Chancellor of Cyprus, who joined the Celestine Order in 1380 and who had proposed a new crusading Order of the Passion. This miniature shows him presenting his book to King Richard and carrying a banner of the Lamb (symbolizing his new Order). Note the courtiers' long pointed shoes, their wide sleeves and parti-coloured hose.

43
Thomas Occleve, *De Regimine principum* (B.M. MS. Harley 4866, f. 88; English, early fifteenth century)

This portrait of Chaucer is the only one generally accepted as authentic. Occleve had it painted from memory after Chaucer's death and had it placed opposite these lines in his poem:

> Although his lyfe be queynt the résemblaunce
> Of him hath in me so fresh lyflynesse
> That to putte othir men in rémembraunce
> Of his persóne I have heare his lyknesse
> Do makë to this ende in sothfastnesse
> That thei that have of him lest thought and mynde
> By this peynturë may ageyn him fynde.
>
> (ll. 4,992–8)

(For a full discussion of this and the other so-called portraits of Chaucer, see M. H. Spielmann's *Portraits of Geoffrey Chaucer*, Chaucer Society, 1900.)

44
The Luttrell Psalter (B.M. MS. add. 42, 130, f. 202^v; for general description of MS. see note under [7] above)

Sir Geoffrey Luttrell is here shown mounted on his horse and attended by his wife, Agnes Sutton, and his daughter-in-law, Beatrice Scrope, the former of whom is handing him his helmet, while the latter holds his shield. The ladies' gowns and the trappings of the horse repeat the Luttrell martlets of the shield.

45
The Fall of Richard II, by Jehan Creton (B.M. MS. Harley 1319, f. 57; French, early fifteenth century)

This MS. tells in French verse the events of 1399 and ends with the deposition of Richard and the accession of Henry IV. The sixteen miniatures which illustrate it include representations of Richard's expedition to Ireland, his return to Conway, Henry's landing and reception of the Dukes of Exeter and Surrey at Chester, the capture of Richard, the meeting of Richard and Henry at Flint, and the final scene (illustrated here) where Henry claims the throne on Richard's abdication. The scene is laid in the Parliament at Westminster, the bishops on the left, the nobles on the right. Henry can be seen in the background beside the vacant throne, he is wearing a high black cap.

46

Troilus and Criseyde, by Geoffrey Chaucer (Corpus Christi College, Cambridge, MS. no. 61; frontispiece; English, *c.* 1400)

This full-page miniature shows the poet reading his poem to an audience of courtiers in a garden. Note the rich elaborate dress and the fantastic background of crags and castle. Though English in execution the style betrays an ultimate Italian influence.

47

The Luttrell Psalter (B.M. MS. add. 42, 130, f. 164^v; for general description of MS. see note under [7] above)

This medieval walled city is labelled 'Constantinus Nobilis' (Constantinople), but the artist has drawn an English city as he knew it with battlemented walls, a church (its spire topped by a weathercock), an inn (with its sign of a bush on a pole), and gabled shops and houses with signs. A group of people at the city gate are dancing to the music of pipe and tabor.

48

Le Livre de Rusticon des prouffiz ruraulx etc. (B.M. MS. add. 19, 720, f. 165; for general description of MS. see note under [23] above)

This shows a walled herb garden in the town. Gardeners are at work and the master appears to be discoursing to one of them on a plant which he has plucked.

49 and 50

Oxford and Cambridge (from engravings from Loggan's *Oxonia Illustrata*, 1675, and *Cantabrigia Illustrata*, 1690, respectively, from copies in the Cambridge University Library)

These are of particular interest in showing that enclosure and open fields flourished at the same time. It so happens that the enclosures can be seen on the hills behind Oxford, while open-field cultivation proceeds in the foreground of the Cambridge view. Note in the latter that the land has been opened as pasture directly after the harvest has been gathered.

51
Geoffrey of Monmouth, *Historia Regum Britanniae* (B.M. MS. Royal 13 A. iii, f. 14; English, early fourteenth-century drawings, though the MS. itself was written in the late thirteenth century)

These drawings have been added in the lower margins of the pages, and represent a number of cities, among them London, Winchester, and York. In this sketch of London there seems to be some attempt to represent Westminster and the many spires of the city.

52
The Pageants of Richard Beauchamp, Earl of Warwick (B.M. MS. Cott. Julius E. iv, art. 6, f. 18^v; for general description of MS. see note under [2] above)

This illustration shows a fight in the Channel between two ships, one of which is ramming the other, while the crews oppose each other with bows, arrows, and spears, as if on land. The man at the mast top of the further ship has been transfixed by an arrow in the very act of hurling a missile himself.

53
Jean de Wavrin, *Chronique d'Angleterre*, vol. iii (B.M. MS. Royal 14 E. iv, f. 169^v; Flemish, late fifteenth century)

This chronicle is based on Froissart and this particular volume deals with Richard II's reign up to 1387. It was executed for Edward IV, probably at Bruges. The scene depicted in this miniature illustrates the status of the Master of the Staple at this time.

54
William Grevel's House, Chipping Campden, Gloucestershire (from a photograph in the Library of the Central Office of Information; Crown copyright reserved)

Contrast this early fifteenth-century stone-built Cotswold house of a great wool merchant with that [119] of the Essex cloth merchant, Thomas Paycocke, with its richly carved timber work.

55
High Street, Chipping Campden, Gloucestershire (from a

photograph in the Library of the Central Office of Information;
Crown copyright reserved)

Chipping Campden was a great medieval wool centre. The
present market house, from whose arches this photograph was
taken, is Jacobean.

56
Flemish Weavers' Cottages, Lavenham, Suffolk (from a photo-
graph in the Library of the Central Office of Information;
Crown copyright reserved)

Lavenham, with its great Perpendicular church, Guild Hall,
and Wool Hall (see [121] below), its plaster cottages and fine
timber houses (see [163] below), retains today many evidences of
its position as a medieval wool town. The cottages in this illustration are some of the oldest in the town and were inhabited by
Flemish weavers, whose introduction (in the fourteenth century)
into England contributed so largely to the growth of our cloth
trade.

57
The Merchant Adventurers' Hall, York (from a drawing by
E. R. Tate, September 1912, reproduced in *Country Life*)

This interior dates from about 1370. Note the fine original
roof.

58
Pictorial Illustrations to the Book of Genesis (B.M. MS. Egerton
1894, f. 2^v; English, fourteenth century)

The outline drawings in this MS. show great vigour and
assurance, especially perhaps in the variety of facial expressions.
Note the careful delineation of detail in this scene of a woman
weaving at a loom.

59
Des Proprietez des choses (French translation by Jean Corbechon
of the *De Proprietatibus rerum*; B.M. MS. Royal 15 E. iii, f. 269;
the first part of this work is contained in Royal 15 E. ii, see [62]
and [153] below; Flemish, late fifteenth century)

This MS. was written at Bruges in 1482 by Jean du Ries,
possibly for Edward IV. The miniatures which illustrate it are
often in a coarse, unattractive style but cover a wide variety of
scenes and activities. In this illustration the cloth is being
dipped in the dye vat. Note the faggots for keeping the fire
going underneath the vat.

60

John Lydgate, *Life of St Edmund* (B.M. MS. Harley 2278, f. 28ᵛ; English, *c.* 1433)

This MS. was presented to Henry VI in 1433 by Lydgate. In the prologue (ff. 6–10) which precedes the life, Lydgate tells of King Henry's visit to Bury St Edmunds at Christmas 1433 and a couple of miniatures illustrate this. The miniatures throughout the MS. are of course devoted to the events of St Edmund's life, and this one is intended to illustrate the Saint on his first landing in England superintending the building of his royal town at Hunstanton.

61

Book of Hours of John, Duke of Bedford (the so-called *Bedford Missal*) (B.M. MS. add. 18, 850, f. 17ᵛ; French, early fifteenth century)

This sumptuous MS. is lavishly illustrated with many miniatures, rich in gold and colour, as well as with elaborate borders of flowers, birds, and foliage to every page of text. It was probably executed for the marriage in 1423 of John of Lancaster, Duke of Bedford, and Regent of France from 1422 to 1435, to Anne of Burgundy. On Christmas Eve 1430, the Duchess gave it, with her husband's consent, to the young King Henry VI at Rouen. Portraits of the Duke and Duchess are introduced towards the end of the MS.

The present illustration shows the building of the Tower of Babel. The artist has introduced all the paraphernalia of the medieval builders' craft. The man to the left of the tower is mixing some kind of mortar, those on the right are sending up blocks of stone by means of a wheel and pulley. On the top of the tower itself is some rather unsafe looking scaffolding, from which one workman has already fallen. In the foreground masons are at work measuring and fashioning the stone.

62

Des Proprietez des choses (French translation by Jean Corbechon of the *De Proprietatibus rerum*; B.M. MS. Royal 15 E. ii, f. 265; the second part of this work is contained in Royal 15 E. iii, see [59] above; Flemish, late fifteenth century; for general description of MS. see note under [59] above)

In this illustration the guild master is apparently judging the work of a mason and a carpenter.

63 and 64

Decretals of Gregory IX (B.M. MS. Royal 10 E. iv, ff. 222ᵛ and

49^v – commonly called *The Smithfield Decretals*, since it belonged at one time to the Priory of St Bartholomew, Smithfield; written in Italy but illuminated in England in the early fourteenth century)

This MS. is full of rough, vigorous drawings of scenes from English social life – crafts and sports are illustrated side by side with story pictures and numerous grotesques.

These two illustrations are of interest in showing a monk undergoing punishment in the stocks – actually for robbing a church – and the animal fable of the fox attired in a bishop's mitre and holding a staff, preaching to a congregation of geese and hens. There is a strong anti-clerical flavour in the animal fable literature of the time.

65
Queen Mary's Psalter (B.M. MS. Royal 2 B. vii, f. 131; for general description of MS. see note under [5] above)

The showman is apparently leading his bear along the street when it turns upon a woman; its master seems about to beat it to heel.

66–9
The Luttrell Psalter (B.M. MS. add. 42, 130, ff. 32, 53, 78^v, and 70^v; for general description of MS. see note under [7] above)

[66] This figure of St James (the patron saint of pilgrims) is shown carrying a pilgrim's staff, and wearing a white cockle-shell in his hat and a wallet at his side.

[67] Two of the grinders are occupied in turning the grind-stone, while a third sharpens the knife.

[68] This beggar woman carries her child on her back and a rosary on her left arm.

[69] This tinker carries his bellows slung on his shoulders. He takes no notice of a vicious little dog which seems to be biting his ankle.

70 and 71
Li romans du boin roi Alexandre (ff. 1–208 of Bodleian MS. 264; these illustrations are on ff. 54^v and 76; for general description of MS. see note under [22] above)

In these two illustrations the artist depicts puppet shows in progress. The audiences seem to be segregated according to sex, although the shows would appear to be identical in type with much display of cudgels. The curtained booths and the attitude of the players (especially in that watched by the group of women) recall the later Punch and Judy.

72

Decretals of Gregory IX (B.M. MS. Royal 10 E. iv, f. 58 (*The Smithfield Decretals*); for general description of MS. see note under [63] and [64] above)

A woman is juggling on two swords to the music of a pipe and tabor.

73
The Luttrell Psalter (B.M. MS. add. 42, 130, f. 176; for general description of MS. see note under [7] above)

These musicians are playing the nakers (i.e. kettledrums) to which the player appears to be dancing, a symphony, and the bagpipes.

74
Book of Hours (B.M. MS. add. 29, 433, f. 89; French, with strong Italian influence, early fifteenth century)

This miniature is a graphic representation of the medieval idea of hell. The damned are being brought to hell's gate in carts and wheel-barrows by horned and sooty demons; unbaptized children arrive by the basketful slung on a demon's back or are flown direct clutched in the talons of winged monsters. Beneath the ornate roof of hell, Satan, surrounded by his devils, torturing the newest arrivals, himself swallows one victim whole, the while he seizes another.

75
'Doom', Pickworth Church, Lincolnshire (this illustration is from a measured water-colour drawing made by Mr E. Clive Rouse from the painting over the chancel arch, which he uncovered in 1947)

This newly discovered Doom or Last Judgement is of particular interest in that it is an example of a medieval wall painting preserved since the late fourteenth century without modern re-painting or restoration. It is painted above the chancel arch of the fourteenth-century church and unfortunately suffered mutilation by the lowering of the roof in the late fifteenth century.

In the centre can be seen the pierced feet of Christ resting upon the sphere. On either side are the Virgin and St John and probably angels holding the cross and pillar, with traces of Apostles or Evangelists beyond. Below, the dead, rising from their graves, are being led away in two directions, the blessed (on the left) being conducted to heaven by St Peter, carrying his keys, while the damned are dragged by a chain into hell's mouth by attendant demons. The subject is continued on the south clerestory wall, with a demon stirring three souls in a cauldron. The rest of the church is lavishly decorated with wall paintings of the Ascension, the weighing of souls, and the familiar medieval motif of the Three Living and the Three Dead (I am indebted to Mr E. Clive Rouse for these descriptive details as well as for the photograph itself).

76
Li romans du boin roi Alexandre (ff. 1–208 of Bodleian MS. 264; this illustration is on f. 79; for general description of MS. see note under [22] above)

This illustration shows a friar preaching from an open-air pulpit.

77 and 78
Pilgrimage of the Life of Man, translated in 1426 by John Lydgate from G. de Deguileville's *Pelerin de la vie humaine* (B.M. MS. Cott. Tiberius A. vii, ff. 90 and 99; English, early fifteenth century)

This allegorical poem of the pilgrim's life is illustrated by crudely executed scenes showing his adventures. The two selected here are of interest as indicating the type of lodging that travellers and pilgrims to such shrines as Bury St Edmunds might meet with. The first shows them satisfying their hunger, while in the second the beds are being prepared for the night. The stick was apparently used to beat and smooth the bedding.

79
Plan of Bury St Edmunds engraved by R. Collins after a drawing by T. Warren (1776) (from the copy in the Map Room of the British Museum)

This beautiful eighteenth-century plan with its elevations of notable Bury buildings (including that of the Abbot's palace as it was in 1720) is reproduced here in order to illustrate the extent of the former abbey grounds in relation to the town. The great court of the abbey can be seen to the left of the abbey church and the gateway, with dormitory and refectory between, while across the River Lark lies the vineyard of the abbey. The Abbot's palace stood at the top of the great court, flanked on the left side by the Abbot's brewhouse and stables.

80
Exeter Cathedral, the nave, looking west (from a photograph in the library of the Central Office of Information; Crown copyright reserved)

The nave is of fourteenth-century work and was completed under Bishop Grandisson (1327–69); note the elaboration of the ribbed vaulting.

81

York Minster, from the south (from an air photograph by Aerofilms Ltd)

The fabric was largely rebuilt in the fifteenth century, initially under William Colchester (master mason of Westminster Abbey). Note the amount of space occupied by the windows by this date.

82

Winchester Cathedral, the nave, looking west (from a photograph by Walter Scott, Bradford, in the possession of the library of the National Buildings Record)

The rebuilding of the nave was begun by William of Wykeham with William Wynford as his architect. It is fine Perpendicular work of late fourteenth- and fifteenth-century date. The west window (late fifteenth century) was apparently glazed as a great triptych, but most of the glass was destroyed in the seventeenth century during the Civil War.

83

William of Wykeham's chantry chapel, south aisle of Winchester Cathedral (from a photograph by Walter Scott, Bradford, in the possession of the Library of the National Buildings Record)

This chapel was built by Wykeham himself, who was Bishop of Winchester from 1367 to 1404, and was responsible for rebuilding the Norman nave of the Cathedral in Perpendicular style. He also founded New College, Oxford, and Winchester College. His tomb (shown here) has three figures at the foot, representing three clerks.

84

Winchester College; engraving from Loggan's *Oxonia Illustrata* (1675) (from a copy in the Cambridge University Library)

William of Wykeham founded his college of St Mary's at Winchester in 1382. A grammar school (at which Wykeham was himself educated) already existed in Winchester, but in founding his college Wykeham had in view the building up of a secular clergy. From this college at Winchester were to be drawn the scholars of his New College at Oxford (see note for [85] below). The buildings of Winchester College – the outer and middle gateways, the inner quadrangle, the chapel, and the cloisters are substantially the same in Loggan's view as at their

first building, except for the tower, which had been rebuilt
between 1473 and 1481.

85

New College, Oxford; engraving from Loggan's *Oxonia Illustrata* (1675) (from a copy in the Cambridge University Library)

William of Wykeham founded New College in 1379, most of
the building taking place between 1380 and 1400; his seventy
scholars were to be drawn from his college at Winchester (see
note for [84] above).

In Loggan's view the gateway and tower, together with the
chapel, hall, and cloisters are much as they were in their founder's
day, but a storey had been added to the front quadrangle in
the seventeenth century. We can thus see Wykeham's College as
it was before the unhappy additions and restorations of the
nineteenth century. Note in the background the old city wall
(thirteenth century) (see [132] below).

86

John Lydgate's *Troy Book* and *Story of Thebes* (B.M. MS. Royal
18 D. ii, f. 148; illuminations partly English fifteenth century and
partly Flemish sixteenth century)

This particular miniature is sixteenth-century Flemish work
and is supposed to portray John Lydgate, monk of Bury St
Edmunds, leaving Canterbury 'by a mery conseyte' with the
Canterbury Pilgrims, the while he adds his version of the Siege
of Thebes to the Canterbury Tales. Note the girdling wall of the
medieval city, with its bastions.

87

Tattershall Castle, Lincolnshire (from a photograph in the
Library of the Central Office of Information; Crown copyright
reserved)

This tower, built of narrow bricks by Ralph, Lord Cromwell
(1394–1456), is all that remains of the great castle in which he
lived as Lord Treasurer to Henry VI. Its walls, some sixteen
feet thick, contain noble fireplaces with rich heraldic mouldings
(see [100] below).

88

Bible History, in Flemish (B.M. MS. add. 38, 122, f. 78^v;
Flemish, mid fifteenth century)

This MS. is illuminated with fine pen-and-ink drawings; the
one reproduced here illustrates a Flemish brickworks with work
in progress.

89

Queens' College, Cambridge (from a photograph by A. F. Kersting)

Founded under the patronage of Queen Margaret of Anjou in 1448, and, after intermission during the Wars of the Roses, continued about 1465, under the patronage of Edward IV's queen, Elizabeth Wydville, and thereafter known as Queens' College, since it commemorates two queens. The principal court (shown here) was almost complete when the Civil Wars broke out. The gateway of red brick has octagonal turrets. (The dial on the old chapel wall on the left is eighteenth century.)

90

Jean de Wavrin's *Chronique d'Angleterre*, vol. iii (B.M. MS. Royal 14 E. iv, f. 195; for general description of MS. see note under [53] above)

This fifteenth-century illustration shows an English expedition arriving at Lisbon in 1385 and being received by John, King of Portugal. The occasion (as described by Froissart) was that of the departure of the King of Castile from the siege of Lisbon and the arrival of three English men-of-war with 500 archers. They were made up mostly of adventurers from Calais, Cherbourg, and Brest, who, hearing of the war, had assembled in Bordeaux and set out under three English captains eager to join in the fight. Their coming was hailed with joy in Lisbon and the King of Portugal sent for them, thinking that John of Gaunt might have sent them to help him, since Gaunt (believing himself to be the rightful King of Castile) was eager in protestations of friendship to John of Portugal, who might be expected to help him against Spain. 'Sir,' quoth Northbery [one of the English captains], 'it is a long season sith he [John of Gaunt] had any knowledge of us or we of him. Sir we be men of divers sorts seeking for adventures: here be some are come to serve you from the town of Calais.' John of Portugal accepted them gladly, dined them in his palace, had lodgings found for them, and ordered their wages to be paid them for three months. The adventurers gave him good counsel afterwards and helped him to win the Battle of Aljubarrota.

91

The Court of the King's Bench (from *Archaeologia*, XXXIX, 1863, p. 357; English, early fifteenth century)

This miniature is one of four vellum leaves surviving from a law treatise of Henry VI's reign. The other three leaves represent the Courts of Chancery, Common Pleas, and Exchequer. The present illustration shows at the top the five judges of the Court; below them are the king's coroner and attorney, etc. On the left are the jury and in front in the dock is a prisoner in fetters, with serjeants of the law on either side of him. In the foreground more wretched prisoners, chained together, wait their turn, watched over by gaolers. On the centre table stand the ushers, one of whom seems to be swearing in the jury.

92

Roman de la Rose (B.M. MS. Harley 4425, f. 12ᵛ; Flemish, late fifteenth century)

This elaborately illuminated MS. of the well-known allegory illustrates the medieval idea of chivalry and all that it entailed. Here (in the miniature shown) is the walled formal garden, with its gushing fountain, flowering shrubs, and trees full of fruit. On the lawn beside the fountain sit the ladies with their attendant knights making music.

93

Parade Shield (Dept of British and Medieval Antiquities, British Museum; Flemish, late fifteenth century)

This exquisite shield of parade would be displayed at tournaments and was not of course for protection in combat. The whole spirit of medieval chivalry is incarnate in the decoration: the pale delicate elegance of the lady in her rich brocaded gown, the steadfast armoured knight kneeling before her with Death at his shoulder, and his vow on the scroll above him 'VOUS OU LA MORT', all express the mystic rapture of the love poetry of the Middle Ages.

94

'The Ballad of the Nut-Brown Maid', as printed in R. Arnold's *Customs of London* (Antwerp, 1503) (from a copy in the British Museum)

95

Boccaccio, *De Claris mulieribus* (French version; B.M. MS. Royal 16 G. v, f. 56; French, early fifteenth century)

This miniature shows a royal lady weaving at a loom, with her women spinning in company. It illustrates well the kind of activity that went on in palace and manor all through the Middle Ages. Thread was spun, materials woven and embroidered, while tapestry reproduced the stories that were told to the accompaniment of busy fingers.

96

Oeuvres de Virgile, frontispiece to the Georgics (Holkham MS. 311; from *Les MSS. à peintures de la Bibliothèque de lord Leicester à Holkham Hall, Norfolk*, par Leon Dorez, Paris, 1908, plate LI; Flemish, late fifteenth century)

Every manor depended on its farm for food and fuel. The artist has crowded into this miniature the labourers with their farm implements, the woodsmen and the hedgers and ditchers, all the cattle and horses, and has not forgotten Virgil's bees. One realizes how busy the ladies of the household would be kept dealing with the products of all this activity.

97

Tapestry at St Mary's Hall, Coventry (from a painted photograph, 1881, in the Victoria and Albert Museum, Dept of Textiles; Flemish, late fifteenth century or possibly early sixteenth century)

This tapestry hangs beneath the north window in St Mary's Hall, Coventry, and appears to have been woven for the space it occupies, since it fills it precisely. It is divided into compartments, the scenes representing the Assumption of the Virgin, with the twelve Apostles kneeling on either side. Above, angels flank a central figure of Justice, which is a later insertion probably replacing a Christ in Majesty or the Trinity. In the lower compartments (to left and right) are the figures of a king and queen attended by courtiers. These are variously identified as Henry VI and Margaret of Anjou or Henry VII and Elizabeth of York; the tapestry may have been woven to commemorate a visit of either to Coventry.

98

Domestic wall-paintings at Longthorpe Tower, near Peterborough (photograph by courtesy of Mr E. Clive Rouse; English, second quarter of the fourteenth century)

These wall-paintings were discovered early in 1947 in the Great Chamber of this late thirteenth-century fortified house. They are amongst the earliest known domestic wall-paintings in England and reveal the hitherto unimagined richness of decoration which might be found in the home of a country gentleman of Chaucer's time. The Tower (which contains the Great Chamber) appears to have been a later addition to the manor-house itself, to which it is connected by a passage in the wall at first-floor level. The whole of the walls to floor level and the vault of this chamber were found to have been covered with mural paintings. Only two of the scenes are purely religious, the remainder being moral and secular, embracing what appear to be moral or allegorical subjects, such as are associated with the medieval teaching of youth. The present illustration shows the north wall and gives some idea of the comprehensive scheme of decoration including even the window recesses – the window itself has been altered. The Seven Ages of Man are depicted above a Nativity, while on either side of the window recess are figures of the Apostles with scrolls bearing sentences from the Creed, which are continued round the room above a border of birds grouped in pairs.

For a full preliminary description of the discovery and the decoration itself, reference should be made to Mr E. Clive Rouse's article in *Country Life* (4 April 1947).

99
The Great Hall, Penshurst Place, Kent (from a drawing by Edward Blore, 1787–1879, architect and artist, and son of the topographer Thomas Blore; B.M. MS. add 42, 017, f. 70)

The Great Hall of Penshurst built by Sir John de Pulteney in the fourteenth century is a substantially untouched feudal hall with open hearth in the centre, screens and minstrels' gallery, and a raised dais for the high table.

100
Fireplace at Tattershall Castle, Lincolnshire (from a photograph by *Country Life*; see general note under [87] above)

This is a fireplace on the ground floor of the brick tower in [87] and illustrates Ralph, Lord Cromwell's love of richly ornamented chimney-pieces. This one has an ogee arch with crocketed finial, below which appears his shield, while on either side are the shields of his family alliances, alternated with the Lord Treasurer's purse.

101 and 102
King Henry VI's Psalter (B.M. MS. Cott. Domitian A, xvii, ff. 175^v and 122^v; English, *c.* 1430)

This MS. was probably a gift to Henry VI from his mother on his coronation at Paris in 1430; his portrait appears in six of the miniatures. The miniatures are executed with great delicacy – the architectural detail being especially fine in the two illustrated here of nuns and monks in choir. Note the lively treatment of the faces.

103
The Warwick or Rous Roll (MS. in the possession of the College of Arms; English, 1477–85)

This Roll of the Earls of Warwick is illustrated with coloured drawings executed between 1477 and 1485 by John Rous, whose self-portrait (on the back of the Roll) is shown in this illustration. He is seen seated in his carved chair at work on his Roll.

John Rous (1411–91) became in 1445 chaplain or chantry priest of Guy's Cliffe, near Warwick, which had been built in 1423 by Richard Beauchamp, Earl of Warwick. Besides his duties in this capacity Rous busied himself in antiquarian and historical work.

104
Chantry Chapel, Wakefield Bridge, Yorkshire (from a photograph of a nineteenth-century engraving in the possession of the Library of the National Buildings Record)

This fourteenth-century bridge chapel was restored in the mid nineteenth century. It was first endowed as a chantry by Edmund, Duke of York, in 1398, but had already been in receipt of a grant under Edward III for the singing of masses.

105
Waynflete Chantry, Winchester Cathedral (from a photograph by Dr Weaver, Trinity College, Oxford, in the possession of the Library of the National Buildings Record)

This is an example of the side-chapel type of chantry within a cathedral. The tomb of William of Waynflete, Bishop of Winchester from 1447 to 1486, lies within its carved and canopied chapel in the retrochoir. He was the founder of Magdalen College, Oxford, and Provost of Eton.

106   'At school'
Woodcut from John Stanbridge's *Parvulorum Institutio*, printed by Wynkyn de Worde, 1512–13 (from a copy in the British Museum)

This illustration from a school-book by one of the first teachers at Magdalen Grammar School (see [110] below) shows a schoolmaster (his birch ready to hand) with eight pupils who are studying their books, the ones in the background not very attentively it appears.

107   'Field sports'
Woodcut from the *Boke of Hawkynge*, printed by Wynkyn de Worde in 1496 (from a copy in the British Museum)

This shows a nobleman setting out with his huntsmen, falcons, and hounds. Education in field sports of this kind played an important part in the training of the young nobleman and went on side by side with his tuition in book-learning.

108 'Students'
Woodcut from *Compotus manualis ad usum Oxoniensium*, printed by Charles Kyrfoth, 5 February 1519 (from *English Woodcuts (1480–1535)*, by Edward Hodnett, Bibliographical Society, 1935)

This illustration also shows a schoolmaster with his pupils but they are older than those shown in [106] – 'At school' – above, though the birch is still in evidence. Note the books and globes, the lamp and hour-glass, the master's desk with its book cupboard, and the knife and 'penner' (or pencase) on the left-hand side, as well as the book-stands on either side.

109 'A scholar'
Woodcut from *Stans puer ad mensam*, by Joannes Sulpitius, printed by Wynkyn de Worde in 1518 (from a copy in the British Museum)

This cut shows a scholar in his study; note his reading-desk and bookshelf, and his pencase.

110
Grammar Hall, Magdalen College, Oxford (from a photograph in the Library of the Central Office of Information; Crown copyright reserved)

In 1480 William of Waynflete founded a grammar school for his College of St Mary Magdalen at Oxford. It was set up within the precincts of the College and had a grammar master and usher appointed. Its purpose was to provide a preliminary grounding for university courses, and one of its first teachers was John Stanbridge, the author of the *Parvulorum Institutio* (a woodcut from which in Wynkyn de Worde's edition is reproduced on page 155. The building in the centre of this photograph is all that remains of the grammar school and the old Magdalen Hall.

111
Magdalen College, Oxford (from a photograph in the Library of the Central Office of Information; Crown copyright reserved)

The roofed cloister with stone figures (illustrated here) was built about 1480 (for a note on the founder, William of Waynflete, see under [105] above).

112
Duke Humphrey's Library in the Bodleian, Oxford (from a photograph by A. F. Kersting)

Humphrey, Duke of Gloucester, gave to the University of Oxford many of the books he had seized from the Louvre and elsewhere during his French campaigns. In 1444 the University asked his permission to use his name as founder of the building they intended to erect to house his gifts. This building now forms part of the Bodleian and is still known as Duke Humphrey's Library, although almost all of Duke Humphrey's books have long since been dispersed.

113

King's College Chapel, Cambridge (from a photograph by A. F. Kersting)

Founded in 1440 by King Henry VI (possibly in emulation of William of Wykeham's foundations at Winchester and Oxford) King's College possesses a Perpendicular chapel, which is far loftier and more spacious than the usual college chapel. The work came to a standstill with Edward IV's accession in 1462 but was resumed by Richard III in 1483, though two years later it was again abandoned until Henry VII became its patron in 1508. The fabric was completed by 1515 under Henry VIII and the work of glazing the great windows then began.

While the actual building was spread over some seventy years, the whole design appears to have been chiefly the work of Reginald of Ely, who had been appointed by Henry VI in 1443 to secure workmen for building the chapel and remained in charge of the work until the King's deposition. The chapel was completed under John Wastell (who had already been working at Canterbury) as master mason and designer of the vaulting.

114

From Sanderus's *Flandria Illustrata* (1641) (reproduced from William Blades's *William Caxton* (1882), plate 11)

This shows the House of the Merchant Adventurers in Bruges where Caxton lived as Governor of the 'English nation' as the Merchant Adventurers were known in the Low Countries. From being a merchant of the Mercers' Company, Caxton seems to have become Governor of the English merchants at Bruges between June 1462 and June 1463.

In this house each merchant lived under rules as strict as a monastery's, since the foreign merchant in the Low Countries had to endure many restrictions in his manner of trading and in his way of life.

115

The oldest known representation of a printing-press, from the title page of Hegesippus's *Historia de Bello Judaico*, printed by Judocus Badius Ascensius in Paris (1507) (reproduced from William Blades's *William Caxton* (1882), plate VII)

116

A German printing-press from Jobst Amman's *Stünde und Handwerker* (1568) (reproduced from William Blades's *William Caxton* (1882), plate IX)

117

Poems of Charles, Duke of Orleans (B.M. MS. Royal 16 E. ii, f. 73; executed in England in Flemish style *c.* 1500)

Charles, Duke of Orleans, father of Louis XII of France, was captured at Agincourt and imprisoned in England from 1415 to 1440 (cf. text, p. 67, for the life of French prisoners in England). This splendid miniature shows the Pool crowded with ships, old London Bridge in the background with its medieval houses, and in the foreground the Tower of London. The medieval practice of showing several episodes in a man's life side by side in one miniature is followed here – the Duke can be seen seated within the Tower writing, at a window, and in the courtyard handing a letter to a messenger.

118

Brass of Thomas Pownder and his wife in the Church of St Mary Quay, Ipswich, Suffolk (from a rubbing in the British Museum, add. MS. 32,489, EE. 5; Flemish, 1525)

This brass, engraved in Renaissance style, is a good example of Flemish work. It shows Thomas Pownder, merchant bailey of Ipswich, his wife and family. The shield in the centre bears upon it his merchant marks, with his initial T in the middle of it. The shields on either side bear the arms of Ipswich and of the Merchant Adventurers.

119

Thomas Paycocke's House, Great Coggeshall, Essex (from a photograph in the Library of the Central Office of Information; Crown copyright reserved)

The village of Great Coggeshall lay in the centre of the great cloth-making district of Essex, and here the clothier Thomas Paycocke built (about 1500) the house shown in this illustration. Its timber is rich in carving; note the leaf and flower decoration of the bressumer supporting the upper storey, the linen-fold panelling of the door on the left, and the figure on the right side of it.

120

Little Sodbury Manor, Gloucestershire (from a photograph in the Library of the National Buildings Record)

This stone manor-house was originally held by the family of Stanshaws in the fifteenth century. The porch and the part to the left of it are fifteenth century, while that to the right (with corbelled bay window) is early sixteenth. The manor has a fine fifteenth-century hall with an open timber roof.

121

Wool Hall, Lavenham, Suffolk (from a photograph in the Library of the Central Office of Information; Crown copyright reserved; cf. note on Lavenham under [56] above)

This was probably the Hall of the Guild of St Mary the Virgin and dates from about 1480.

122

The Passion Play of Valenciennes (Paris, Bibliothèque Nationale, MS. franc. 12,536; French, 1547)

This water-colour drawing well illustrates one kind of medieval stage, in which the various scenes against which the action took place are ranged in order across the stage from Heaven to Hell-mouth. The various 'mansions' are labelled Nazareth, Jerusalem The Palace, etc.

123

Book of Hours: executed for Étienne Chevalier by Jehan Fouquet (Musée Condé, Chantilly; French, fifteenth century)

This miniature (Miniature no. 44 according to Henri Martin's classification) shows a typical mystery play of the fifteenth century being acted on a wattled stage (the mansions of heaven and hell appearing to left and right). The play is that of the Martyrdom of St Apollonia, an aged deaconess of Alexandria, alleged to have suffered martyrdom in A.D. 248–9. Her teeth were pulled out with pincers and on being threatened with death by burning she cast herself on the pyre 'by supernatural impulse' according to St Augustine. Her aid as patron saint was invoked against the toothache!

124

The Plays of Terence (Paris, Bibliothèque d'Arsenal, cod. lat. 664, f. 1ᵛ – the so-called Térence des ducs; French, early fifteenth century)

This richly illuminated M S., which owed its name to its having belonged first to the Duke of Guyenne (d. 1415) and then to his uncle, the Duke of Berri (d. 1416) is of great importance for the history of the drama of the Middle Ages and its costume. This miniature (the frontispiece) shows the miming of a classical comedy by masked actors, the book being apparently recited from a draped box, before a crowded audience, the whole being enclosed in a circle labelled 'Theatrum joculatoris'. Below, the author is seen presenting his book to his patron.

125
Map of the Manor of Feckenham, Worcestershire (reproduced by courtesy of the owner, Dr Edward Lynam)

This map was drawn by John Doharty the Younger (1677–1755) in 1744 from an earlier map surveyed and drawn by John Blagrave in 1591. It shows a typical Tudor manor; the chief buildings, court house, church, mill, etc., can be easily identified, but the map is of special interest in showing the common lands and the gradual encroachment on these and on the 'lord's wastes' by different land-holders who are named in the key (for fuller details see Dr Lynam's 'The Character of England in Maps', *Geographical Magazine*, June 1945).

126
Cardinal Wolsey (1475 ?–1530) (from the portrait by an unknown artist in the National Portrait Gallery)

127
William Tyndale (d. 1536) (from the portrait by an unknown artist in the National Portrait Gallery)

128
Sir Thomas More (1478–1535) (from the portrait after Hans Holbein in the National Portrait Gallery)

129
Title-page of the Fourth Great Bible (printed in London by Edward Whitchurch in November 1540, but not published until 1541; from a copy in the British Museum)

A royal proclamation was made on 6 May 1541, ordering 'that in al & syngular paryshe churches, there shuld be prouyded by a certen day now expired, at the costes of the curaytes & paryshioners, Bybles Conteynge the olde & newe Testament, in the Englyshe tounge, to be fyxed & set up openlye in euery of the said paryshe Churches. . . . By the which Iniunctions the kynges royall maiestye intended that his louynge subjectes shulde have & use the commodities of the readyng of the said Bibles . . . humbly, mekely, reverently & obediently. . . . '

After 1541 Bible printing ceased for the rest of Henry's reign, since Bishop Gardiner condemned the translation which the Church had been so lately ordered to procure. A new translation (closer to the Vulgate) was decided on, but not proceeded with.

130

Edward VI's coronation procession (commonly known as 'The Riding from the Tower') (from a water-colour copy made for the Society of Antiquaries by S. H. Grimm in 1785 from the picture, c. 1547, at Cowdray, destroyed by fire in 1793)

The procession is shown passing down Cheapside on its way to Westminster. In the centre can be seen Cheapside Cross, on the extreme left is the Tower, and on the right old St Paul's. Note the tall gabled houses and the rich hangings which decorate the balconies in honour of the procession.

131

Joris Hofnagel's 'Tudor Wedding' (1590) (from a water-colour copy made by S. H. Grimm, 1788, for the Society of Antiquaries from the original painting at Hatfield House)

This probably represents a wedding feast by the old Church of St Mary Magdalen at Bermondsey, though the scene has been variously described as a 'Tudor masque' and 'Horsleydown Fair'. The vigour and incident of the scene with its feasting and dancing is a lively portrayal of Tudor England at the end of the sixteenth century.

132

The old city wall (thirteenth century) in the gardens of New College, Oxford (cf. [85] above) (from a photograph by A. F. Kersting)

133

The ruins of Bury St Edmunds Abbey, Suffolk, as engraved by R. Godfrey in 1779 (from the copy in the Map Room of the British Museum)

The Abbey was dissolved in 1540 and this print is of interest as showing the extent to which the buildings had been despoiled some 230 years later (cf. also [134] below).

134

Bury St Edmunds Abbey, as engraved by S. Kendall (1787)

(from the copy in the Map Room of the British Museum) (cf. [133] above).

135
Castle Acre Priory, Norfolk (from a photograph in the Library of the Central Office of Information; Crown copyright reserved)

The Priory was surrendered to Henry VIII in 1537 and was granted to the Duke of Norfolk. On the left can be seen the ruins of the west end of the Priory church – a fifteenth-century Perpendicular window above a Norman doorway and arcading. On the right lies the Prior's lodging built by Prior Winchelsea at the beginning of the sixteenth century.

136
Fountains Abbey, Yorkshire (from an air photograph by Aero-films Ltd)

This great Cistercian house was founded in 1132 and its ruins still exhibit the typical Cistercian arrangement of the church, cloisters, and conventual buildings. The Perpendicular tower was not built until the early sixteenth century, and thus only shortly before the Dissolution (cf. note under [166] below).

137
Trinity College, Cambridge (from an engraving by Loggan in his *Cantabrigia Illustrata*, 1690; from a copy in the Cambridge University Library)

Founded by Henry VIII in 1546 the College absorbed King's Hall (1336), Michael House (1323), and Physick's Hostel (belonging to Gonville Hall), together with some minor hostels. The Great Court (as shown by Loggan) owed its form to Neville (appointed Master in 1573); the chapel was finished about 1564; the Library (in the far distance) by Wren was just being completed at the time of Loggan's engraving.

138
Christ Church, Oxford (from an engraving by Loggan in his *Oxonia Illustrata*, 1675; from a copy in the Cambridge University Library)

Founded by Cardinal Wolsey in 1525 as Cardinal's College, and converted after his fall into 'King Henry VIII's College at Oxford' in 1532, it did not become Christ Church until 1546. The lower part of the tower, Tom Quad, the hall, and kitchens are of Wolsey's time, while the cloisters are fifteenth century. The rest is of seventeenth- and eighteenth-century date.

139

Much Wenlock Abbey, Shropshire (from a drawing by Edward Blore, for whom see note under [99] above; B.M. MS. add. 42,018, f. 31)

This Cluniac priory was surrendered in 1539, when the Prior's lodging (which had only been built at the end of the fifteenth century) together with the Infirmary building (of Norman date) were taken over by the Lawley family and used as a dwelling house, although the Priory church and St Milburga's shrine were destroyed.

140

Titchfield Abbey, Hampshire (from a photograph in the Library of the Central Office of Information; Crown copyright reserved)

Passed at the Dissolution to Thomas Wriothesley, Earl of Southampton, who cut through the middle of the nave to erect the great gate of his mansion.

141

The Chained Library, Hereford Cathedral (from a photograph in *Cathedrals*, 1926, by courtesy of British Railways)

This medieval library still contains over 2,000 chained volumes. Note the rail to which the chains are fastened and the placing of the books with fore-edges facing outwards.

142

The Abbot's Kitchen, Glastonbury (from a photograph in the Library of the Central Office of Information; Crown copyright reserved)

Built entirely of stone in the late fourteenth or early fifteenth century, this kitchen has a vaulted roof and four enormous fireplaces. In the lantern hung the bell to call the poor to the almonry which adjoined the kitchen on the north side.

143

St Augustine's Abbey, Canterbury (from a photograph in the Library of the Central Office of Information; Crown copyright reserved)

The Great Gate was built by Abbot Fyndon between 1300 and 1365. The upper part formed a lodging for distinguished guests.

144

The 'carrels' in the south cloisters, Gloucester Cathedral (from a photograph by Mrs J. P. Sumner, in the Library of the National Buildings Record)

This cloister was completed by Walter Froucester, who was Abbot from 1382 until his death in 1412.

145
The refectory, Chester Cathedral (from a photograph in *Cathedrals*, 1926, by courtesy of British Railways)

Built by Abbot Simon de Whitchurch 1265-90.

146
The Chapter House, Wells Cathedral (from a photograph by A. F. Kersting)

Begun probably under William de Marchia, Bishop (1293–1302), who built the walls, it was finished about 1319 under John de Godelee, Dean (1306–33), when the vaulting and windows were built. The vaulting ribs branch out from the cluster of shafts which form the central pillar of this octagonal chapter house. The carved and canopied stalls are ranged round the room as a wall arcade above the stone bench which forms the seats of the stalls.

147
The Abbot's Tribunal, Glastonbury (from a photograph in the Library of the Central Office of Information; Crown copyright reserved)

Built by Abbot Beere, *c.* 1493.

148
The Guild Hall, King's Lynn (from a photograph in the Library of the Central Office of Information; Crown copyright reserved)

Built about 1423 this guild hall has a chequered front and entrance porch of flint and freestone. It was the Hall of the Trinity Guild. The arms above the porch are of Edward VI and Elizabeth.

149
Edward VI granting the Charter to Bridewell (from an engraving by George Vertue, published 16 February 1750, after a contemporary picture at Bridewell Hospital; from Vertue's *Nine Historical Prints*, republished by the Society of Antiquaries, 1776)

The King is shown giving the Charter to the Lord Mayor and Sheriffs of London. Those surrounding the King are identified by Vertue. Among them the Master of the Rolls and the Earl of Pembroke, with ' in the corner the face of Hans Holbein the painter'. The granting of the Charter took place, however, in 1553, ten years after Holbein's death.

150

Sir Nicholas Bacon (1509–79) (from the portrait by an unknown artist in the National Portrait Gallery)

Bacon was Lord Keeper of the Great Seal (1558) and High Steward of St Albans, the friend of Matthew Parker and benefactor of Corpus Christi College, Cambridge.

151

Gorhambury, St Albans (from an eighteenth-century water-colour drawing, by courtesy of *Country Life*)

The house shown here was built by Sir Nicholas Bacon between 1563 and 1568, partly with stone from the abbey of St Albans. The abbey, after its surrender in 1539, was granted in 1541 by Henry VIII to Ralph Rowlett, Merchant of the Staple at Calais (d. 1543). It passed thence to his brother who sold it in 1561 to Sir Nicholas Bacon.

152

The Grammar School, Stratford on Avon (from a photograph in the Library of the Central Office of Information; Crown copyright reserved)

Built about 1473 as the Guild House, its 'over hall' or 'dorter' was converted into a schoolroom by Shakespeare's father, and became the grammar school. The hall beneath housed the Court of Records and was also the scene of plays performed before the Bailiff for his approval by companies coming to the town, before they gave public performances in the inn yards. It was probably also the scene at other times of the Latin plays acted by the boys of the grammar school.

153

Des Proprietez des choses (B.M. MS. Royal 15 E. ii, f. 165; the second part of this work is contained in Royal 15 E. iii; for general description of this MS. see note under [59] above; Flemish, late fifteenth century)

This illustration shows patients arriving for treatment by a physician and waiting their turn to be seen. The first man is being bled.

154

The Dance of Death, by Hans Holbein the Younger (Cologne, 1573) (from the copy in the Cambridge University Library)

155

William Cecil, Baron Burghley (1520–94) (from the portrait attributed to Marc Gheerhaerdts in the National Portrait Gallery)

This great Tudor statesman held the lucrative office of *custos brevium* in the Court of Common Pleas from 1547 to 1561; after a period in the Tower consequent upon his having been secretary to the Lord Protector Somerset (who was disgraced in 1549), he became Secretary of State in 1550, was created Baron Burghley in 1571, becoming Lord High Treasurer from 1572 to 1598 and Elizabeth's chief Minister (for his building of Burghley House, see note under [158] below).

156
Edward Seymour, first Duke of Somerset (1506?–52) (from the portrait by an unknown artist in the National Portrait Gallery)

Brother of Henry VIII's third wife, Jane Seymour, Edward Seymour was closely associated with the King's household and was made Lieutenant of the Kingdom during Henry's absence in France in 1544. The next year he was active and successful in the war with France, becoming Lieutenant-General in 1546. On Henry's death he was appointed Lord Protector to the young Edward VI and Duke of Somerset the same year. His fall in 1549 was brought about by the measures he advocated, which stirred up much opposition against him and brought him to the Tower. After a brief period of pardon and readmission to the King's favour he was arrested again in 1551 and beheaded on Tower Hill in 1552.

157
From a portrait of two unknown sitters (formerly thought to be William Cecil, Baron Burghley, and his second wife, Mildred) by an unknown artist (1596) (in the possession of the Hon. Michael Astor, M.P.)

(Cf. text, pp. 261–2, for comments on Elizabethan portraiture. Note the stiff attitudes, the white faces, the attention to the rich detail of the dress.)

158
Burghley House, Northamptonshire (from a drawing by Edward Blore, for whom see note under [99] above; B.M. MS. add. 42,019, f. 82)

Cecil (for whom see note under [155] above) began to build Burghley House in 1556, on the site of the old manor-house. Subsequent portions were added between 1577 and 1587 from designs by John Thorpe (who also designed Kirby Hall, Northamptonshire, about the same time). This great Tudor house provides an example of one paid for 'by money made in the Courts of Law' (cf. text, pp. 243–4).

159

Dover Harbour at the time of Henry VIII (B.M. MS. Cott. Augustus I, i, 22 and 23)

This roll shows the fortifications of the harbour with the gun emplacements at the ends of the mole. The town can be seen in the background, with the castle above. Note the ships, their high poops, their spread of sail, and their guns. This roll bears precise descriptive notes upon the condition of the harbour and its main features.

160
'The Anne Gallant', from *The Second Roll declaring the Number of the Kings Majestys own Galliases*, by Anthony Anthony (1546) (B.M. MS. add. 22,047; the first roll is in the Pepysian Library at Magdalene College, Cambridge)

This coloured drawing shows the *Anne Gallant* of 450 tons. Her complement was 250 men, of whom 220 are described as soldiers and mariners and 30 as gunners; the last were to handle 7 guns of brass and 38 guns of iron. The roll also gives details of the gunpowder and shot (of iron, stone, and lead), the weapons, etc.

161
St Mawes Castle, Cornwall (from an air photograph by Aerofilms Ltd)

This castle formed part of Henry VIII's scheme of coastal defence. It was designed with Pendennis Castle about 1540 to defend Falmouth Harbour. It is actually a small massive blockhouse, consisting of a central tower with bastions pierced for guns; similar examples are Deal and Walmer Castles, and Camber Castle, near Rye.

162
Tudor cottages at Chiddingstone, Kent (from a photograph in the library of the Central Office of Information; Crown copyright reserved)

163
Tudor House, Lady Street, Lavenham, Suffolk (from a photograph in the library of the Central Office of Information; Crown copyright reserved)

Note the doorway and the fine timber work (for general note on Lavenham, see note under [56] above).

164
Gringoire's *Castel of Laboure*, printed by Wynkyn de Worde, 1506 (from the copy in the Cambridge University Library)

This woodcut illustrates the simple arrangements for cooking and eating which one would expect to find in a poor inn or small yeoman's house in early Tudor times. Note the scanty array of pots and pans, the rough bench, settle, and trestle table.

165

Compton Wynyates, Warwickshire (from a photograph in the library of the Central Office of Information; Crown copyright reserved)

This early Tudor house was much restored by Sir William Compton in Henry VIII's reign, partly (according to Leland) with material from the ruined Fulbrooke Castle, near Warwick.

166

Fountains Hall, Yorkshire (from a drawing by Edward Blore, for whom see note under [99] above; B.M. MS. add. 42,019, f. 95)

At the Dissolution Sir Richard Gresham bought Fountains Abbey from the King. It was sold in 1596 to Sir Stephen Proctor, who in 1611 used material (including stained glass) from the ruined abbey to build this mansion.

167

West Stow Hall, Suffolk (interior) (from a photograph by *Country Life*; cf. note on West Stow Hall under [170] below)

The interior of the gatehouse has a Tudor wall-painting of four of the seven ages of man, with an elaborate frieze above and traces of ornamentation on either side. From left to right the scene depicts:

A boy with a hawk who is saying: 'Thus do I all the day.'
A pair of lovers: 'Thus do I while I may.'
An older man (looking on): 'Thus did I when I myght.'
A very old man: 'Good lord, will this world last ever?'

168

The Abbot's Parlour, Thame Park, Oxfordshire (from a photograph in *Country Life*)

The Tudor block of Thame Park was built by Abbot King between 1530 and the dissolution of the Abbey in 1539. His parlour has fine linen-fold panelling with a frieze above of richly carved wood suggestive of Italian workmanship. Note also the elaborate carving of the ceiling beams in similar style. The fireplace is contemporary.

169

East Barsham, Norfolk (from a drawing by Edward Blore, for

whom see note under [99] above; B.M. MS. add. 42,019, f. 59)

This manor is a fine example of ornamental brickwork and was built by the Fermors in the reigns of Henry VII and VIII. The detached gatehouse bears the royal arms in moulded brick above the entrance. Note the terracotta ornament and the elaborate turrets.

Henry VIII visited here in 1511 and is reported to have walked barefoot from the house to the Shrine of Walsingham, some two and a half miles distant.

170
West Stow Hall, Suffolk (from a photograph by *Country Life*)

Another type of brick gateway is illustrated here. The Hall was rebuilt by Sir John Crofts between 1520 and 1533. It is plainer in style than the East Barsham gateway (see note under [169] above), although it also has turrets, topped in this case with ornamental figures.

171
Henry VIII jousting before Katherine of Aragon (from the Westminster Tournament Roll in the possession of the College of Arms)

On 12 and 13 February 1509/10 (O.S.) Henry VIII held the jousts at Westminster to celebrate the birth of his son Henry (who, however, only lived from 1 January to 22 February). The roll is richly though crudely illuminated and records the procession, the tournament itself, and the return to court. This illustration shows Henry himself riding in the lists before the Queen and her ladies.

172
Psalter (B.M. MS. Royal 2 A, xvi, f. 63^v; for general description of MS. see note under [173] below)

This illustration shows Henry VIII playing on his harp. His jester, William Sommers, stands on the right. 'It was the fashion at the Court, from the King downwards, to compose musical tunes and verses to go with them' (see text, p. 262).

173
Psalter (B.M. MS. Royal 2 A, xvi, f. 3; English, sixteenth century)

This psalter, written in Italian style for Henry VIII by John Mallard ('*regius orator*'), has many marginal notes in Latin by Henry himself. This illustration shows Henry seated reading in his bedroom. The influence of the Renaissance can be seen in the ornamentation of the bed and the chair in which the King is seated, as well as in the vista through the archway, perhaps also in the fact that he is engaged in studying richly bound MSS.

174–7 TUDOR PORTRAITS

174
The Darnley Brothers (from the portrait by Hans Eworth, c. 1520–after 1578, at Windsor Castle)

175
Henry VIII (from the portrait in the National Portrait Gallery after Hans Holbein's painting at Althorp)

176
The Princess Elizabeth (from the portrait by an unknown painter working in England, c. 1546, at Windsor Castle)

177
Thomas Howard, third Duke of Norfolk (1473–1554) (from the portrait by Hans Holbein the Younger at Windsor Castle)

The above four portraits have been selected to illustrate different styles of portraiture which flourished in Tudor England. Those of Henry VIII and the Duke of Norfolk are in typical Holbein style, shrewd in characterization, paying full attention to the importance of robes of state and insignia of office; that of the Princess Elizabeth (the only certain contemporary portrait of her as Princess) exhibits a calm assurance and warmth of treatment which make it unique, while that of the young Darnley brothers (the taller of whom became husband of Mary, Queen of Scots), with its background of panelled gallery, is a variation of the stiff, white-faced, family portrait.

[174, 176, 177] are reproduced by gracious permission of H.M. the Queen.

178
Li Livres du graunt Caam . . . , by Marco Polo (Bodleian MS. 264, ff. 218–71ᵛ; this miniature is on f. 218; English, c. 1400)

This scene depicts Marco Polo's embarkation at Venice; in the background is a view of Venice itself, while in the foreground are scenes from his voyages. The ships are the type of trading vessel which brought Venetian goods to England during the fifteenth century in return for wool.

179
'Chart of the Southern Ocean . . . from a Portolano', by Diego Homem (B.M. MS. add. 5415 A, ff. 13ᵛ–14; Portuguese, 1558)

This map, executed for Philip II, illustrates in pictorial scenes the natives and animals of the Guinea Coast in 1558, that is, a little later than the period at which William Hawkins 'had traded in friendly fashion with its natives for ivory'.

180
The Fuller's Panel: bench-end at Spaxton Church, Somerset (from a drawing by Alfred Clarke, 1859, in the *Somersetshire Archaeological Society's Proceedings*, vol. viii, pt 1, for the year 1858)

This bench-end exhibits some of the implements in use by a sixteenth-century Somersetshire cloth-weaver. He appears to be pressing a piece of cloth.

INDEX

INDEX

MORE ABOUT PENGUINS
AND PELICANS

Penguinews, which appears every month, contains details of all the new books issued by Penguins as they are published. From time to time it is supplemented by *Penguins in Print*, which is a complete list of all available books published by Penguins. (There are well over four thousand of these.)

A specimen copy of *Penguinews* will be sent to you free on request, and you can become a subscriber for the price of the postage. For a year's issues (including the complete lists) please send 30p if you live in the United Kingdom, or 60p if you live elsewhere. Just write to Dept EP, Penguin Books Ltd, Harmondsworth, Middlesex, enclosing a cheque or postal order, and your name will be added to the mailing list.

Note: *Penguinews* and *Penguins in Print* are not available in the U.S.A. or Canada

THE PELICAN GUIDE TO
ENGLISH LITERATURE

EDITED BY BORIS FORD

What this work sets out to offer is a guide to the history and traditions of English Literature, a contour-map of the literary scene. It attempts, that is, to draw up an ordered account of literature that is concerned, first and foremost, with value for the present, and this as a direct encouragement to people to read for themselves.

Each volume sets out to present the reader with four kinds of related material:

(i) An account of the social context of literature in each period.

(ii) A literary survey of the period.

(iii) Detailed studies of some of the chief writers and works in the period.

(iv) An appendix of essential facts for reference purposes.

The *Guide* consists of seven volumes, as follow:

1. *The Age of Chaucer*
2. *The Age of Shakespeare*
3. *From Donne to Marvell*
4. *From Dryden to Johnson*
5. *From Blake to Byron*
6. *From Dickens to Hardy*
7. *The Modern Age*

RELIGION AND THE RISE OF CAPITALISM

R. H. TAWNEY

Religion and the Rise of Capitalism is a study of religious thought on social issues during the three centuries from the later middle ages to the early eighteenth century. Starting with an account of medieval theories of social ethics, it goes on to examine the impact on traditional doctrines of the new forces released by the economic and political changes of the age of the Reformation. The social backgrounds and teaching of Luther, Calvin, and the English divines from Latimer to Laud, receive attention in turn. A chapter on the Puritan Movement discusses, among other topics, the theory that Capitalism had Puritanism as one of its parents.

Turning to the practical realities of history, Professor Tawney explains the conditions which gave point to prohibitions of usury and to the insistence on a just price; describes the social consequences of the Tudor land question; and touches on the impetus to economic speculation given by the price-revolution, the expansion of foreign commerce, and the growth of the money-market.

ENGLAND IN THE LATE MIDDLE AGES

(1307–1536)

A. R. MYERS

During the last generation a vast amount of research has been done on all aspects of the late Middle Ages in England, and this has radically modified previous views; yet no general synthesis has hitherto been attempted. Moreover, the period has suffered undue neglect and disparagement in comparison with the preceding 'Age of Faith' or the subsequent triumphs of Elizabethan England. But our generation may well find a particular interest in an England afflicted by war and disillusionment – from which it eventually recovered; and the late Middle Age in England was a time not merely of violence and decay but of growth and creativeness. Its *Canterbury Tales* and its *Paston Letters*, its ballads and its carols, its Perpendicular churches and its unsurpassed wood-carving, are still an essential part of English culture. It was an age of decisive importance for the future – the time of a developing Parliament and common law, of a government learning how to cooperate with the governed, of the rise to political and social importance of the middle classes, of a new pride in the English tongue, English ways, and English nationality.

This is Volume 4 in *The Pelican History of England*.

A SHORTENED HISTORY OF ENGLAND

G. M. TREVELYAN

In this brilliant chronicle one of the greatest writers of English history tells the story of the building of 'this realm, this England' from the remote days of the Celt and the Iberian to just before the Second World War. By abbreviating his narrative in dealing with periods of minor importance he is able to give pace and proportion to this exhilarating history of the British people.

What the reader may look forward to in *A Shortened History* is shown by the high praise of its parent volume:

'The text, with its easy style, beautiful clarity, and mastery in summarizing, will always deserve and win new readers' – *The Times Weekly Review*

'This elegant narrative is the outstanding twentieth-century example of the "Whig interpretation" of history. . . . As a synthesis, this is a book which will always be read' – Asa Briggs in the *New Statesman*

BRITISH HISTORY IN
THE NINETEENTH CENTURY
AND AFTER: 1782–1919

G. M. TREVELYAN

Between 1780 and 1920 Britain underwent the most rapid change of character any country had ever experienced until then. Despite the most stable political structure in Europe the nation changed with startling speed. The first industrial state was created; the world shrank under the impact of steam power and the electric telegraph; man's scientific, social, and political attitudes were revolutionized; an Empire grew at the same time as a parliamentary aristocracy transformed itself into a parliamentary democracy. And Britain, almost alone, was without violent revolution.

G. M. Trevelyan's famous study of the period is focused on the political stage, on which the central themes of the century were played out by such actors as Pitt and Gladstone, Wellington and Queen Victoria, Disraeli and Parnell. The author employs his gift for divining the logic of events to show how developments in science, industry, economics, and social theory made themselves felt on the conduct of the nation's affairs.

ILLUSTRATED ENGLISH
SOCIAL HISTORY
(in four volumes)
G. M. TREVELYAN

'The illustrations are chosen with a wholly admirable freshness
and originality; and, together with Mrs Wright's helpful notes,
they are a fitting enhancement of the pleasure and instruction
afforded by this recently established popular classic' – *History*
(in a review of Volume 2)

The contents of the other three volumes are as follows: